'Step up' to cha
Ideas from practice writter

'Step up' to change:
Ideas from practice written by students

Edited by
Graham Ixer

w&b
MMXVIII

© Whiting & Birch Ltd 2018
Published by Whiting & Birch Ltd,
Forest Hill, London SE23 3HZ
ISBN 9781861771414
Printed in England and the United States by Lightning Source

Contents

Foreword by Professor Jonathan Parker vii

Preface by Dr Ray Jones xi

The Contributors xiii

1. 'Step up' to change: Ideas from practice written by students
   Graham Ixer 1

2. How fear, generated by client violence, impacts on child protection social workers
   Stephen Brearley 11

3. A contemporary discourse of social work decision-making
   Leo Harverson 31

4. The role of emotional containment in a child protection workforce
   Stella Vincent 46

5. A feminist analysis of mothers' involvement in child abuse
   Alison Love 62

6. Key issues arising from practice under section 17 of the Children Act 1989
   James McCullough 75

7. Key issues in the involvement of fathers in child protection
   Jacqueline Pilgrim 88

8. The issue of physical touch with children and young people
   Joanna Genter 102

9. The re-victimisation of women in domestic violence
   Samantha Belbin 117

10. Online grooming: A consideration of everyday practice in child protection
    Billy Hughes 132

11. Reunification of looked after children with their birth parents
    Samuel Tolerton.. 146

12. Meaningful contact between the child and social worker:
    A critical review
    Clair Lockyer..160

13. Life story work in promoting strong attachments
    and identity in children
    Gary Castle 180

14. Talking Mats as a tool to hear voices of disabled children
    Peter Holland 193

15. 'Seeing the Child Alone'
    Jacqui Gaunt 211

16. Exploring digital technology and its potential to improve outcomes
    Anthony McMurdo 226

Foreword

There has been over a century of growth, develop and turbulence in social work education in Britain and throughout the world. The early university courses and diplomas in social administration set the foundations for education that was rigorous, recognised and worthy of inclusion within our bastions of learning. The fluidity and, to an extent, incoherence of social work education was addressed following the implementation of the Local Authority Social Services Act 1970 and the creation of the Central Council for the Education and Training in Social Work (CCETSW) in 1970 under the auspices of the Health Visiting and Social Work Act 1962 which consolidated the diverse range of training bodies.

CCETSW operated from 1970 until its replacement by the Care Councils for the UK administrations in 2001, recognising and approving programmes and providing research and advice. Although many of us railed against aspects of CCETSW and its bureaucratic functions, it was perhaps a victim of its own success in serving social work's development in the UK and fiercely brandishing its independence from party political influences and rather promoting the centrality of values and radical political challenges. Acknowledging the importance of race and ethnicity in social work education and practice, CCETSW's black perspectives committee championed the inclusion of challenging racism in social workers' training and education. Government has, as we may note, always been suspicious of too much independence and the need for the control of potentially radical elements – something we see today in respect of the *Prevent* agenda. We can trace an increasingly governmental and surveillance approach to social work education from the challenges and reviews of CCETSW and its 'political correctness' from the early to mid 1990s resulting from these politically important and radical agendas that aimed to raise awareness of the unseen or unacknowledged discrimination and oppression of a range of groups outside mainstream society.

From this time onwards, we may surmise that the die was cast. Governments wanted to ensure that social work education served the welfare state as defined by the state and, alongside economic pressures, that social workers practised as state employees. Thus it was inevitable that along with representative social work bodies the qualifications underpinning social work were also reviewed. The move towards degree level qualifications, firstly implemented in England in 2003 and taken up by the other three nations and administrations in the subsequent two years, was presented as a means of ensuring standardisation in qualification and a means of enhancing quality across the programmes. Contextualisation, specialisation and expertise in education and research was, to a large extent, side-lined and silenced, and a paean to mediocrity potentially created. Greater levels of prescription were given and higher education institutions and social work academics were subject, from that time, to greater gaze and scrutiny that has been adopted as self-monitoring technologies that now often unquestioningly accept the interference of government in challenging, reviewing and changing social work education practices.

Since 2003, social work education has not been left to mature and develop, which could have allowed the desired professionalisation and quality enhancement to become embedded within programmes. Questions raised by some employers have allowed social work education to become associated more with vocational training for a specific purpose rather than as an education for a critically demanding human profession. And following the politically charged situation arising around the tragic death of Peter Connelly (Baby P), politicians cynically employed the soft targets of social work education and practice to deflect attention from other pressing matters taking social work into yet further rounds of costly review and reform without solid evidence on which to move forward.

The change to degree level awards and subsequent reforms have been a two-edged sword, therefore, with one blade carving out a path towards greater professionalisation, higher educational attainment and coherent standards in provision, and a second blade slicing away aspects of individualism, specialist pathways and in-depth study, and damaging the confidence of social work academics to undertake their roles in the ways they know best – not as arrogant individualists but as collaborative partners in the human world. The challenges to university education have continued in the development of 'fast-track' and elitist approaches to child care and mental health social work education. Before these more, possibly, insidious threats to education were forged, the Step-Up to social work qualifications in child care social work have been piloted and further rolled out to university/local authority partners. These too aroused suspicion and debate and calls for wider evaluation but have become part of the panoply of programmes that reflect collaborative working and the fused nature of social work as theory in practice.

This brief and somewhat jaded review of social work education in the UK may appear to be a little at odds with a book that derives from one of the new pathways to education – Step-Up to Social Work. However, whatever misgivings I may have about the directions and tangents taken by social work education in the years since 2003 what is heartening and important to see is the level of insight and criticality developing in social work students' accounts of their work and demonstration of their learning from this programme. The alliance of academy and practice is most clearly shown through these case reflections and studies that exemplifies Professor Graham Ixer's commitment to excellence in social work education, and the importance of developing criticality for contemporary practice. There has not been a book like this since my old professor, Robert Harris, edited a, long out of print, collection of practice placement case studies of probation students in the late 1980s. It is well overdue.

The sixteen chapters of the book address areas of immediate import to beginning professionals. After Graham Ixer's initial chapter setting the policy context and scene for the work the book offers chapters that address the importance of looking after or caring for oneself as a social worker including dealing with fear and containing the strong emotions that arise especially in child protection work. There are chapters also relating to practice issues that offer bright rays of sunshine in promoting direct work that is so highly skilled and yet so often relegated to marginal positions in contemporary practice. Questions of emotional and individual contact, meaningfulness and 'being human' or physical contact abound and are addressed by students grappling with these complex issues. Thirdly, as regards a thematic grouping of the chapters, although these are not so structured within the book, there are chapters concerning some of the academic issues relating to mothers, fathers, ways in which grooming occurs, the complexities of domestic violence and the application of the law that show these students wrestling with feminist theories, contemporary elements of abuse and how this may have an impact on their practices. The chapters represent a welcome challenge to me and my concerns at the direction of social work education in England: there is still a critical and insightful edge to those qualifying as social workers and long may this remain.

There are still concerns regarding the ways in which social work education is moving. Perhaps Step-Up represents a form of partnership to be reflected more fully in the roll-out of teaching partnerships in the future. Perhaps, if a more generic approach to the programmes could be developed, this would allow universities to contribute their expertise and, so importantly, their research skills and knowledge into the future education of social workers – in a way that maybe the 'fast-track' approaches do not permit. However, the current focus in Step-Up - solely on children's social work - is problematic and is indicative of an underlying privileging of social work in this area and the relegation of adult social work to the margins – something that is both political and economic. However, given the critical thinking shown by these contributors there is hope that social work education and practice in England will be able to re-establish its place in the world and offer contributions that resonate widely and reflect our professions' international values.

The authors of these chapters are to be commended for their work and the commitment which have shown to their studies and their personal development as social workers. They are moving into their careers as qualified workers and taking with them published contributions to the field that will hopefully allow them to develop further and more deeply in the future as they take positions of leadership and education themselves.

Professor Jonathan Parker
Bournemouth University

x

Preface

In his Foreword Professor Jonathan Parker sketches out an informed and critical appraisal of social work education in England over the past 50 years. It is a story of a profession which through its education and practice has championed the value base of social work, with a concern for social justice, anti-discrimination and staying alongside those who are minimised and marginalised by much of mainstream political, press and public discourses.

It is a value-base which is under challenge from within current national government policies, where the financial crisis created by powerful bankers in the early 2000s has been used as a rationale not too restrict the excesses of the rich but to penalise the poor. Inequality is increasing and those who are disadvantaged are being moved from deprivation to destitution. The welfare state, created at a time of post-war austerity in the 1940s, is being replaced by the demeaning insecurity of food and clothing banks and with those in poverty – children and adults of all ages - neglected and rejected.

What shines through in this collection of papers by those now entering the social work profession is that the commitment to social work's value base is still seen as important, impressive and integral to social work practice. These papers are by a new cadre of Step-Up to Social Work students, and Parker in his Foreword is right to challenge the too early specialisation being generated by new government-sponsored routes into social work.

But criticising and being concerned about the privileged entry routes into social work being promoted by the government at the expense of the greater majority of social work students is not to lessen in any way the acknowledgement of the commitment and passion of those, through whatever route, are starting to build the foundations of hopefully social work careers of longevity.

Nor is it to fail to recognise the intellectual competence of the students, a competence required of practising social workers in all settings as they have to create an understanding of complex, chaotic and confusing situations of major life changes or personal conflict and threat and, alongside service users, undertake assessments and action planning which may be crucial to well-being and safety. It is a task which is intellectually and emotionally demanding, and of considerable importance for children and adults in difficulty.

What also shines through in this book is the reach, range, richness and relevance of social work for those who are in the midst of difficult life experiences, and the issues faced by social workers themselves as they are immersed in but not to be overwhelmed by lives of others which may be distressing and disrupted.

Whether it is engaging directly with children, keeping in sight all in a family, and staying alert to wider community and societal influences, including now the opportunities and dangers for children and others of social media and new technologies, the task is to stay head-up and continually thinking and reflecting but not to be frozen and paralysed into inactivity because of uncertainty.

One of the professional requirements of social workers is to stay inquisitive, intrigued and indeed investigative but not to be deterred from taking action because all is not certain. It is a pity that the press and politicians cannot tolerate or understand uncertainty and with the benefit of hindsight look back when something terrible has happened to pile blame on to those who have been brave enough do at the time what seemed best when all inevitably was not known and the future could not be predicted.

So we should be thankful that the new generation of social workers at Winchester University, and their social work student colleagues elsewhere, are still fired up to help children, adults and families, to apply their intellectual and emotional capacity and competence, and are champions for the value-base.

And thank you also to those more experienced social workers who are now their educators and practice mentors, sharing their knowledge, experience and expertise.

Social work is a collaborative exercise across the generations of experience within the profession, with other professions, and with service users and their communities. It is reassuring and to be celebrated that, as demonstrated by this book, despite its trials and threats social work should look forward to a new cohort of its champions. I wish them well.

Dr Ray Jones
Emeritus Professor of Social Work
Kingston University and St George's, University of London

The Contributors

Leo Harverson Prior to completing the Step-Up to Social Work Post-Graduate Diploma at the University of Winchester, Leo Harverson worked in NHS mental health services, initially as service-user involvement lead for NHS Isle of Wight. Leo also holds a Post Graduate Certificate in Mental Health Studies from Southampton University and he has previously worked as a Psychological Wellbeing Practitioner and academic library assistant. Leo is currently employed as a Social Worker with a Children in Need team for the Isle of Wight Council Children's Services.

Sam Tolerton works in a children in care team for a local authority and has a Background in welfare to work, focusing on young adults with various social disadvantages to gaining employment.

Stephen Brearley is currently a social worker working for Wokingham Borough Council Children's Services. He graduated from the 'Step Up to Social Work' course in March 2015. Prior to this Stephen graduated from Southampton University in 2008 with an LLB in Law. Stephen has worked residentially for children's charities such as Barnardos and CHICKS and has set up youth groups and football teams in his role as a Personal Advisor to Care Leavers. Stephen is also currently a Trustee for CHICKS children's charity; a national charity giving disadvantaged children from around the UK free respite activity breaks

James McCullough graduated from Plymouth University in 2006 having read Psychology with Criminal Justice Studies. Following this he co-ordinated a resettlement project for adult offenders, which led him to work with young and adult offenders for Hampshire Youth Offending Team and Hampshire Probation Trust respectively. James left his career in the justice system in 2014 to complete the acclaimed Step Up to Social Work programme at The University of Winchester and has worked in frontline Children's Services as a qualified social worker since 2015

Jacqui Gaunt I completed a degree course at Winchester in Philosophy and Psychology and then took an MA in Philosophy at Southampton. I worked in the Early Years Sector in various roles in Portsmouth and Southampton. A change of career from early 2014 led me to undertake the 'Step Up To Social Work' course, again at Winchester University. Since then I have been employed by HCC as a social worker, working in the Children in Need Team in Fareham and Gosport.

Stella Vincent Stella studied Criminal Justice and Criminology in the School of Law at the University of Leeds, where she volunteered with the Leeds Youth Offending Service. Following her graduation, Stella took a job as a Restorative

Justice Officer with national charity Catch22 before being transferred into Hampshire Youth Offending Team. Here, she worked with 10-18 year olds involved in the Criminal Justice System and the victims of their crimes, supporting all those involved to find a positive way to move forward and repair the harm caused through offending. After qualifying as a social worker through the government funded Step-Up programme now works as a Children's Social Worker with Wokingham Children's Services in the Duty, Triage and Assessment Team.

Samantha Belbin After completing the Step Up to Social work programme Samantha qualified as a children and families social worker in 2015 in the Referral and Assessment team in statutory Children's Services. She has a background working in a Local Authority Children's Home for young people, as well as working as an Intensive Support Worker for children on the edge of care.

Clair Lockyer Having gained a Psychology degree I moved into the Probation Service delivering interventions to offenders with a Cognitive Behavioural approach. I then developed an interest into the impact offending behaviour had on children and families and went on to work as a family support outreach practitioner within an early years setting supporting vulnerable children and families. I took the opportunity to train as a Social Worker in 2014 and in 2015 was awarded a Postgraduate Diploma in Social Work, following the successful completion of the Step-Up to Social Work programme. I am currently working as a registered Social Worker in a statutory child protection team.

Billy Hughes progressed his interest in social functioning by studying BSc (HONS) Sociology at the University of Portsmouth. He was successful in securing employment with the Local Authority's Substance Misuse Service which provided him with invaluable knowledge and insight. Four years into this post, Billy embarked on a new challenge and successfully achieved a place on a Step Up to Social Work course. Since qualifying, Billy has been working within Children's Services and he is continuing to promote the importance of keeping children safe online.

Jacqueline Pilgrim After several years in the corporate industry, I changed careers. During 2005-2008 I completed a degree course in Criminology at Southampton Solent University. I achieved a First Class and Outstanding Achievement Award. I then specialised in the area of 'Rights of Women and Children' with a specific focus on: Child Sexual Exploitation, Human Trafficking, Domestic Violence and Sexual Abuse; this included multi-complex, high risk, holistic needs, support and advocacy; operational and strategic co-ordination and facilitation. This led me to undertake the Step-Up to Social Work programme at University of Winchester (2014). I was awarded the Post-Graduate Diploma in Social Work. I now work with Hampshire County Council as a Social Worker, working in the Children in Need Team in Eastleigh & Winchester District and have successfully passed my ASYE and I am due to start the EPD in September 2016.

Peter Holland Prior to starting the Step Up to Social Work Programme in 2014 Peter worked in Children's Services on the Isle of Wight from 2009. It was during Peter's 100 day student placement on the 'Step Up' programme with the Disabled Children's Team on the Isle of Wight during Step Up that inspired his interest in Talking Mats. He now works as a qualified Social Worker in 'Children in Need Team' on the Isle of Wight and continues to use the 'Talking Mat' tool as a means of hearing the voice of the child.

Jo Genter is a qualified Social Worker working in a front-line Child Protection team in Hampshire. Prior to completing the Step-Up to Social Work programme, Jo spent 13 years working at the Foreign and Commonwealth Office and was made an MBE in 2009 for services to the Foreign and Commonwealth Office. Prior to studying Social Work, Jo experienced working in residential settings with children and with adults with disabilities.

Gary Castle Gary works in the Children in care team with the Isle of Wight local authority since he qualified on the Step Up programme. Previously he worked with challenging young people and their families for 10 plus years, supporting them through difficulties such as drugs and alcohol, homelessness, domestic violence, child sexual abuse and sexual health. He is now about to move into a role as a supervising social worker within the Isle of Wight fostering team.

Alison Love Whist completing my first degree in Social Sciences with Social Policy through the Open University I began to work with an organisation undertaking Restorative Justice with young offenders and trained as a conference facilitator. Through this work I began to realise the importance of early intervention and took other roles in supporting young people at early stages and before behaviours become too entrenched. I worked in the early intervention side of the Youth Offending Team and as a support worker in Motiv8 before taking my first step into Children's Services as a Child and Family support Worker. After qualifying Alison initially went to work as a Social Worker in a Children in Need Team in Hampshire to complete her Assessed and Supported Year in Employment before moving to Child and Adolescent Mental Health (CAMHS).

Tony McMurdo obtained a BA Hons Degree in Childhood and Youth Studies from The University of Portsmouth in 2014 which led him to taking a role providing pastoral care to teenagers in a school setting. Tony then completed his Post Graduate Diploma in Social Work in 2017 through the Step Up To Social Work Programme, and is currently exploring ways to harness digital technologies transformative power to support vulnerable children.

Tony McMurdo obtained his Post Graduate Diploma in Social Work in 2017 at The University of Winchester, through the Step Up To Social Work Programme. This was following a period of time providing support to vulnerable teenagers in a school setting after completing his BA Hons Degree in Childhood and Youth Studies, which was obtained from The University of Portsmouth in 2014.

Graham Ixer is Professor of Social Work and Social Policy at the University of Winchester where he has been responsible for three cohorts of the social work programme 'Step Up.' Previously he was head of Social Work Education at the General Social Care Council for England regulating all qualifying and post qualifying programmes. He has many interests in policy and research. He has published widely on reflective practice and worked in many countries including USA, Sweden and Japan. His career in social work practice, policy and education spans over 30 years.

Jonathan Parker is Professor of Society & Social Welfare and Director of the Centre for Social Work and Social Policy at Bournemouth University. He moved to Bournemouth in 2006 after 11 years at the University of Hull where he was one of the founders and director of the Family Assessment and Support Unit, a practice placement agency attached to the University and awarded the Queen's Anniversary Prize for Higher Education in 1996, and latterly Head of Department of Social Work. Jonathan's research projects focus on disadvantage and marginalisation, cross cultural aspects of social work, research ethics and violence, conflict and religion. He has also researched and published in theories and methods in social work and dementia care. He has recently conducted cross cultural research on learning and practice with colleagues in Southeast Asia. He is currently working on projects concerning the meanings constructed during church visiting, constructions of adult safeguarding, gendered rituals in professional practice, and research ethics and learning disabled people.

Ray Jones is emeritus professor of social work at Kingston University and St George's, University of London. From 1992 to 2006 he was director of social services for Wiltshire, and he has been the deputy chair and chair of the British Association of Social Workers and chief executive of the Social Care Institute for Excellence. The second edition of his most recent book, *The Story of Baby P: Setting the Record Straight*, was published in 2017.

I
'Step up' to change:
Ideas from practice written by students
Graham Ixer

Introduction

This book is about contemporary social work and is different to most because instead of being written by subject specialists or academics the book is written by students as experts by experience. Each chapter is a contribution to practice as an outcome of a student's social work placement in front line children's services in England. Most post-graduate students studying social work in the UK will normally complete their study by undertaking a thesis or large written project. For students at the University of Winchester (UK) undertaking the government's flagship training policy 'Step up to Social Work' Postgraduate Diploma in social work, they complete a final piece of work as a major project derived from their placement. It must achieve innovation or challenging ideas in either policy, practice or specialist social work knowledge. Each student writes about the outcome of his or her project as a final piece of assessed work. All students passed with Distinction or Merit and were immediately employed in front line children's services. In addition a number of their projects were implemented in practice in either changing policy or ideas towards innovative change. The purpose of these projects were to develop sound ideas for change that emerge from their practice experience to be harnessed and developed further in benefitting front line children's social work. It is a two way investment into enhancing social work practice and with whom will become our future practitioners.

The following chapters are a selection of the best projects produced in 2015 and 2017, which have been edited into short standalone monographs to stimulate debate, argument and an exchange of ideas. Not all the projects were related to the specific service from the student's placement but was inspired by their experience in front line consequently, led to their research investigation into an area of interest that potentially will achieve better outcomes for children's services. We hope that their contributions will inspire others to debate and extend discussion on these important topics that are rarely covered in social work education. They are a practical demonstration of how others such as students make a useful contribution to professional and expert knowledge. Moreover, to disband the myth that professional knowledge is only the preserve of experts and academics.

Contextualising social work training

Why is the 'Step Up' programme so different to any other form of social work training and education output? Training social workers in the UK is regulated and each approved programme must adhere to minimum standards to ensure every student who graduates has achieved the same basic standards of competence. The issue for government and the public is a lack of confidence in social work training, which has led to many discussions on the nature of training relevant to preparing students for front line contemporary practice. In a Select Committee Report (DCSF, 2010) and numerous reviews on social work education (Munro 2011, DoE, 2014, DoH 2014), conclude that social workers are not sufficiently trained to make them 'fit for practice.' The evidence to support this assertion was never published only the conclusions so it is difficult to challenge the government's hypothesis that standards of training create incompetent social workers in their first year of employment. Through a plethora of initiatives to improve social work education across four governments since 1997 and inspired by experience from teacher training, social work education was subject to direct control and influence by central government. Although in England there is an independent body for social work education (the Health and Care Professions Council), government ensured control through economic influence in changing the way future funding would be dispersed to ensure maximum control of the profession over education providers. Government linked the availability of funding to specific government initiatives to ensure the transfer of power shifted away from the sector to meet specific Ministerial imperatives to improve standards. The national bursary scheme allocation for example, was available to everyone that trained but began to decrease the budget for undergraduate routes whilst increasing postgraduate routes such as 'Step Up'. This was not new money but the same money dispersed differently. The 'Step Up to Social Work' initiative was brought in during the Labour government in 2009 based on teacher training, the 'Teach First' initiative. Again there is no real evidence that this approach is any more successful than any other approach as the main outcome employers want is effective and well prepared newly qualified social workers. The evidence in the evaluative report (DoE 2013) fails to address this but rather records data on progression and satisfaction rates on the course, which compares similarly to social work.

The government has invested considerably into 'Step Up' which has seen five cohorts of students trained and another in process. Unlike other forms of training they are paid a generous tax free bursary and consequently, attract graduates from other professions such as psychology, law and teaching. We know from the evidence (CWDC 2010) that graduates do well in going into employment but what we do not know is how better these graduates are in the task of social work. The government's current evaluation is measuring this. Although there is no independent evidence about the impact 'Step Up' students have on practice, what we know from our own programme and what other programmes share with us - do 'Step Up' students come to training with an already developed maturity and emotional resilience that gives them considerable advantage in being prepared for the demands of the task? Is this because they have already developed these skills in their previous established career? Step Up students come with qualities that are attractive to employers who need practitioners to cope from day one with the complex and heavy demands of front line children's social work. Employers want people who can manage complexity, prioritise efficiently, independently and take responsibility. Step Up students appear to deliver this although there is not any independent evidence to support such an assertion.

Unlike many other professions such as medicine, law or engineering, new recruits must complete an apprenticeship in practice and undertake specialist training that is independently assessed before they can proceed into their chosen area of practice. If successful the individual professional is able to enter that part of the professional Register and legally practice in a specialised area. Social work does not have reserved functions therefore a newly qualified social worker can still be given the full range of duties and tasks of a senior social worker who has the benefit of many years of experience. Although wholly wrong and unethical, this is the environment that in whatever route an individual takes to qualification is the reality for all newly qualified social workers in England. Despite this employers not only expect but, continue to demand the full range of specialist expertise from such graduates who have only just qualified to a basic and generic level qualification. Previous governments have colluded with this false illusion. In the absence of a professional body such as the British Medical Association for doctors, social work's lack of a voice allows for a political free for all from anyone in the sector who wishes to pursue their own self-interest of critical bias. In the absence of a strong body to counter the lack of evidence to support self-serving political ideology of the day, social work becomes a 'political punch bag' making it vulnerable to constant change that is not always in its best interests and so often hidden under the banner 'we are changing to make social workers more effective' without really defining what that means. However credit must be given to government for continuing its policy on Step Up which now brings benefits of stability and consistency to local authority recruitment in children's social services.

In essence the sector wants specialist and experienced social workers in children's services who can cope with the full range of tasks but instead have generically trained social workers at the basic level of entry into the profession. This creates a tension with no easy solution. The current system of 'Assessed and Supported Year in Employment (ASYE) is a local system managed by employers with no independent verification of meeting required standards. It is the alternative of a regulated licensing system similar to doctors, which restricts practice until properly assessed and qualified. Because the system for social work is managed locally it fails to deliver national consistency and moreover, lacks a gate keeping role across the profession for example, a newly qualified social worker in one employer who fails their NQSW training can easily move to another. The new system of accreditation recently announced by UK government will be no different (Morgan 2016). Therefore we retain a system of training and education dictated by an ineffective system of minimum standards at a generic level. This is in conflict with employers who require specialization and advanced level practice at the point of qualification. The situation continues a negative tension between those who train and the type of training being delivered, and those who employ and hold unrealistic expectations of newly qualified social workers in what they should do from day one in their employment.

There is no easy answer and this cycle of change and political interference continues. In 2012 the government decided to transfer the functions of the bespoke social work regulator the General Social Care Council to a health regulator the Health Professions Council renamed the Health and Care Professions Council. The GSCC closed and the profession lost the only social work body that represented the regulatory interest of the social work profession. However because of criticism that the HCPC was weak and failed to provide the type of training employers want (DoE, 2014) despite the type of training never being clearly defined, a new change was announced to yet again, transfer the functions to another body specific to social work but yet undefined (Morgan 2016). This change came about in less than 4 years. Although I am sure social workers would welcome their own specific professional regulator again there is no clear evidence supporting why such a policy is required as there was during the 2010 debate to transfer the functions from the GSCC to the HCPC. To find an answer to this interesting dilemma one is left to ponder and speculate on such emerging assumptions. However whatever thinking there is about the way social work education is developing it is clear the 'Step Up' programme is producing effective graduates as part of employer's effective recruitment strategy, albeit expensive compared to other routes.

Analysis of change

To appreciate why social work education is so vulnerable to change one has to look further into the political environment that social work inhabits. During the past 30 years there has been a gradual decline in public services towards private organisations either owning social care services or taking over large contracts to manage social work and social care. The neoliberal agenda of the right sees the

UK government implement its policy of 'market forces' as the best way to deliver quality in the social work and the social care sector. However there is no evidence this works but to the contrary, social care presents a good case for failure (CQC, 2011) in the way large corporate financial industries have invested heavily in social care as they see an ageing population ripe for profit as more and more people live longer whilst needing care. During the health debate in the House of Lords in 2010 major changes in the National Health Service were being introduced that saw health services being opened up further to market forces. NHS leaders were being allowed for the first time to contract private companies to provide to parts of the NHS that since 1948 was always a free public service. A coalition government pushed through these reforms into the Health and Social Care Act 2012. However a journalist published data that two thirds of the government peers who voted for the Bill had a financial interest in the health contracts to be awarded by government because they sat on large private companies waiting in the wings to tender for this new business (McClenoghan, 2012).

Care and profit are ideals that when set together work in conflict. More and more of our public services are now being run by four or five of the largest corporate companies that do not have a back ground in care but rather the prioritising of profit. Companies such as the large accountancy firms of Deloites and Price Waterhouse-Cooper and others in Serco and G4S hold large government contracts for all aspects of public care. Although one may argue there is no problem with global capitalist profit per se, the issue we have seen in the UK is how everyone including government and organisations collude with the dominant sound bites when things go wrong because of weak regulation. The banking crisis in 2008 is a good example where it saw the UK Prime Minister David Cameron say 'We are all in this together' as part of the 'Big Society' (Garrett 2013:96) and how we all assumed this is 'our problem' (society) rather than the few powerful institutions who made mistakes on risky lending. Conversely when the banks have their good times and large institutions invest well and make significant profits for their shareholders society is excluded and the phenomenon of profit is only the business of these powerful institutions and the sharing of profits is limited to the few whilst the rest of us remain in the barren land. This one way blame is best exemplified in the Republic of Ireland's financial collapse where it blamed the public sector for of its problems, similar to England and projected how we are 'in this together' (Garrett, 2013).

In this sense society becomes an all-consuming mechanised industry of production. Workers become part of the production line that have developed automated attitudes that strip away their individuality and human content in work. Workers become part of the modernity that Gramsci was critical when challenging the ideas associated with Americanism, Fordism and Taylorism. These economic arguments explaining society give weight to a new world order of social welfare where Cameron's government steers a pro-marketisation agenda that seeks to destroy the welfare state and therefore, social work. If this analogy is true then it is easy to see how Gramsci and others could view how global hegemony is achieved. Consequently the concept of care is irrefutably a challenge to the neoliberal agenda of the conservative government whose ambition for 'capital' and power undermines the values of social work. The aim of social work is about sharing rather than accumulating power, which for most social workers will always experience as a tension. It is with this tension that we now focus because to understand us this dilemma will help understand why social work and therefore social work education is constantly in a state of flux and ambivalence in pursuing its agenda for change.

In order to develop and maintain hegemony in social work the controlling interest of the powerful influence the political and neo-intellectual agenda to sustain a domination of power. Jones (2011) stated over 30 years ago in his portrait of radical social work, we do not want social workers to think for themselves but rather do what they are instructed. This enlightened thought is important to social work today. Through decades, governments have been critical of social work education for providing what they saw as too much non-relevant intellectualisation on subjects that do not matter such as sociology. But to understand why people behave in the way they do social workers need to enquire into the reasons behind the behavior legitimising sociology teaching. Many see the subject of sociology for example, as knowledge that is not relevant. The more sinister reason behind this admonishment of the profession may be the need to control what and how people think to manage their passive following rather than a more critical challenge, which such thinking encourages and develops, a theme Jones warned of (Jones, 2011). In this sense it is even more worrying as the controlling agents of government, the few social work directors who sit in the exclusive club of government with other special advisers, dictate the social work curriculum and place pressure on programmes to deliver a politically led curriculum that will deliver social workers who rather than think for themselves, obey commands. This dichotomy is best exemplified in recent relevant reviews on social work education (DoE , 2012, 2014, 2016) where it is clear that the rhetoric calls for critical thinkers the policy says something else in practice as it oppresses such criticism through subtle compliance. Government will only support programmes with funding that follow their policy therefore, control the outcome they desire.

This approach creates a manageable workforce that can easily hide and mask the failings of care as there are few practitioners who are able to stand up and resist the inevitable outcomes of privatised social work. Moreover, there is no one to challenge the evidence base for policy and operational decision making but rather a closed door allowing only those few senior officers such opportunity and only if they are minded to do so. When whistle blowers have attempted to shout out in the past they have been muzzled (Jones, 2014). This is the inevitable consequences of what government likes to think is transparent policy making. We are led to believe that we own and are all part of making public policy but in reality merely manipulated into believing this false hope as a form of cultural hegemony in the way Gramsci predicted. Social workers like most public servants are cogs in a large tight wheel with little ability to deviate let alone create the counter-hegemony needed to hold government and their aids to account.

However whilst this might be an argument against Step Up, it shows that if you invest heavily in recognised talent, nurture and develop it you are more likely to bring into the profession capable and effective individuals to become our future social workers. This route of course denies those who do not meet the requirements of 'Step Up' and who might equally make good social workers. Step Up is clearly an exclusive route similar to other routes such as 'Front Line' (based on 'Teach First' teacher training and implemented by government in May 2013). However, for employers it is an effective recruitment policy that sustains their supply of effective practitioners who have a well-developed emotional maturity and resilience However, will the evidence from the government's longitudinal study on impact support this conclusion?

Introduction to the chapters

The following chapters have been separated into three parts. **Part 1** explores a range of specific areas that highlight contemporary debates in social work and looks to extend the discussion.
In chapter 2, Stephen Brearley investigating the fascinating area of fear in social work and how this impacts on their ability to make sound judgments in their decision-making. This is an eloquent and thought provoking chapter that leads the reader to practical conclusions based on research from an area of complexity and density within the literature.

Chapter 3 starts with an analysis of decision making by Leo Harverson. The phenomenon of good decision making is an intrinsic part of good social work.

Stella Vincent then looks at emotional containment in chapter 4. She analyses research from serious case reviews and criticism from Ofsted about the shortcomings of local authorities in how they use emotional containment to keep children safe and secure. She makes some key recommendations such as critical reflection on one's work is not self-indulgent but essential to effective social work practice.

Alison Love in chapter 5 presents an interesting analysis from a feminist perspective on mothers and how they are often demonised in the child protection system and can lead to being criminalised.

James McCullough in chapter 6 explores an interesting issue arising out of Sec 17 of the Children Act 1989 and the ethical dilemma of parental involvement.

Under such a section families must agree to local authority involvement as this is meant to enhance partnership in working to support families outside of court directions. He explores how so often in practice families are not informed or asked for their agreement, but instead are coerced to social work intervention as they believe not to will have detrimental effect on their family.

Part 2 explores a range of practice issues that are rarely discussed or viewed as mainstream social work.

Chapter 7 looks at key issues and consequences in not involving fathers in assessment. Jacqueline Pilgrim highlights key issues and the impact on the family when fathers are not involved in plans for their children. This is not only pertinent to social work but other professions as well.

Jo Genter's work on the use of physical touch with children in chapter 8 is an outstanding example of how fear, anxiety and confidence undermine this important area of communication with children in distress. She makes some interesting findings about how we deny children comfort that leads the reader to understanding the impact this can have on children whilst recognising the dilemma for the professional whose fear for getting it wrong or having false allegations made about them heightens their risk adverse approach. In essence the refusal to physically hold a small child in distress does no more than give the child a feeling of rejection.

In chapter 9 Samantha Belbin analyses whether child protection services contribute to female victims of domestic violence as their judgment on the inaction women take to remove themselves from a dangerous situation is wholly wrong and misguided. This is an area that has attracted little attention and becomes entwined in the patriarchal agenda of power.

In Billy Hughes's chapter 10 he looks at on-line grooming. In todays' world society has not caught up with the advancement of technology. Children at very young ages have access to smart phones and computers and put themselves at risk. Clear messages and learning are presented for all social workers to help protect children from this new phenomenon.

Chapter 11 analyses the complex issue of reunification of looked after children with their birth parents. Samuel Tolerton makes an insightful analysis of this interesting area in reviewing important literature and identifying areas where social work could make a significant difference to 'looked after' children.

Clair Lockyer investigates meaningful contact with the child in chapter 12. What does contact mean and how much is sufficient? Serious care reviews and other evidence identify this as a qualifying major area of failing in child protection. The problem with any term that is proceeded by a qualifying word such as 'meaningful,' is left to subjective interpretation. This can mean anything or nothing, creating confusing and inconsistency in the type of contact social workers make in their duty to protect children.

Part 3 gives a range of practice examples of skills intervention where social workers can make a difference by simply changing their approach. Although this section could easily have taken up the entire book it was important to include the preceding chapters that develop social work knowledge to help enhance social work skills and values in this chapter and in particular taking account of the political environment of change and vulnerability.

Gary Castle presents an interesting account of how identity is strengthened through the use of life story work in chapter 13. Life story work is a tool that helps build bridges of fact to help children who have experienced multiple attachments understand who they are and where they come from. Past histories are an essential part of our identity that help to make new attachments as we come to terms with the past to face the future. Although a well-established technique in adoption services Gary takes a new approach to how this can be also incorporated as an established and mandatory function in working with all 'looked after' children.

Chapter 14 presents a fascinating account of the use of 'Talking Mats' in working with disabled children by Peter Holland. Talking Mats is a tool that provides disabled children with a voice to enable professionals to understand their needs and concerns. The Children Act 1989 requires the voice of the child as paramount but how is the voice physically heard. Talking Mats is an example of a technique using an aid to help children communicate their thoughts and feelings in a simple, visual and practical way. They could provide agencies with an effective platform to understand the child. Peter recommends that Talking Mats could also be used with all children as an aid to communication.

In chapter 15, Jacqueline Gaunt explores the technique of contact and seeing the child alone. Social workers need confidence to assert their requirement and see the child alone in a situation of potential conflict or violence. However, we know from research and inspection reports, social workers rarely speak to the child alone. What is it that social workers need to enable them to see the child alone? This is something that Jacqueline investigates and concludes with sound advice.

In the final chapter, Anthony McMurdo explores the power and effectiveness of digital technology in assessment and working with vulnerable children. This is a neglected area of research and practice. Despite the earlier chapter on on-line grooming exposing risks presented to children because of technology, McMurdo presents the alternative positive side. He shows how you can help children engage in difficult discussions through video games where other modes of communication have failed. This is a truly innovative idea to end this book and provide readers with more than mere thoughts but hopefully, good ideas for action.

References

CQC (2011), *Review of Compliance of Winterbourne View*. Regulatory review carried out on the 12th May 2011. London: The Care Quality Commission. July 2011.

DoE (2016) *Children's Social Care Reform: A vision for change*. Department of Education January 2016. Ref. 00008-2016

DoE (2014) *Making the Education of Social Workers consistently Effective*. An independent report by Sir Martin Narey. 13th February 2016. Ref 00082-2014. Department of Education.

DoE (2012) *Safeguarding Children and schools, colleges and Children's Services*. A collection of 7 reviews by Eileen Munro at www.gov.uk/doe

Garrett, P. (2013) *Social Work and Social Theory*. Bristol: Policy Press

DoE (2013) *Step Up to Social Work Programme Evaluation 2012: the regional partnerships and employers perspectives*. Department of Education, DFE-RR290 4th June 2013

DoH (2014) *Social Work Education Review*. An independent review by Professor David Croisdale-Appleby. 27th February 2914. Department of Health.

DCSF (2010) *Children's Select Committee Seventh Report on the Training of Children and Family Social Workers, Session 2008-09*. Department of Children, Schools and Families. 9th March 2010.

Jones, C. (2011) The best and worst of times: reflection on the impact of Radicalism in British social work education in the 1970's in M. Lavalette (ed) *Radical Social Work: Social work at the crossroads*. Bristol: Policy Press.

Jones, R. (2014) *The Story of Baby P: Setting the record straight*. London: Policy Press

McClenoghan, Maeve (2012) *NHS Reform*. The Bureau of Investigative Journalism 12th July 2012

Morgan, N. (2016) *Nicky Morgan unveils plans to transfer children's social work – Press Release*. The Rt Hon Nicky Morgan MP, 14th January 2016. Department of Education

2

How fear, generated by client violence, impacts on child protection social workers

Stephen Brearley

'The oldest and strongest emotion of mankind is fear, and the oldest and strongest kind of fear is fear of the unknown.' (Lovecraft, 1973)

Child protection social workers are frequently put in situations that evoke fear and face the unknown. Given its powerful primordial roots why is fear given so little attention in social work practice?

Introduction

This chapter aims to explore how fear is generated by client violence and the extent to which this impacts on child protection social workers. Is there a need to get to know fear more intimately? Do child protection social workers fear the right thing to the right extent, at the right time and in the right way (Smith, 2005)? If not, then what can be done in the future to address these issues?

In a *Community Care* survey (2011) during a period of 12 months 91% of social workers reported that they held caseloads with hostile parents, 68% stated threats were made to their person, 50% were intimidated on a weekly basis and 26% had threats made to their family. However, despite its prevalence, client violence to social workers is an aversive subject that many prefer not to discuss (Criss, 2009, p. 70). The impacts of which have been relatively neglected and are only recently starting to be addressed in literature (Wosu & Stewart, 2010) (Braescu, 2012). Very few studies concentrate on the social worker's experiences and emotions after experiencing client violence (Macdonald & Sirotich, 2013). But if anger, aggression and hostility feature so frequently in the experiences of social workers should we not engage with this than deny it (Smith, 2010, p. 102)?

Studies have shown that a common effect of direct client violence is an increased feeling of fear (Littlechild, 2008) (Dwyer, 2007) (Smith, 2000). This is a powerful emotion that has the potential to 'irretrievably wound' (Criss, 2009, p. 3) social worker's physiological and psychological health (Macdonald & Sirotich, 2013). The 'culture of silence' (Kleban, 2008) serves to collude to its denial, rather than working with it to achieve better outcomes. (Braescu, 2012)? I came to concentrate on this subject area after experiencing client violence first-hand over the years in numerous settings from residential child care to child protection social work.

Literature review : Client violence

What is client violence?

The definition of what actually constitutes client violence is a contentious issue and presents many challenges (Denney, 2010, p. 1301). The disparity in defining the subject itself is one limitation on the validity of the existing data.

The most commonly used definition within the literature is:

> 'Intentional personal or agency property damage, threats, verbal abuse, attempted physical harm, actual physical harm on social workers by individuals in receipt or formally in receipt of those services' (Newhill, 2003)

Though this is a widely used definition in a range of studies (Song, 2005) (Horwitz, 2008) it must be highlighted that it is not the only definition used. The major difficulty is in encapsulating the full range of potential qualifying behaviours in a concise manner which can produce reliable generalisations. The same violent act may have differential impacts on individual employees (Bowie, 2000) and is thereby received, perceived, processed and potentially reported in vastly contrasting manners (Ringstad, 2005). Alternative definitions include Kemshall & Pritchard's (1996) who defined client violence as 'behaviour that has damaging effects either physically or emotionally on other people'. I prefer Wynne, et al. (1997) definition as 'any incident where a person is abused, threatened or assaulted in circumstances relating to work involving an explicit or implicit challenge to their safety well-being or health'. The broader perspective of this definition shifts the focus from the purely physical and recognises damage done by psychological forms of violence.

There is a growing range of literature on client violence within social work (Macdonald & Sirotich, 2013) (Norris & Kedward, 1990) (Guy & Brady, 1998). An emergent theme is that client violence has become a real yet overlooked part of direct social work practice (Ringstad, 2005). The majority of the literature indicates that it is a regular occurrence and a serious concern in child protection (Spencer & Munch, 2003) (Harris & Leather, 2012). The precise statistics produced from each study vary. NASW (2006) carried out one of the biggest surveys by interviewing 5000 social workers. 47% reported experiencing concerns over their personal safety whilst 30% felt employers did not adequately address these concerns. Rowett (1986) conducted the first major UK study into client violence and found that directors/managers reported very low concerns about this topic. However, when social workers were asked directly ¼ reported to have been assaulted. Leadbetter (1993) also reported on the mismatch of perceptions between managers and front line social workers.

Rey (1996) further added to the issue by reporting that out of a sample 300 interviews 82% of social workers were concerned about client violence with 89% being verbally abused and 23% physically assaulted. Additionally, an OSHA survey (2004) suggested that 48% of non-fatal work place injuries occur in health or social care settings. Whilst the workplace injury rate for social workers is 7 ½ times higher than in private sector (Criss, 2009, p. 10). Newhill (1996) found that from a sample of 1,129 78% of social workers agreed that client violence is significant issue and 52% worried about own safety. .

Students

Studies have shown that there is a high prevalence of client violence experienced by students (Mama, 2001). Criss (2009, p.1) reported 41% of social work students directly experienced client violence during their practicum with 37.5% verbal aggression and 3.5% physical assault. Star (1984) found that client violence was one of the three most worrying issues confronting students on placement. Whilst Lyter and Abbott (2007) reported that 66% of students were fearful of their clients whilst 33% had actually been threatened. However, in contrast Tulley, et al. (1993) found students less likely to experience violence as they were afforded greater protection and were frequently shielded from potentially dangerous practice situations.

Gender

Criss (2009, p. 1) reported that being male is the most significant predictor of client violence. She found that male social workers experienced almost twice the rate of violence for threats of physical harm and verbal abuse. Newhill (1996) supported this stating that male staff may be involved in situations of violence more frequently as males are picked by their managers with more frequency for potentially dangerous situations. This has been a common finding (Brockmann, 2002) (Jayaratne, et al., 2004). Only Song (2005) found contradictory results finding that from his study women are more likely to experience verbal assaults then men.

Experience/Age

Jayaratne (2004) and Beaver(1999) found that the younger the worker the greater the risk. Koritsas (2010) found that workers under the age of 45 were more likely to experience violence. However, Elwood & Rey (1996) found that age did not affect the likelihood of violence.

Settings

Residential social workers were consistently found to be the highest risk of violence with child protection home visits often close behind (Ringstad, 2005) (Leadbetter, 1993). Interestingly, rural locations were more likely to lead to a greater risk of intimidation then metropolitan settings. Koritsas, et al (2010) attributed this to its more subtle application of violence and the social worker's increased likelihood of knowing that service user in the rural setting.

Limitations

However, there are many limitations to these studies which make it difficult to generalise the findings. The majority of these studies rely on self-reporting which may skew the statistical outcome. The studies are also limited by race and gender because most are white, and female between 40-50 years old (Astor, et al., 1998) (Song, 2005).

Self-reporting via questionnaires often rely on small regionalised returns and samples (Macdonald & Sirotich, 2013). Client violence is a particularly subjective and emotive topic whereby individual workers often underreport to give more socially and professionally 'accepted' responses. Additionally, some studies (Song, 2005) (Newhill, 1996) have greater validity due to their larger sample (Mama 2001) . Therefore, is it possible to rely on what the data tells us?

Studies into client violence to social workers also cross national boundaries, for example, from Australia (Maidment, 2003) to Korea (Shin, 2011) Highlighting this as a global phenomenon (Criss, 2009, p. 18)

The common theme running through the literature is the prevalence of client violence and its influence on fear, which is further reinforced by the work of (Huxley, et al., 2005), Littlechild (2005) (Smith, et al., 2004) (Smith, 2006) and Criss (2010). Despite this, existing literature rarely attempts to address the resultant impact on the emotional wellbeing of child protection social workers (Denney, 2010). Therefore, it is important to further explore the influence of fear generated by client violence.

Literature review: Fear

Harris and Leather (2012, p.851) purported that fear needs to be addressed in theory and practice in tackling violence in social care. Fear generated via client violence has been identified as a potentially damaging influence, especially if left unchecked (Schat & Kelloway, 2000) (Barling, 1996). Associated responses include depression, anxiety, high turnover rates and job neglect (Criss, 2009) (Astor, et al., 1998). This highlights the significant relationship between exposure to client violence and the creation of fear (Huxley, et al., 2005) (Littlechild, 2008). But what is fear and what impact does it actually have on the individual child protection social worker?

Fear is a question of degree, perception and use. It can be perceived as a life restricting and diminishing emotional shackle (Cohen, 2003). However, if it is acknowledged and explored it can be a life preserving gift with potential ability to both teach and enrich in equal measure (Smith, 2005, p. 29). The Department of Health (1995) has highlighted the relationship between service user and worker as the most fundamental tool in social work practice. So to what extent does the impact of fear generated from client violence obstruct the individual worker's effectiveness when interacting with service users? Is fear intricately interwoven into the client and practitioner relationship (Stanford, 2010, p. 1072)?

Fear is a complex, multifaceted and multi-layered emotion requiring an interdisciplinary approach from neurobiology, psychology and sociology (Braescu, 2012) but cannot be viewed as disparate discussions but rather overlapping and interlinked.

Neurobiological

Fear is normal and adaptive in neurobiology for human survival and is elicited by internal or external stimuli (Scherer, 2005). It is an unconscious evaluative process that establishes the most appropriate answer to an identified danger. The amygdala is the part of the brain found deep in the temporal lobes within the limbic subcortical system and is said to control the brain's emotion response to stimuli (Fellous, et al., 2002). In response to intense fear the amygdala responds faster than the prefrontal cortex which usually moderates its demand. Emotional actions take place before we know what happens (Braescu, 2012, p. 6). This is evidence of the biological power of the emotion and concept of fear. Goleman (1996) acknowledged that although it is impossible to effectively control this there is a need for more attention to be given to it as a subject within social work (Smith, 2010) (Bion, 1994).

From a biological perspective fear is often automatic and unconscious creating an intuitive response. De Becker (1997) argues that intuition should always be carefully listened to because it arises in response to perceived dangerous stimuli.. Smith (2005) reinforced this by stating that fear has the primary evolutionary purpose to protect us.

So what are the impacts of fear from a neurobiological perception? When frightened the amygdala signals to the adrenal gland to release the hormone cortisol. The hormone is the catalyst for common feelings such increased heart rate, becoming sweaty and that familiar sinking feeling in the stomach (Braescu, 2012). These immediate physiological responses are often not readily distinguishable from one another (Smith, et al., 2004). LeBlanc, et al. (2012) states these responses are associated with impairments in verbal, social and declarative memory. This suggests that stress responses may influence the social worker's appraisal of risk. However, this study also concluded that these responses are reduced when a social worker rapidly habituates to a situation. Therefore when faced with a fearful situation these physical responses lead to the social worker to make an intuitive decision between fight, flight or freeze. The option to freeze is interesting as Bion (1994) has described thalamic fear as being so powerful that it can make thinking impossible. This highlights the link between this response and the evolutionary defence mechanism of some animals who 'play dead' when faced with danger.

De Becker (1997) argued that the inherent nature of child protection social work is in direct conflict with our biological responses to fear. She made a comparison to the animal kingdom by asking which animal would ignore all these biological instincts and yet still enter dangerous situations? Yet this is a situation that child protection social workers have to wrestle with frequently. A common theme in the literature is the need to use this primal biological fear as a positive power to aid preparing, motivating and developing courage (Battersby, 2008) (Brosch, et al. 2008). However, discussion of biological primal fear creates dialectical tensions between its positives and negatives.

Evolutionary theory suggests that fear is needed and natural (Giddens, 1991). However, a singular focus on the biological aspects and effects of fear is crude as it does not consider powerful psychological influences (Smith (2005).

Psychological literature review

'In the mental life nothing that has once been formed may perish... everything is somehow preserved and can be bought back to light in suitable circumstances' (Freud, 1909)

If this is true then intense emotional experiences of fear generated by client violence may be evoked at any time. Therefore, not addressing the individual's ability to psychologically process these emotions will make social workers vulnerable

Several studies have highlighted the importance of how fears are psychologically received and processed as being critical (Smith, 2003) (Crotty, 1998). Whilst Braescu (2012) has stated that neurobiological perspectives of fear are not sufficient alone to explain what human fear is. It has been established that fear generated by client violence is a topic that crosses many layers of the human psyche; from the deep primal responses to the unconscious mind. This is reinforced by Ledoux (2000) who purported that fear has its roots in unconscious process leading to conscious experiences..

From a psychological perspective the relevant stimulus is not the essential piece of information. Instead it is how the stimulus is perceived and psychologically processed that is crucial. Lazarus (1984) reinforces this stating that what is stressful and fearful to one person may not be to another and it is the appraisal of the situation that ultimately determines the outcome for the individual. Not all dangers elicit fear it is only those that resonate personally with us in terms of our needs, values and goals that do (Oatley & Johnson-Laird (1998). Rime (2009) stated that the consequences of fear need to be analysed in the broader context of social interactions. He purported that key to a psychological understanding of fear is the art of negotiating its socially constructed reality.

Power of the imagination

'Fear is pain arising from the anticipation of evil.' Aristotle (384-322 BC)

The argument that psychological fear is a question of personal construction is not a new one. For example, Shakespeare's Hamlet exclaimed 'there is nothing either good or bad but thinking makes it so' (2:2:11). This is a pithy example of the importance of psychological perception in face of fearful or potentially fearful situations. Academic studies support the suggestion that often the worst fear is the imagined fear e.g. the fear of future violence that may occur (Littlechild, 2008). Therefore it becomes even more difficult to create a universal definition of client violence.. This highlights the need for child protection social workers to acknowledge and respect the power of the imagination (Smith, 2005).

Psychodynamics

Established psychodynamic models are used as explanatory vehicles to expand upon the psychological processing of fear generated from client violence (Smith, 2000). Smith, et al. (2004 p. 544) reported that people often refer to themselves in the third person when asked to recall emotions of fear generated in response to an incident of client violence. They suggested that individuals do so to distance themselves from the fear; as if they were acting out a role to keep a 'performing self' distinct from an 'essential self'. This third party disassociation is used to distance themselves from the physical and psychological impacts of the emotion of fear.

The above is an example of a self-created and often unconscious form of psychological defence. A further example includes the perception of splitting your personality so that when faced in a fearful situation a social worker may face a fight to balance their 'coping' and their 'non -coping' self (Smith, 2006). For example, in this type of situation the individual often faces an initial confused rush of tumbling thoughts generated in partnership with their innate biological responses. The worker is left feeling that they have forgotten all that they know even if this is only temporarily until their 'coping self' can come to the forefront and act as rational and logical response to the fearful stimuli (Smith, et al., 2004, p. 545).

Expanding on Freudian concepts of projection Bion (1977) and Klein (1946) suggested that it is possible to split off temporarily undesired parts of the personality and project them into another person. This is called projective identification where an individual unconsciously forces parts of them self into others. Could this be one explanation why the service users sometimes respond with aggression to social workers; projecting and focusing their fear and anger onto them?

Winnicott (1992) purported that projective identification is bidirectional and that social workers themselves may respond to their psychological fears by unconsciously forcing parts of their personality onto the service user. Therefore, perceiving them as more fearful stimuli then is perhaps realistic. Winnicott referred to this as hate transference; a common theme in psychodynamic counselling. Using this concept a social worker may perceive to feel 'hatred' towards their service users. Ringstad's (2005) research reinforced this stating that 23.4% of social workers had committed an aggressive act to a service user in the past year with 4% committing an actual assault. These figures were surprisingly high and may demonstrate projective identification via hate transference. However, Ringstad's research is limited by the small sample size of participants and its reliance upon self-reporting.

Effects of psychological fear

Numerous studies have concluded that fear generated by violence compromises the effectiveness and standards of care provided (Koritsas, et al., 2010). Linking this relationship to negative outcomes ranging from feeling frightened, detached and emotionally exhausted (Rowett, 1986) to being disempowered and intimidated (Littlechild, 2008) to anxiety, loss of confidence, flashbacks and traumatic memories (Smith, et al., 2004). The psychological impact of fear can have dilapidating effects on the individual in both short and long term.

However what appears as a strong theme from the literature is the dangers of long term vicarious trauma due to prolonged and unchecked exposure to fear generated from client violence. Horwitz, (2008, p. 14) has described this as a 'toxic' process that can lead to significant cognitive distortions for the individual overwhelming their adaptive capacities. This is reinforced by Averett & Soper (2011, p. 359) who warn of the dangers of fear limiting an individual's ability to participate in their life, leading to a loss of autonomy and emotional isolation. Further studies by Schat and Kelloway (2000), Guy and Brady (1998) and

Norris (1990) all highlighted the role fear plays in long term damage to the individual social worker if they are not supported to psychologically process their experiences in a positive manner.

The supervision of fear

> 'A thing that has not been understood inevitably reappears like an un-laid ghost... it cannot rest until the mystery has been resolved and spell broken' (Freud, 1909, p. 122)

If individual social workers are unable to deal with the impacts of fear generated from client violence then they may experience a type of 'professional vertigo' (Loughlin, 1992) resulting in feeling deeply unskilled and a loss of professional confidence. After these experiences they are left trying to regain a version of the belief in themselves they once had.

This is where supervisors/managers are critical. Winnicott (1958) stated that the function of the person listening is to believe what they hear so that the teller feels that they have been heard to a level which matches the emotional intensity of their experience. Arguably, the individual does not want superficial reassurances but a combination of availability and attention to a thoughtful consideration of the situation (Smith, 2000). Mere reassurance from the supervisor is not accepted as a successful technique by psychodynamic writers due to the need to trace the patient's anxieties to their source, not drive them underground by reassuring them (Malan, 1979). However, this view is not universally shared, as Phillips (1988) argued there are differentiated types of reassurance and that 'normal reassurance through reality' is better and different from reassurance as abnormal defence which arrest the process of constructive thinking as recognised by Klein (1946).

However, the ideal qualities of a hypothetical supervisor depend on how willing the supervisee is to welcoming acceptable attempts to think about the experiences (Smith 2000). Additionally Horwitz (2008) and Criss (2009) have both highlighted the need for further exploratory research into the impact of factors such as age, ethnicity and gender have on the effectiveness of the supervisory relationship.

There is a need for further research into the impact of vicarious trauma on the supervisors and managers themselves. As humans they cannot be immune to the psychological impacts that front line workers experience. There is a lack of knowledge on the psychological impact on the supervisor and how this may hinder their ability to display the 'ideal' qualities highlighted by Smith (2000).

Sociological aspects of fear

The final aspect to consider is how wider sociological concepts influence fear generated from client violence. Fear is not just neurobiological or psychological it is also shaped by different cultural and historical factors (Furedi, 2007). It is only when all these aspects are considered that a rounded perspective can be obtained..

Throughout our lives we are instructed by society about what to and not to fear e.g. from fairy tales to films (Averett & Soper, 2011, p. 369). This may create a 'cultural script' reflecting specific rules about feelings and meanings which direct the way individual's experience and express fears (Braescu). For example, fears are not just generated from specific dangers but can be elicited via socially constructed means. Glassner (1999) gave the example of widespread hysteria created by the AIDS virus in the 1980s. However, Braescu (2012) has questioned the extent to which cultural scripts are relevant. He argued that individualisation in terms of personal ethics and judgements are more important. This paper suggests these cultural scripts are important in the child protection considering how culturally and politically charged this arena is. Collective socially constructed, yet politically fuelled, 'dangers' such as David Cameron's recent warning of the imprisonment of social workers who fail in cases of child sexual exploitation could be one such example. Fear generated through these influences can have serious repercussions on responses and decisions made by individual child protection social workers.

The media is one driving force for these cultural scripts. Kish-Gephart, et al. (2009) stated that the media is a powerful influence over fear and that this issue is exacerbated by the rapid increase of the effectiveness and availability of technology. With Orwellian undertones, Averett & Soper (2011) warned of media and broadcasts potentially acting as control agents of fear. Building from comments on collective scripts, Jung (1978) purported that there is not only the personal individual unconscious but also a collective unconscious that is socially constructed by societal norms and ingrained expectations. Fear is imprinted in children from the earliest age. Archetypal images found in creative arts, religious beliefs and mythologies were suggested as catalytic examples behind the creation of fears originating from the collective unconscious (Smith, 2005).

The individual and the system: Can we learn from fearful situations?

Serious case reviews (SCRs) evoke the most fearful situations and emotions in child protection. However, it is surprising how SCRs view violence with some ambivalence (Smith, 2005, p. 43). For example, in the SCR of Kimberley Carlile it was concluded that it was 'a fact that he (social worker) was blinded by his incompetence' (Department of Health, 1991). This paper questions the validity of this statement and questions whether the worker was 'in fact' scared. Do failures to address fears on both an individual and organisational level perpetuate events that sadly lead to SCRs?

In later SCRs the propensity and prevalence of client violence is more openly acknowledged and attributed as a catalytic factor. In the aftermath of Baby P Lord Laming specifically discussed the dangers of unpredictable people in the parenting role (UNISON, 2008). The Q family SCR (2015, p 27) explicitly stated that fear was the 'single most pervasive factor' in this case. However, despite acknowledging fear generated from client violence as an orgnaisational failing, its impact on the individual worker's emotions is still not fully acknowledged.

To what extent is this approach compatible with the Health & Safety at Work Act 1974? How many other professions would you be expected to ignore all neurobiological, psychological and sociological fear indictors and continue regardless? Despite fear generated by client violence in child protection there is a cultural expectation, twinned with a statutory responsibility that the relationship with the aggressors will somehow continue. It is hard to think of another profession where the relationship is so inextricably indivisible (Kleban, 2008, p. 27). Does this add to the social worker's psychological emotional isolation?

Fear and ethics

So what drives individual social workers to continue despite these fears? Arguably, social workers often individually operate within the paradigm of virtues ethics (Webb, 2006). Whereby they have the ethical disposition to try and do the best for their service user. This ethical stance operates in contrast and competition to the emotional feelings and responses that are highlighted to be evoked by experiencing fear generated through client violence. This stance is then reinforced by the HCPC code of ethics which stipulates the professional ethical base for individual workers (HCPC, 2008. S1) but fails to specify taking responsibility for one's own safety and well-being.

The power of fear

How does fear generated from client violence interact with situational power dynamics and therefore principles of anti-oppressive practice and anti-discriminatory practice? It is clear that fear generated from client violence has a real and distinct impact on the individual social worker. But this impact, especially if left unchecked, also has the potential to spill over in the relationship between the social worker and the service user. Therefore, altering the already delicate power dynamics of the situation (Dalrymple & Burke, 2008).

Howe (2008) argued that fear generated from client violence in child protection work can lead to both the individual worker and the organisation as a whole operating to a deficit model of risk assessment. This perpetuates and exacerbates the fundamental barriers in engaging in relationships with families. To what extent do social workers counteract their fears by 'hiding' behind paternalistic practice thus becoming more cautious in their practice (Wosu & Stewart, 2010) (Rodgers, 2001)? It is acknowledged that this is likely to be an organisational/governmental response after high profile child deaths (Turbett, 2014). These controlling manageralist policies create anxiety and fear throughout the whole system (Turbett, 2014).. This creates a self-perpetuating and interdependent cycle of fear in the child protection arena as shown by the self-penned model below:

This cycle continues unless something happens to break the loop and increase the emotional understanding, intelligence and awareness of the personal impacts of fear generated from client violence.

Karpman's drama triangle (1968) can be used to compliment the above diagrammatical explanation to enhance the understanding of how the individual social worker is affected. This model can be used to show how quickly and easily fear can alter the power dynamics of the situation leading to perceived oppressive practice. It shows how the social worker can flip from being perceived as being a rescuer to victim to persecutor due to the powerful, dynamic and amorphous influence of the emotion of fear generated through client violence (Smith, 2010, p. 104).

Conclusions and suggestions for practice

1. Practical measures

An increased attention should be given to the small daily practical measures that can reduce the regularity of social workers being in positions where they experience client violence.

These measures include regularly updating colleagues of movements, the use of alarms and phones, buddy systems and increasing the regularity of joint visits. These are simple considerations but have been reported to be often flouted (Braithwaite, 2001, p. 78). These measures should be in place anyway but this paper highlights their importance and link with the creation of a psychologically 'safe base'.

Organisational policy and direction on these issues may increase their individual effectiveness (Newhill, 2003). Especially as some studies have reported social workers to have a lack of confidence and knowledge of their organisations ability to respond to their concerns and fear regarding their own safety (Criss, 2009) (Littlechild, 2008). This may be achieved through involving front line workers in senior management prevention strategies giving prominence to self-care strategies. Koritsas (2010) has even reported how improving client waiting times and reading materials in the office/waiting rooms can decrease likelihood of client violence and reduce fears.

2. Training/Education

Strongly linked to the above call for intervention strategies at an organisational level is the need to develop and implement specific prevention programmes on education and treatment for social workers who have experienced fear generated by client violence (Shin, 2011).

This includes a recommendation for fear generated by client violence to receive greater attention in social work education. Newhill (1996) found that only 4% of students interviewed recalled receiving training on their graduate programme regarding client violence whilst 79% said they felt they needed more training. Similar findings were reported by Elwood and Rey (1999). Reeser and Wertkin (2001) conducted a study and found that 77% of child protection directors felt that safety content should be fully integrated in the curriculum to a great extent. Faria & Kendra (2007) found 68% of social work schools taught safety in their curriculum. This chapter calls for client violence and fear to receive more attention in training and education programmes with a greater effort to coordinate these across the social work curriculum and on placement.

3. Supervision

It is important that social workers need skilled and sensitive supervision more than ever when faced with serious threat and fearful situations (Denney 2010). A clear theme running through the literature is the need for a greater emotional intelligence and understanding around violence and fear. This chapter agrees that making sense of these feelings help to ameliorate the negative effects (Atkinson, 1991).

Kadushin's (1976) model of supervision identified the three functions of social work supervision as administrative, educational and supportive. I would recommend using supervision as the professional platform to explore the biological, psychological and sociological aspects of fear generated by client violence impacts on the individual child protection social worker. There is a greater need for research into how the individual aspects of the supervisor/supervisee impact on their relationship e.g. ethnicity and gender. However, Kleban (2008) has suggested that this type of supervision may be best addressed and provided outside of the organisations themselves.

4. Cultural organisational shift

There is a need for a cultural shift in the way the child protection system interacts with and perceives the emotion of fear generated by client violence. The recommendations made above cannot be used in isolation and this paper is

Cycle of fear

- Child protection intervention: Creates fear in the service user
- Client violence
- Creates fear in individual social worker
- Creates fearful response from organisation
- Paternalistic and oppressive practice responses

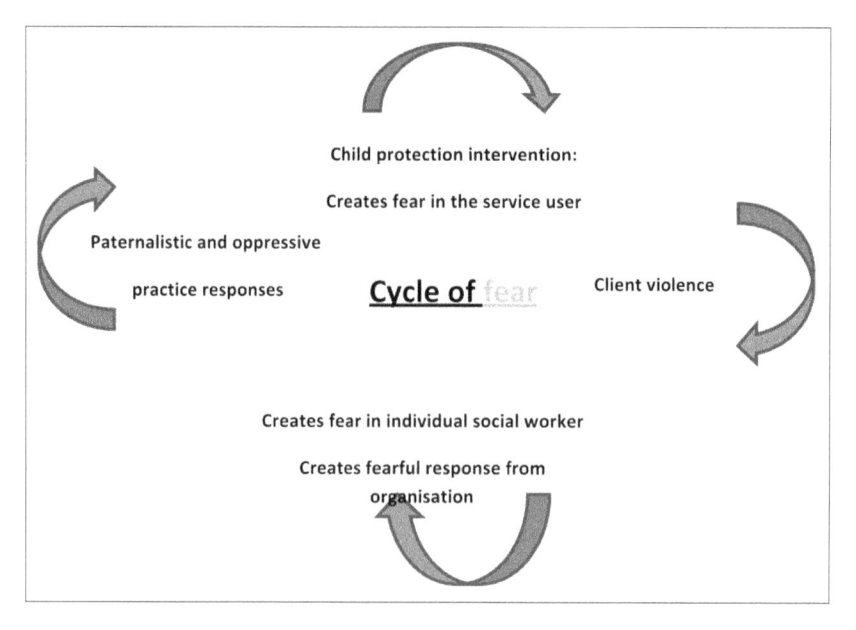

hopeful that they can be used in tandem to change the present culture towards fear; from one of silence to one of support (Kleban 2008). Perhaps the child protection system needs to shine a light on itself to expose its own 'monsters' first before the cycle of fear has a chance of being broken? Perhaps, like in many horror movies, once the 'monster' is seen in the cold light of day it is not anywhere near as scary?

To ignore the irrational, emotional and psychological relationship between violence and fear, and ultimately in human relationships, is to severely limit the scope of child protection practice (Dwyer, 2007, p. 53). This chapter is hopeful that the above collation of findings from literature and subsequent recommendations will highlight the importance of understanding the relationship between client violence and fear. Although it is acknowledged that client violence is not the only way fear is generated a clear correlation between the two has been established.

Fear is a layered and complex emotion involving rational and irrational human behaviours and is therefore impossible to reliably predict or eliminate (Smith 2005). Therefore, the goal is not to eradicate fear but to harness its positive and protective qualities by at first taking the time to understand it.

Fear has been shown to be a powerful and complex emotion that is responsive to biological, psychological and sociological stimuli. If left unchecked it has the potential to be a destructive and obstructive influence on child protection social workers. However, although there is a clear tension between the positive and negative use of fear generated through direct experience with client violence (Folkman & Mosowitz, 2000). It is impossible to eradicate this primal force

(Brockmann, 2002) but this chapter supports the need to act upon this topic to generate a greater awareness and understanding amongst child protection social workers. This may prove beneficial to their emotional wellbeing, effectiveness and longevity in the job and ultimately on the service they can provide to those who need it most.

Though first quoted 171 years ago individual workers and even the child protection system itself may benefit from the wisdom of Kierkegaard (1844):

'He therefore who has learned rightly to be in dread has learned the most important thing'

References

Aristotle, 384-322bce. *Unknown.* s.l.:s.n.

Astor, R., Behre, W., Wallace, J. & Fravil, K., 1998. School social workers and school violence: personal safety, training and violence programs. *Social Work,* 43, 223-233.

Atkinson, J., 1991. Worker reaction to client assault. *Smith College Studies in Social Work,* 62, 34-42.

Averett, P. & Soper, D., 2011. Sometimes I am afraid: an autoethnography of resistance and compliance. *The Qualitative Report ,* 16(2), 358-376.

Barling, J., 1996. The prediction, experience and consequences of workplace violence. In: E. Bulatao & G. Vandenbos, eds. *Violence in the workplace.* Washington DC: American Psychological Association , 29-49.

Battersby, D., 2008. *www.ezinearticles.com.* Available at: www.ezinearticles.com/?the-positive-power-of-fear&id=1235324 [Accessed 27th March 2015].

Beaver, H., 1999. *Client violence against professional social workers: frequency, worker characteristics, and impacts on job satisfaction, burn out and health,* s.l.: University of Arkansas.

Bion, W., 1977. Attention and interpretation . In: W. Bion & J. Aronson, eds. *Seven Servants.* New York: s.n., p. 124.

Bion, W., 1994. *Clinical Seminars and Other Works.* London: Karnac.

Bowie, V., 2000. Defining Violence. In: M. Gill, B. Fisher & V. Bowie, eds. *Violence at Work.* London: Macmillan.

Braescu, P., 2012. The blind side of mild fear. *Journal of social work practice,* 26(1), 5-13.

Braithwaite, R., 2001. *Managing aggression.* London: Routledge .

Brockmann, M., 2002. New perspectives on violence in social care. *Journal of Social Work,* 2, 29-44.

Brosch, T., Sanders, D. P. G. & Scherer, K., 2008. Beyond fear: rapid spatial orienting toward positive emotional stimuli. *Psychological Science,* 19(4), 362-370.

Cohen, P., 2003. *Fear busting: a proven plan to beat fear and change your life.* London: Element.

Community Care, 2011. *Community Care Inform*. [Online] Available at: http://www.communitycare.co.uk/2011/09/30/social-workers-struggle-with-hostile-and-intimidating-parents/ [Accessed 3rd March November].

Criss, P., 2009. *Prevalence of client violence against social work students and its effects on fear of future violence, occupational commitment and career withdrawal intentions*, s.l.: University of South Florida .

Crotty, M., 1998. *The foundations of social research: meaning and perspective in the research process*. London: Sage.

Dalrymple, J. & Burke, B., 2008. *Anti-oppressive practice: social care and the law*. 2nd ed. Maidenhead: Open University Press.

De Becker, G., 1997. *The Gift of Fear: survival signals that protect us from violence*. London: Bloomsbury.

Denney, D., 2010. Violence and social care staff: positive and negative approaches to risk. *British Journal of Social Work*, 40, 1297-1313.

Department of Health, 1991. *Child abuse: a study of inquiry reports* , London: HMSO.

Department of Health, 1995. *Child Protection: messages from research*, London: HMSO .

Dewey, J. & Tufts, J., 2012. *www.gutenberg.org*. [Online] Available at: http://www.gutenberg.org/files/39551/39551-h/39551-h.htm [Accessed 27th March 2015].

Dwyer, S., 2007. The emotional impact of social work practice. *Journal of Social Work Practice*, 21(1), 49-60.

Elwood, A. & Rey, L., 1996. Awareness and fear of violence among medical and social work students. *Family Medicine*, 28, 488-492.

Faria, G. & Kendra, M., 2007. Safety education: a study of undergraduate social work programs. *Journal of Baccalaureate Social Work*, 12, 141-153.

Fellous, J., Armony, J. & Ledoux, J., 2002. Emotional circuits and computational neuroscience. In: M. Arbib, ed. *The Handbook of Brain theory and Neural Networks*. s.l.:MIT Press, 356-361.

Folkman, S. & Mosowitz, J., 2000. Positive affect and the other side of coping. *American Psychologist*, 55(6), 647-654.

Fordham, F., 1966. *An introduction to Jung's psychology*. London: Penguin.

Freud, S., 1909. *Analysis of a phobia in a five year old boy*. 1955 ed. London: Hogarth Press.

Freud, S., 1953. *Three essays on the theory of sexuality in:*. London: Hogarth Press.

Furedi, F., 2007. *www.frankfuredi.com*. [Online] Available at: http://www.frankfuredi.com/pdf/fearessay-20070404.pdf [Accessed 27th March 2015].

Giddens, A., 1991. *Modernity and self identity*. Cambridge: Policy Press.

Glassner, B., 1999. The construction of fear. *Qualitative Sociology*, 22(4), 301-309.

Goleman, D., 1996. *Emotional Intelligence*. London: Bloombury.

Harris, B. & Leather, P., 2012. Levels and consequences of exposure to service user violence: evidence from a sample of UK social care staff. *British Journal of Social Work*, 42, 851-869.

Health and Care Professions Council, 2008. *http://www.hpc-uk.org/*. [Online] Available at: http://www.hcpc-uk.org/assets/documents/10003B6EStandardsofconduct,perform

anceandethics.pdf [Accessed 27th March 2015].

Health and Safety at Work Act, 1974. *www.legislation.gov.uk*. [Online] Available at: http://www.legislation.gov.uk/ukpga/1974/37/contents [Accessed 27th March 2015].

Horwitz, M., 2008. Work related trauma effects in child prorection social workers. *Journal of Social Service Research*, 32(3), 1-18.

Howe, D., 1995. *Attachment Theory for Social Work Practice*. 1st ed. Basingstoke: Palgrave.

Howe, D., 2008. Child abuse and the bureaucratisation of social work. *The Sociological Review*, 40(3), 491-508.

Huxley, P. et al., 2005. Stress and pressures in mental health social work: the worker speaks. *British Journal of Social Work*, 40, 1063-79.

Isle of Wight Children's Safeguarding Board, 2015. *Q Family Serious Case Review*, s.l.: IOWSCB.

Jayaratne, S., Croxton, T. & Mattison, D., 2004. A national survey of violence in practice of social work. *Families in Society*, 85, 445-454.

Jung, C., 1978. *Man and his symbols*. London: Picador.

Kadushin, A., 1976. *Supervision in social work*. New York: Columbia University.

Karpman, S., 1968. Fairy Tales and script drama analysis. *Transactional Analysis*, 26, 39-44.

Kemshall, H. & Pritchard, J., 1996. *Good practice in risk assessment and risk management*. London: Jessica Kingsley.

Kierkegaard, S., 1844. *The Concept of Anxiety: A Simple Psychologically Orienting Deliberation on the Dogmatic Issue of Hereditary Sin*. Copenhagen: s.n.

Kish-Gephart, J., Detert, J., Klebe-Travino, L. & Edmonson, A., 2009. Silenced by fear: the nature, sources and consequences of feat at work. *Research in Organisational Behaviour*, 29, 163-193.

Kleban, I., 2008. *The effects of critical incident stressors on front line child protection workers*, Hamilton, Ontario: McMaster University.

Klein, M., 1946. *Notes on some schizoid mechanisms in: envy and gratitude and other works*. London: Virago Press.

Koritsas, S., Coles, J. & Boyle, M., 2010. Workplace violence towards social workers: the Australian experience. *British Journal of Social Work*, 40, 257-271.

Laird, S., 2013. *Child Protection: managing conflict, hostility and aggression*. 1st ed. Bristol: The Policy Press.

Laming, L., 2003. *The Victoria Climbié Inquiry: report of an inquiry report by Lord Laming*, London: TSO.

Lazarus, R. F. S., 1984. *Stress, appraisal and coping*. New York: Springer.

Leadbetter, D., 1993. Trends in assaults in social work staff: the experience of one Scottish department. *British Journal of Social Work*, 23, 613-628.

LeBlanc, V., Regehr, C., Shlonsky, A. & Bobo, M., 2012. Stress responses and decision making in child protection workers faced with high conflict situations. *Child Abuse and Neglect*, 36, 404-412.

Ledoux, J., 2000. Emotion circuits in the brain. *Annual Review of Neuroscience*, 23, 155-184.

Littlechild, B., 2008. Child Protection Social Work: risks of fears and fears of risks - impossible tasks from impossible goals. *Social Policy and Administration*, 42(6), 662-675.

Littlechild, B., 2013. *Community Care Inform*. [Online] Available at: www.ccinform.co.uk/research/professional-dangerousness [Accessed 3rd March 2015].

Local Safeguarding Children Board Haringey , 2009. *Serious Case Review: Baby Peter*, London: LSCB Haringey .

Loughlin, B., 1992. Supervision in the face of no cure - working on the boundary. *Journal of social work practice*, 6(2), 111-116.

Lovecraft, H., 1973. *Supernatural Horror in Literature*. New York: Dover.

Lyter, S. & Abbott, A., 2007. Home visits in a violent world. *The Clinical Supervisor*, 26, 17-33.

Macdonald, G. & Sirotich, F., 2013. Violence in the social work workplace. *International Social Work*, 48(6), 772-781.

Maidment, J., 2003. Problems experienced by students on field placement: using research findings to inform curriculum design and content. *Australian Social Work*, 56, 50-60.

Malan, D., 1979. *Individual psychotherapy and the science of psychodynamics*. London: Butterworth-Heinemann.

Mama, R., 2001. Violence in the field: experiences of students and supervisors. *Journal of Baccalaureate Social Work*, 7, 17-26.

NASW, 2006. *Workforce Studies & Centre for Health Workforce Studies*, New York : NASW & University of Albany .

Newhill, C., 1996. Prevalence and risk factors for client violence towards social workers. *Families in Society*, 77, 488-496.

Newhill, C., 2003. *Client violence in social work practice: prevention, intervention and research*. New York: Guilford Press.

Newhill, C. & Wexler, S., 1997. Client violence towards children and youth services social workers. *Children and Youth Services Review*, 19, 195-212.

Norris, D. & Kedward, C., 1990. *Violence against social workers: the implication for practice*. London: Jessica Kingsley.

Oatley, K., 2009. Communication to self and others: emotional experience and its skills. *Emotion Review*, 1(3), 206-213.

Oatley, K. & Johnson-Laird, P., 1998. The communicative theory of emotions. In: J. Jenkins, K. Oatley & N. Stein, eds. *Human emotions: A Reader*. Oxford: Blackwell, 84-98.

Occupational Safety and Health Administration, 2004. *www.osha-slc.gov.com*. [Online] Available at: www.osha-slc.gov/SLTC/workplaceviolence/healthcare [Accessed 27th March 2015].

Phillips, A., 1988. *Winnicott*. London: Fontana.

Reeser, L. & Wertkin, R., 2001. Safety training in social work education: a national survey. *Journal of Teaching in Social Work*, 21, 95-113.

Rey, L., 1996. What social workers need to know about client violence. *Families in Society*, 77, 33-40.

Rime, B., 2009. Emotion elicits the social sharing of information: theory and empirical review. *Emotion Review*, 1(1), 60-85.

Ringstad, R., 2005. Conflict in the workplace: social workers as victims and perpetrators.

Social Work, 50(4), 305-313.

Rodgers, A., 2001. Nurture, bureaucracy and rebalancing the mind and heart. *Journal of Social Work Practice*, 14(1), 17-26.

Rowett, C., 1986. *Violence in Social Work: a research study of violence in the context of local authority social work*, s.l.: University of Cambridge.

Schat, A. & Kelloway, K., 2000. Effects of perceived control on the outcomes of workplace aggression and violence. *Journal of Occupational Health Psychology*, 5, 386-402.

Scherer, K., 2005. What are emotions? How can they be measured?. *Social Science Information*, 44(4), 695-729.

Shakespeare, W., n.d. *Hamlet*. s.l.:s.n.

Shin, J., 2011. Client violence and its negative impacts on work attitudes of child protection workers compared to community service workers. *Journal of Interpersonal Violence*, 26(16), 3338-3360.

Smith, M., 2000. Supervision of fear in social work. A re-evaluation of reassurance. *Journal of Social Work Practice*, 14(1), 17-26.

Smith, M., 2000. Supervision of fear in social work: a re-evaluation of reassurance. *Journal of Social Work Practice*, 14(1), 17-26.

Smith, M., 2003. Gorgons, cars and the frightful fiend: representations of fear in social work and counselling. *Journal of Social Work Practice*, 17(2), 153-162.

Smith, M., 2005. *Surviving Fears in Health and Social Care*. London: Jessica Kingsley.

Smith, M., 2006. Too little fear can kill you. Staying alive as a social worker. *Journal of Social Work Practice*, 20(1), 69-81.

Smith, M., 2010. Sustaining Relationships: working with strong feelings. In: G. Ruch, D. Turney & A. Ward, eds. *Relationship Based Social Work*. London: Jessica Kingsley, 102-117.

Smith, M., Nursten, J. & McMahon, L., 2004. Social worker' responses to experiences of fear. *British Journal of Social Work*, 34, 541-559.

Snow, K., 1994. Aggression: Part of the Job? The psychological impact of aggression on child and youth workers. *Journal of Child and Youth Care*, 9, 11-29.

Song, K., 2005. *Prevalence of client violence toward child and family social workers and its effects on burnout, organisational commitment and turnover interntion: a structural equation modelling approach*, s.l.: Columbia University.

Spencer, P. & Munch, S., 2003. Client violence towards social workers: the role of management in community mental health programs. *Social Work*, 48, 532-545.

Stanford, S., 2010. 'Speaking back' to fear: responding to the moral dilemmas of risk in social work practice. *British Journal of Social Work*, 40, 1065-1080.

Stanley, J. & Goddard, S., 2002. *In the firing line: violence and power in child protection work*. Chichester: Wiley.

Star, B., 1984. Patient Violence/Therapist Safety. *Social Work*, 29, 225-230.

Taylor, C. & White, S., 2006. Knowledge and reasoning in social work educating for humane judgement. *British Journal of Social Work*, 36, 937-954.

Turbett, C., 2014. *Doing Radical Social Work*. 1st ed. Basingstoke: Palgrave.

UNISON, 2008. *Summary of Unison's memorandum to Lord Laming inquiry into safeguarding of children*, London: Unison.

Webb, S., 2006. *Social work in a risk society.* Basingstoke: Palgrave.

Winnicot, D., 1992. Hate in countertransference. In: D. Winnicot, ed. *Through Paediatrics to psychoanalysis.* London: Karnac.

Winnicott, D., 1958. *The capacity to be alone in the maturational process and the facilitating environment.* 1990 edition ed. London : Karnac.

Wosu, H. & Stewart, J., 2010. *Engaging with involuntary service users: a literature review and case study* , Edinburgh : The Local Authority Research Council Initiative .

Wynne, R., Clarkin, N., Cox, T. & Griffiths, A., 1997. *Guidance on the prevention of violence at work,* Luxembourg : European Commission.

3
A contemporary discourse of social work decision-making

Leo Harverson

Introduction

This chapter focuses on the theme of decision-making in social work. Decision-making is an important aspect of social work practice because the actions or inactions that arise from social workers' reasoning processes have a direct impact on service users (Taylor, 2013). I will not define what constitutes a 'good decision' in terms of social work. The term 'good decision' is intrinsically subjective, dependent upon circumstances and the respective standpoint of the individual social worker, family, child and organizational contexts. However it is a phenomenon often heard when the media reports on social work performance.

Instead, the aim is to examine and review the development of social work's contemporary discourse around the decision-making process. The purpose of doing so is not only to critically consider implications for practice, but also to consider factors that are not sufficiently articulated or well developed. Given the extensive and contested nature of this topic, it is acknowledged that in addressing this issue, no claim has been made to it being authoritative or definitive. For the purpose of consistency, the terms 'him'/'he'/'his' are used to refer to a social worker.

The practice context of decision-making in social work

The social worker's role is led by statutory guidance and operates within a context of legal, professional and bureaucratic expectations, all of which may impact on his reasoning. In addition, the families and children who use services are likely to have expectations of consistency in social worker's decision-making, and also expect the subtleties of their problems demand unique sensitivity. The newly revised document *Working Together to Safeguard Children (2015)* sets out pivotal guidance to assessment practice.

At base level, decision-making in social work has relevance to the statutory framework, legislation and case law that underpin the professional task. Although a process of constant revision means that law continually changes and evolves, the equitable application of the law is a basic expectation within democratic society and service users should expect fair treatment (Dale et al, 2005). In this sense, social workers need to ensure their decision-making reflects and corresponds to the legal framework (e.g. balancing Parental Responsibility against the individual Human Rights of the child). This is affirmed by a code that endorses a principle for social workers to

> '...make judgements based on balanced and considered reasoning, maintaining awareness of the impact of their own values, prejudices and conflicts of interest on their practice and on other people' (BASW, 2014:10).

Through a Professional Capabilities Framework (TCSW, 2012), standards in respect of professionalism, ethical decision-making, rights, justice and judgement in intervention further embed a principle of decision-making that corresponds to an equitable application of law.

In addition, the professional conduct standards of the regulating body for social workers in the UK also places a clear emphasis on registrants to make 'informed and reasonable decisions' (HCPC, 2012:5).

Due to the potential legal and ethical implications of his reasoning, the social worker's decision-making should be consistent yet flexible enough to take account of changing conditions. For example, differences in decisions made under The Children Act at Child in Need (1989:s17) and Child Protection (1989:s47) levels (Platt and Turney, 2014, Spratt, 2000).

The ethics of decision-making: An elemental problem

At an early stage, student social workers are encouraged to consider the potential interplay between law, ethics, professionalism and bureaucracy. Through examination of this interplay, the student develops an understanding that the best interests and welfare of the child (The Children Act, 1989) are fraught with ethical and value dilemmas that conflict with practice expectations. It is therefore accepted that the ethics of decision-making are an intrinsic feature of social work.

A social worker might adopt a 'consequentialist approach' to their practice in which the outcome or implications of an act determines it's virtue, or they may seek to employ a utilitarian stance, acting in the least detrimental way or to maximise good. An essential point remains: ethical approaches in themselves do not necessarily provide the 'answer'.

One of the most pertinent examples of this can be found in the controversial decision to remove a child from their family. When taking the decision to seek or recommend the removal of a child, a social worker must consider whether the removal will have a greater impact on the child than the potential harm resulting from the alternatives. It is possible that neither option is ethical or satisfactory, either for the child, family, social worker or Local Authority. In part, this is due to the difficulty of predicting the outcome of alternatives (i.e. what might have happened if a different decision had been made).

Although propositions have been made that such dilemmas can be negotiated through the considered application of advocacy and critical reflection in social work practice (Houston, 2003), the same basic issue prevails:

> '...often there is no outcome that satisfies everyone and that some people feel destroyed by what social workers have to do is a painful truth ...' (Ferguson, 2011:150)

Ethical decision-making does not therefore bring about definitively 'right' decisions, and furthermore, leads us to an inherent and existential problem: Social work decision-making is not about arriving at an objectively correct decision. Instead, it is about achieving the best possible decision in the prevailing circumstances at a given time.

Contemporary discourse around decision-making in social work has focussed on the analytical and intuitive processes of reasoning. The argument I put forward here is that the focus on the discourse between analytical and intuitive reasoning is a consequence of the same existential dilemma. As such, it potentially represents a false quest for an empirical approach to decision-making in social work.

The discourse of decision-making in social work

As with debates about the ethics of decision-making, insights drawn from social psychology have provided significant material relevant to the development of studies in decision-making and reasoning in social work. Before exploring the impact that material from social psychology has had, I will illustrate one particular notion easily overlooked.

Historically the prevailing view among social scientists is that human beings behave rationally (Frank, 1996). That is, (notwithstanding the information available), people make sound and reasoned judgements. However Frank (1996) illustrates that such behavioural models are flawed. A rational model might account for people deciding to buy economical vehicles when fuel prices are high, but the same model does not adequately account for charitable giving.

In addition, a rational model of behaviour does not explain why people fail to evaluate gains and losses when they are paired, and frequently people attach greater importance to losses than gains, even when the net result is an overall gain, as the following succinctly illustrates:

> 'Suppose you get an unexpected gift of $100 and then you return from vacation to find an $80 invoice from the city for the repair of a broken water line on your property. According to the rational choice model, you should regard the occurrence

of these two events as a good thing, because their net effect is a $20 increase in your total wealth' (Frank, 1996:137).

This may seem an unusual example however the tendency to assume people are perfectly rational is introduced as a useful caveat in considering decision-making in social work; by virtue of being human, we cannot assume social workers have an innate capacity to be rational.

Influential research in social psychology has shown that 'heuristic principles' often unconsciously affect decision-making (Kahneman & Tversky, 1982). A heuristic approach seeks to simplify the complexities of a given task to its rudimentary details, thereby allowing a person to reach a judgement or conclusion that is satisfactory with relative ease. Heuristic approaches are therefore essentially about simplifying an issue, and we should note that this might be an uncomfortable truth for service users who would expect thoroughness and rigor. The advantage of this 'rule of thumb' approach is that by reducing the number of factors being considered, the mental effort required in reasoning is much reduced. While a heuristic method has advantages, there is also the potential for heuristics to lead to 'severe and systematic errors' in reasoning (ibid:3).

Kahneman & Tversky (1982) describe three distinct forms of 'bias' that arise through heuristics: Firstly, the 'representativeness' heuristic (ibid:4), in which additional levels of detail that make something statistically less likely, are misconceived as making it more likely. Secondly, the 'availability' heuristic (ibid:11), where people make judgements of likelihood based on the ease of recalling first (or later) examples to mind. Thirdly they describe the 'adjustment and anchoring' heuristic (ibid:14) characterised by people's tendency to make estimates relative to the initial information they are given i.e. the estimates they make in response to an initial value are biased by the initial value itself.

Stein and Rzepnicki (1984) provide an early example of Kahneman & Tversky's research on heuristic biases being applied to Social Work practice. Describing decision-making in relation to child welfare services, Stein and Rzepnicki note that; 'the vividness of information influences recall' (1984:20). Although the vast majority of Social Work interventions may lead to positive outcomes, these cases rarely achieve the detailed media coverage that alleged failings attract. The authors observe that the media is therefore prone to overexposing negative events, and as a consequence, the ease with which we recall these negative cases can contribute to distortions in estimating their prevalence. To some extent, this view may explain significant rises in the number of court applications to protect vulnerable children following media coverage of the second Serious Case Review into the death of baby Peter Connolly (Haringey LSCB, 2009). A net effect of the attention the case received was an increased recognition of chronic neglect (CAFCASS, 2012).

In addition, Stein and Rzepnicki (1984) draw attention to another influence that potentially distorts the reasoning and decision-making of practitioners. The parameters of child welfare and social work are negatively defined or deficit-based. That is, professionals are typically only involved with families where there is something perceived to be wrong. (Stein and Rzepnicki, 1984:20).

More recently, Munro (1999) considered heuristic principles in relation to errors of reasoning by social workers in child protection work. Drawing on the work of Hammond (1996), Munro's paper delineates two forms of thinking that are critical to decision-making: 'analytical reasoning', grounded in clear, methodological process, and 'intuitive reasoning', an often unconscious and seemingly unsystematic approach (Munro, 1999). Although 'often presented as rival forms of thought' (ibid:746), Hammond's alternative contribution describes these processes in terms of a continuum (1996). Also influenced by Hammond (1996), DeBortoli and Dolan (2014) provide a helpfully succinct explanation of this 'Cognitive Continuum Theory (CCT)'.

'The strengths of intuition are displayed in situations needing a rapid digest of numerous factors, such as in human interactions' (Munro 1999:746), but as outlined above, this has the potential to be flawed by associated biases. In contrast, analytical reasoning is thorough and tenable, however a potential criticism of this approach is that; '...there will always be too many unknown variables to disturb the picture and to falsify the precise predictions of analytic reasoning based only on the known variables.' (ibid. p746).

Munro's review began with a hypothesis that mistakes repeatedly occurred, leading to the failings examined in each of the 45 case reviews and inquiries. Key to this hypothesis was a view that such failures were a consequence of common flaws in thinking processes. The review found that in a sizeable proportion of cases, workers did not revise their judgements with sufficient speed and 'the current risk assessment of a family had a major influence on responses to new evidence' (ibid:748). In cases where professionals did revise their judgements or assessment of risk, it was overwhelmingly apparent that this was a result of a significant concern such as injury to a child (ibid:750).

Furthermore, the review found that the professionals' inaccuracy in assessing risk was due to utilising limited information (ibid:751).

The findings outlined above are indicative of heuristic thinking and professionals' preference away from analytic reasoning. Although the research does not condemn either and accepts the necessity to distil the process of reasoning in complex judgements, the conclusion is cautionary: 'One weakness of intuitive reasoning is that it tends to be biased in the information it draws on. It tends to be biased towards that which is vivid, concrete, emotive and either the first or most recent.' (ibid:756).

In subsequent documentary analysis concerning the application of intuitive and analytical reasoning, the methodology of Munro's 1999 review has been questioned. A distinct criticism is that by choosing to examine inquiry findings in cases where errors led to serious consequences (such as child deaths), the cases were not characteristic of *most* social work (Hackett & Taylor, 2014).

Hackett & Taylor (2014) sought to remedy this perceived shortcoming by analysing the decision-making processes in a sample of 98 Core Assessments. Although the authors address issues of analytic and intuitive reasoning, they adopt an integrative approach to the latter, with analytic reasoning being contrasted against 'experiential' reasoning. This is justified by an understanding that increasing expertise & familiarity leads analytic reasoning to be assimilated and thus become part of a worker's intuitive repertoire.

In their analysis of the Core Assessments, the authors found elements of experiential decision-making (Hackett & Taylor, 2014:2188). Furthermore, 45 of the 98 Core Assessments showed evidence of analytical decision-making, and it was noted that this never occurred in isolation (i.e. analytical decision-making occurred in conjunction with experiential decision-making processes).

This led the authors to conclude that 'analytical decision making was used alongside experiential decision making in such a way as to provide evidence for decisions already taken intuitively' (ibid:2192).

The authors were also able to evidence that the intuitive reasoning processes typical of experiential decision-making were predominant in certain conditions. These conditions included (but were not limited to); circumstances where practitioners did not have 'action/feedback loops' to inform them of the consequences of their decisions, and critically; circumstances where the type of case or characterising issue was familiar to the practitioner (Hackett & Taylor, 2014:2196). This latter point emphasises when social work practitioners are less familiar with the defining nature of a case, they are more likely to use analytical reasoning.

Although the research is enlightening to the discourse on decision-making, it does have it's own limitations. In their conclusion Hackett & Taylor acknowledge that due to the methodology of the research partly relying on retrospective interviews, it is possible that the social workers' decisions may be subject to 'post-hoc rationalisation' (2014:2198). If indeed this was the case it may be symptomatic of the anxious 'existential dilemma' social workers have to arrive at an objectively 'right' answer.

The revelation that analytical reasoning was used to substantiate conclusions reached intuitively was used to partially inform DeBortoli and Dolan's critique of the 'Cognitive Continuum Theory' (2014:6) However, both Hackett & Taylor and DeBortoli & Dolan's work appear to have overlooked something significant. An interpretation of this observation is that it substantiates a view that the decisions workers make are susceptible to 'confirmation bias' i.e. 'when professionals search only for information that supports their preferred view' (Burton, 2009:4).

The decision-making process in social work has been examined further still in recent research commissioned by the Department for Education. The research process involved scrutiny of decision-making specifically at the 'front door' of Child Protection services (Kirkman & Melrose, 2014). The research was comprised of site visits to local authorities (and subsequent analysis of findings in the field), together with reviews of literature from behavioural/psychological sciences and literature explicitly pertaining to decision-making in Child Protection work.

Kirkman and Melrose identified four factors 'that complicate or reduce the efficiency' in social workers decision-making (Kirkman & Melrose, 2014:4). In summary, these factors are:

1. Workload and time pressures leading workers to be more reliant on intuition
2. The frequent necessity for consecutive decisions contributing to workers experiencing 'decision fatigue'
3. Opportunity for analysis of information being diminished by the need for workers to spend considerable effort to pore over the low quality of information provided to them
4. Behavioural biases affecting the workers ability to make objective judgements

In response to the first factor, the authors affirm that; 'Contrary to common understanding of the word, intuition is not primarily innate. Intuitive judgements are rapid, automatic and generally unconscious responses to events based on a wide-range of prior knowledge and experience gained over a lifetime.' (Kirkman & Melrose, 2014:18)

In respect of the second factor, the term 'decision fatigue' is used to define the depletion in a social worker's capacity to make decisions (Kirkman & Melrose, 2014:16). This necessity for continual and 'sequential decision-making' is exhausting and may even contribute to professionals becoming averse to making decisions altogether (ibid:29). It is not difficult to comprehend that due to the precedent for social work services typically operating Monday to Friday, 9am to 5pm, decisions taken later in the week or day may not be as robust, with poor outcomes. Furthermore, this of course does not reflect that a significant number of social workers report working considerably more than their contracted hours (Burke, 2012), and that by doing so, this effect might be exacerbated.

The third factor yields additional learning points. One such observation was that 'salient information is often buried' (Kirkman and Melrose, 2014:31) and depending on the priorities of the profession or source providing it, additional efforts are often necessary to extract critical details.

The authors recognise that issues of information quality are inevitable. By way of example they note that this is typified by the limitations of anonymous referral information. However, in my own view this is also an intrinsic feature of a system that emphasises child welfare and safeguarding are everybody's responsibility (4LSCB, 2007). Adopting a social-constructionist approach, we might therefore argue that the criteria used to define what information is passed to social workers will always be subjective and changing, meaning that information quality is always likely to be fallible (Payne, 2005).

The fourth factor has relevance to previously cited work that addresses decision-making. In addition to confirmation bias and the bias associated with availability and ability to recall information, the authors identify several other forms of biased thinking. One of these is described as the 'relative judgement of cases' (Kirkman & Melrose, 2014:25). Here the authors point to the observed practice that social workers judge cases by a process of comparison with other cases. At face value, this method could prove helpful, however the possibility remains that the cases providing the baseline may in turn be biased. Given that this relative judgement bias is remarkably similar to the representativeness and adjustment & anchoring heuristics previously noted by Kahneman & Tversky (1982), it is surprising that Kirkman and Melrose (2014) do not acknowledge this. This apparent oversight may also explain the critical response that the report received from some within the profession of social work who doubted it's relevance and evidence base (Stohart, 2014).

However, the report does introduce other more novel forms of bias. For example, the role of 'affect' bias that leads social workers to make decisions in response to the 'highly emotive nature' of their work (Kirkman & Melrose, 2014:26). In addition, the authors introduce a concept descriptive of another observed bias; 'jargon as a mental shortcut'. Jargon, it is argued, can be a useful tool in exchanges between experts, but it also has the potential to 'mask a lack of understanding and promote less sophisticated thinking' (ibid:27). As part of their examination into this specific form of bias, the authors drew on psychological research that indicates the language we think in has an effect on the reasoning process we engage (Keysar et al, 2012).

Although included by Kirkman & Melrose (2014) because of it's potential relevance to reducing biases associated with jargon, the work of Keysar et al (2012) is arguably relevant to many other aspects of the discussion on social workers decision-making. Drawn from the field of psychological science, it is introduced here as important material in it's own right:

Keysar et al (2012) set out to systematically establish limits that language has on reasoning and decision-making. Constructed around six psychological experiments the research found that contrary to general assumptions, using a foreign language in approaching a problem increases analytical reasoning. This has been termed the 'Foreign-Language Effect'.

As the authors note, this would seem contrary to what we might expect (i.e. that irrespective of the language used, a person would make the same choice or decision). Furthermore, the introduction to the research acknowledges that 'people are usually less proficient in their second language than in their first' and also that developing a second language typically occurs through a purposive taught model (Keysar et al, 2012:661).

The finding that Language has a bearing on analytic reasoning is perhaps surprising because there is an inherent associated difficulty to thinking in a less familiar language; the cognitive effort required to use a second language is greater than would be expected for a native speaker. We might therefore expect the increased cognitive demand of second-language speakers to lead them to compensate or offset the difficulty by utilising more intuitive reasoning.

In part, the research centred on the effect a second language had in mediating and framing decisions concerning risk. The methodology of this section of the research involved participants being presented with a particular problem that was deliberately contrived to emphasise losses rather than gains. The researchers tested the principle that 'willingness to accept risk should be independent of the description of a situation' (2012:662). An adapted version of the following problem was used:

> 'Recently, a dangerous new disease has been going around. Without medicine, 600,000 people will die from it. In order to save these people, two types of medicine are being made.
> If you choose medicine A, 200,000 people will be saved.
> If you choose Medicine B, there is a 33.3% chance that 600,000 people will be saved and a 66.6% chance that no one will be saved.
> Which medicine do you choose?'
> (Keysar et al, 2012)

The problem was however adapted to reflect losses. Thus, where medicine A was described, the emphasis became '400,000 people will die'. Accordingly in the revised version, medicine B emphasised chances that no one will die at 33.3% and a 66.6% chance that 600,000 would die. By random allocation, the revised problem was either presented in a native language or a foreign language form.

Ordinarily (i.e. when presented in a native language), this type of experiment would illustrate that due to the change from lives saved to lives lost, there would be a reversal in the preferences people make regarding the medicine. However, in the foreign language groups the loss/gain (live/die) 'framing effect' was eradicated (Keysar et al, 2012:664). In other words, the participants undertaking the experiment in their foreign language overcame the expected bias.

Together with the results of other experiments in the research, the authors concluded that; '…people rely more on systematic processes that respect normative rules when making decisions in a foreign language than when making decisions in their native tongue.' (Keysar et al, 2012:666).

In addition, the research authors speculate that this effect occurs as a consequence of the 'reduction in emotional resonance that is associated with using a foreign language' (2012:666-667).

Following on from the ground-breaking work of Keysar et al (2012), Costa et al (2014) sought to verify and understand the limitations of this discovery. They examined the Foreign Language Effect relative to other cognitive biases beyond the framing effect of losses and gains. The research found that participants 'gave more objective responses when facing a problem in their foreign language' (Costa et al, 2014:251). It also found that due to the associated decrease in 'emotional resonance' when reasoning in a foreign language, heuristic biases in cognitive processes were reduced (ibid:252). As a consequence, they went on to conclude that thinking in a foreign language 'promotes psychological distance, hence reducing the impact or irrelevant details regarding the way a problem is presented (e.g. framing effects) and helping construct an abstract representation to be used by rational processes' (ibid:252).

These research findings could potentially have a much greater relevance than reducing biases associated with use of jargon: Foreign languages are by nature, less familiar. This reduction in familiarity is now associated with changes in cognition and reasoning which, as both papers illustrate, become more analytical. This potentially tells us something about how 'professional familiarity' can also affect the reasoning of social workers, and how this notion of familiarity might be utilised.

A note of caution is sounded by Taylor & White (2001) in their critique of theories on professional social work judgement. They highlight that social work is both a 'practical-moral' and a 'technical-rational' activity (2001:40). Their critique is levied at the drive towards evidence-based practices within social work, but is equally applicable to any promotion of an analytic rather than intuitive approach to decision-making.

The authors propose that responses to concerns about the adequacy of professional judgement have led to a proliferation of approaches 'with the aim of setting standards and achieving consistency among practitioners' (Taylor & White, 2001:38). These 'technical-procedural' responses would for example include the 'Assessment Triangle' set out in the *Framework for Assessment of Children in Need and their Families* (DoH, 2000) and the increasingly used *Strengths and Difficulties Questionnaire* (Goodman, 1997). The authors argue that these 'technical-procedural' reactions are not in themselves a solution to a problem. While they may provide consistency to a task such as the assessment process, they do not aid 'the process of making better sense of information' (Taylor & White 2001:38), do not necessarily lead to better decisions, and may give rise to unhelpful conventions of practice (Reder et al 1993).

The technical-procedural approach 'offers certainty in the very uncertain and continually changing world of social work' (Taylor & White 2001:39). There might equally be an attraction in the technical-procedural quality inherent to analytic reasoning, and explain why it may be seen by some as a remedy to the 'existential dilemma' of decision-making.

This material prompts one further observation: The reorientation to an evidence-led decision-making approach has the effect of casting intuitive or experiential reasoning in a negative light (Taylor & White, 2001:39-40).

A technical-procedural or analytical approach to decision-making is not entirely unchallenged however. As further testimony to the debate around decision-making at the time of Munro's paper, parallel research by Drury-Hudson (1999) considered the conventions of social workers' decision-making within child-protection. Although limited in it's scope some pertinent points are made.

The research contrasted the decision-making capabilities of experienced and novice social workers and found that the decisions of experienced professionals featured unconscious reasoning, indicative of the intuitive model. The research demonstrated that experienced workers 'tended to have a deeper understanding of theory and a clearer understanding of how social work theories related to practice' (Drury-Hudson, 1999:152) and furthermore, that experienced social workers were; 'more likely to have a clearer understanding of and knowledge of risk assessment and those factors most important in determining risk to the child' (ibid:158).

As previously indicated, we must resist the temptation to take a reductionist view of the contemporary discourse on decision-making by distilling and simplifying the discussion to a question of analytic versus intuitive/experiential approaches:

Helm (2010) is sceptical of analytical reasoning being either consciously or unknowingly advanced as the exclusive, preferred model for decision-making in social work. Helm notes that such is the complexity of social work practice that despite intentions to adopt analytical approaches, practitioners may actually be more reliant on intuition than they acknowledge (2010:123). Furthermore, because of the close association between intuitive reasoning and emotional responses, social workers may be anxious about articulating aspects of problems that are intuitively derived, particularly because 'frameworks for assessment do not usually provide a place for the consideration of feelings' (2010:125).

In part, Helm's view reflects the previously cited continuum model of reasoning (Hammond, 1996, Munro 1999, DeBortoli & Dolan, 2014) with its more holistic perspective of analytic and intuitive reasoning being interdependent. The social work profession 'must seek to embrace the potential benefits of intuitive judgement, rather than merely seek to avoid the perceived costs' (Helm, 2011:895).

The pervasive and dominant view of reasoning relies upon a supposition of 'unbounded rationality', i.e. an assumption that given the right conditions and resources, social workers will make concrete and exact decisions. Helm's answer to this potentially fundamental flaw in the discourse is a model of 'bounded rationality' that acknowledges our intrinsic cognitive restrictions (2011:897).

The nature of decision-making and human judgement affect the way that views of children and young people are conveyed or depicted in assessments by social workers. However, Helm does not explicitly acknowledge that although this effect is undesirable, it is not necessarily unavoidable. This is especially true in circumstances where social workers may exercise authority to make decisions that are in direct contrast to a child's wishes.

In complex circumstances it is argued that intuition comes to the fore (Hammond, 1996). By subsequently using assessment and decision-making models that prioritise analytic reasoning, meanings initially understood through a process of intuition may become neutralised by the analytic process. This would mean that analytical models of reasoning are 'biased to the superimposition of adult views over children's views' (Helm, 2011:902) and run contrary to the professional and ethical objectives of social work.

Although this is a convincing point, a potential criticism lies in Helm's implicit assumptions about the cognitive continuum of analytic and intuitive reasoning: Helm notes that when circumstances overwhelm our capacity to be analytical, intuitive reasoning takes precedence by default, but this is not to say intuition will be any *better* for making decisions.

Conclusion

In summary I have illustrated that as social workers become more familiar with the aspects that characterise the work (i.e. the type of case or concern), there is an associated increase in intuitive reasoning (Hackett & Taylor, 2014). This is no real surprise and it affirms the principle that new learning is incorporated into a knowledge base that informs future practice (Munro, 1999, Kirkman & Melrose, 2014). social workers are less likely to be reliant on analytic reasoning when there are limitations of available information or time pressures (Kirkman & Melrose, 2014, Helm, 2011). Intuitive reasoning is likely to be susceptible to heuristic biases that are not always consciously apparent (Kahneman and Tversky, 1982, Munro, 1999, Kirkman and Melrose, 2014).

Decision-making is more likely to be systemic and analytic when people view problems through the frame of a foreign language (Keysar et al, 2012). Further findings indicate that this effect is due to the associated 'psychological distance' that is achieved by thinking and reasoning in an inherently less familiar way (Costa, 2014).

These insights could potentially inform future social work practice. For example, the research by Costa et al (2014) indicates that unfamiliarity may help newly qualified social workers to construct an 'abstract representation' of a case and therefore promote application of analytic reasoning processes. This may lead us to consider if students or less experienced social workers might be ideally suited to complex casework. The research demonstrates that prior to and after Munro's 1999 paper, social work literature had examined the practices of decision-making. The post-Munro examination involved a critique of a continuum of analytical and intuitive/experiential reasoning. Although decision-making based on analytical reasoning appears more robust (and therefore desirable in social work practice), critics point to the practical problem of the demand it places on workplace resources. Conversely, decisions based on intuitive reasoning are similarly criticised for the opposite reasons.

However, when a social worker approaches a decision informed by the respective pros and cons of analytical or intuitive/experiential reasoning, there is still a potential for him to arrive at an irrational decision (Helm, 2010, Frank, 1996).This truism is paired with another inalienable problem that goes to the very heart of social work. There are no 'right' decisions, and at most there are only the best available decisions at the time given the evidence available to them.

With this understanding the social worker is confronted with uncertainty and a consequent inherent, existential anxiety. As briefly described in the opening section to this chapter, ethical models or approaches to decision-making do not offer any further certainty or resolution to this dilemma. This in turn causes further anxiety, and in my view has fuelled a near-Cartesian longing for ontological certainty in social work. In part this might explain the profession's apparent preoccupation with a discourse that is effectively one of circularity.

In many respects, there could be an unconscious purpose to the indefinite perpetuation of the analytic/intuitive decision-making discourse. For instance, as a profession, we may be more comfortable with having this debate than acknowledging the social worker's fundamental problem – i.e. that there are never likely to be any perfect decisions and therefore the debate is never conclusive. This hypothesis warrants further critical examination, possibly through a psychodynamic approach because the situation could be characterised as one of avoidance.

References

4LSCB (2007), *Safeguarding Children Procedures*, Hampshire/Portsmouth/Isle of Wight/Southampton: 4LSCB [online] Available from: http://www.4lscb.org.uk/documents/4lscbproceduresupdated220708.pdf [Accessed 3 April 2015]

BASW, (2014), *The code of ethics for Social Work*, Birmingham: British Association of social workers

Burke, C. (2012), social workers putting in longer hours, survey finds, *The Guardian*, Tuesday 25 September [online] Available from: http://www.theguardian.com/social-care-network/2012/sep/25/social-workers-longer-hours-survey [Accessed 3 April 2015]

Burton, S. (2009), *The oversight and review of cases in the light of changing circumstances and new information: How do people respond to new (and challenging) information?* London: Centre for Excellence and Outcomes in Children and Young People's Services

CAFCASS (2012), *Three weeks in November… three years on: CAFCASS care application study*, [online] Available from: http://www.cafcass.gov.uk/media/6455/Cafcass%20Care%20study%202012%20FINAL.pdf [Accessed 25 March 2015]

The Children Act (1989) London: The Stationery Office

Costa, A. et al (2014) Piensa Twice: On the foreign language effect in decision making, *Cognition*, 130, 236-254

Dale, P. Green, R. and Fellows, R. (2005) *Child protection assessment following serious injuries to infants: Fine judgements*. Chichester: Wiley

DeBortoli, L. and Dolan, M. (2014) Decision making in social work with families and children: Developing decision-aids compatible with cognition, *British Journal of Social Work*, 1-19 [online, pre-press publication]

DoH (2000) *Framework for Assessment of Children in Need and their Families*, London: The Stationery Office

Drury-Hudson, J. (1999) Decision-making in Child Protection: The use of Theoretical, Empirical and Procedural Knowledge by Novices and Experts and Implications for Fieldwork Placement, *British Journal of Social Work*, 29, 147-169

Ferguson, H. (2011) *Child Protection Practice*, Basingstoke: Palgrave Macmillan

Frank, R. (1996) 'Motivation, cognition and charitable giving' in: Schneewind, J. B. (ed) (1996) *Giving: Western ideas of philanthropy*. (pp130-152). Bloomington/Indianapolis: Indiana University Press

Goodman, R. (1997) The Strengths and difficulties questionnaire: A research note, *Journal of Child Psychiatry and Psychology*, 38, 5, 581-586

Hackett, S. and Taylor, A. (2014) Decision Making in social Work with Children and Families: The use of experiential and analytical cognitive processes, *British Journal of Social Work*, 44, 2182-2199

Hammond, K. (1996) *Human judgement and social policy*, Oxford, England: Oxford University Press

Haringey LSCB (2009) *Serious Case Review: Baby Peter*. [online] Available from: http://www.haringeylscb.org/sites/haringeylscb/files/executive_summary_peter_final.pdf [Accessed 3 April 2015]

HCPC (2012) Standards of Conduct, Performance and Ethics, London: Health and Care Professions Council

Helm, D. (2011) Judgements or assumptions? The role of analysis in assessing children and young people's needs, *British Journal of Social Work*, 41, 894-911

Helm, D. (2010) *Making sense of child and family assessment: How to interpret children's needs*, London: Jessica Kingsley

HM Government, (2015) Working Together to Safeguard Children: A guide to inter-agency working to safeguard and promote the welfare of children. [online] Available from: https://www.gov.uk/government/publications/working-together-to-safeguard-children--2 [Accessed 1 April 2015]

Houston, S. (2003) Moral consciousness and decision-making in child and family Social Work, *Adoption and Fostering*, 27, 3, 61-70

Kahneman, D. and Tversky, A. (1982) Judgement under uncertainty: Heuristics and biases, in: Kahneman, D. Slovic, P. Tversky, A. (Eds) (1982) *Judgement under uncertainty: Heuristics and biases*, (pp3-20) New York: Cambridge University Press

Keysar, B. et al (2012) The foreign language effect: Thinking in a foreign tongue reduces decision biases, *Psychological Science*, .23, 6, 661-668

Kirkman, E. and Melrose, K. (2014) *Clinical Judgment and Decision-Making in Children's Social Work: An analysis of the 'front door' system*, The Behavioural Insights Team/Department for Education

Munro, E. (1999) Common Errors of Reasoning in Child Protection work, *Child Abuse and Neglect*, 23, 8, 745-758

Payne, M. (2005) *Modern Social Work Theory*, 3rd Edn. Basingstoke: Palgrave Macmillan

Platt, D. and Turney, D. (2014) Making threshold decisions in child protection: A conceptual analysis, *British Journal of Social Work*, 44, 1472-1490

Reder, P. Duncan, S. and Gray, M. (1993) *Beyond Blame: Child abuse tragedies revisited*, London: Routledge

Spratt, T. (2000) Decision-making by senior social workers at point of first referral, *British Journal of Social Work*, 30, 597-618

Stein, T. and Rzepnicki, T. (1984) *Decision Making in Child Welfare Services Intake and Planning*, Boston: Kluwer-Nijhoff Publishing/Springer

Stohart, C.(2014) 'Social workers need new models to help them make decisions, finds report', Community Care, 28th April [online] available from http://www.communitycare.co.uk/2014/04/28/social-workers-need-new-models-to-help-them-make-decisions-says-government-report/ [Accessed 1 April 2015]

Taylor, B. (2013) *Professional decision-making and risk in social work*, 2nd Edn. London: Sage

Taylor, C. and White, S. (2001) Knowledge, Truth and Reflexivity: The problem of judgement in social work, *Journal of Social Work*, 1, 1, 37-59

TCSW (2012) Professional Capabilities Framework, [online] Available from: http://www.tcsw.org.uk/pcf.aspx [Accessed 01.04.15]

4
The role of emotional containment in a child protection workforce
Stella Vincent

This chapter aims to explore the concept of *containment* and its uses and effectiveness within child protection practice. I will firstly explore this in relation to children and their caregivers, before drawing inferences with the relationship between service users and social workers and their organisational support networks. I will analyse the current obstacles to effective supervision and reflective space which enables this latter relationship to effectively allow containment to take place. I will discuss the significance of recognising transference and countertransference and the strengths and difficulties in reflection and reflexivity when engaging with children and families. Conclusions will be drawn in an analysis and recommendations to address the issues of staff burnout, fear and anxiety.

Policy context

Amongst the conclusions from Ofsted (2010) in the analysis of 147 serious case reviews between 2009-2010, three overarching shortcomings had relevance to containment and reflectivity. It highlighted that professionals should have been more inquisitive and questioning of their own views, decisions and actions as well as those of families and colleagues. There had been insufficient or ineffective supervision structures or managerial oversight and intervention, which could have monitored good practice. It also suggested that 'professional drift' had taken place and an unjustified 'rule of optimism' had been applied and gone unchallenged (Ofsted 2010).

Munro (2011) in her review of child protection practices criticised the technical-rational approach to social care supervision which had a procedural focus rather than recognising and nurturing personal wellbeing. She suggested that critical appraisal is imperative in recognising the impact of exposure to distress and trauma, which affects relationships and can be at a personal cost to practitioners. Munro (2011: 115) advocates for 'team cohesion' and 'emotional expressiveness' and opportunities to debrief following particularly emotive encounters, in order to support personal resilience and coping strategies. Without this solidarity, she suggested that high staff turnover will lead to further missed opportunities for assisting families.

Social Workers in England are expected to adhere to the BASW Code of Ethics (2012) and HCPC standards of conduct (2012) which provide the ethical principles on which the profession is grounded. It states that social workers must maintain a critical awareness of how their own values and prejudices impact on their practice and advocates for the need for reflective space and supervision to achieve this. The Department for Education (2014a:2) published a Knowledge and Skills statement for Child and Family Social Work, which requires that practitioners exhibit professional ethics by being able to 'critically evaluate the impact of one's own belief system on practice'. Supervision needs to be appropriately utilised and social workers must demonstrate their capability in reflecting on case work, testing and challenging hypotheses.

However, these fundamental messages resonate with the suggestion made by Lord Laming (2003:14) after the death of Victoria Climbié, which stated that 'supervision is the cornerstone of good social work practice'. Yet, 12 years on, supervision is still highly criticised for its bureaucracy, lack of focus on professional subjectivity and practice support and a failure to acknowledge the cumulative impact of stress on frontline workers (Kapoulitsas and Corcoran, 2014; Bradbury-Jones, 2013).

Addressing the concept of containment is therefore pertinent due to the current social work staffing crisis and criticisms regarding inadequacies in social work training. It is also applicable as there is a significant drive within local authorities to improve the quality of the ASYE (Assisted and Supported Year in Employment) programme and reflective learning opportunities. The Department for Education (2014b:1) has reported a national 15% child protection staff turnover rate in the year ending September 2013, with 3390 agency workers filling interim positions and 4% of working days missed due to absence (equating to an average of one day per month, per full time social worker) causing a considerably unstable workforce. This is currently leading local authorities to review their recruitment and retention policies in an attempt to encourage staff to accept or remain in permanent social work posts. McFadden et al (2014:2) defines burnout as 'the experience of physical, emotional and mental exhaustion that can arise from long-term involvement in occupational situations that are emotionally demanding'.

Review of evidence

Containment

Bion (1962) introduced the notion of containment, and suggested that children project onto their caregivers their anxiety, created through their survival instincts in having their basic needs met. When a child recognises that this support is consistently available they are able to feel protected and learn to trust and explore the world with confidence (Douglas, 2007). Bion (1962) concludes that this creates a secure attachment, with the parent providing the secure base from which they can grow. This is supported by Smith (2010a) and Toasland (2007) who suggest that these ideas are underpinned by two separate concepts, and differentiate 'holding', which is a passive act of listening and accepting and 'containment', which is a more active response. The latter involves reacting in a non-threatening way with sensitivity; providing reassurance, comfort and nurturing and meeting their perceptive needs as well as ensuring the child's basic needs for food, shelter and warmth are met (Toasland, 2007).

Ferguson (2011), Winnicott (1953) and Kanter (2004) discuss the attachments formed by children towards objects and people. Although Winnicott (1953) suggests that children cling to, and form dependencies to items of importance, which would indicate that social workers could be used as an 'object' by the child as a form of comfort or distraction, the work of Kanter (2004) indicates that this inaccurately suggests the passivity of the social work role, in which children's experiences and projections are imposed upon the worker. Instead Kanter (2004) proposes that practitioners are 'transitional participants' (Kanter, 2004:75) who support children through difficult episodes in their life and help develop understandings. This relies heavily on the worker's ability to skilfully elicit information, encourage the articulation or demonstration of emotion and be flexible to utilising any opportunity for meaningful interactions. As well as being an 'object' of security to a child, social workers provide consistency and are also 'active participants' in their development (Ferguson 2011:122). However the level of consistency is highly debatable in the current climate of a high turnover of staff and the increased use of interim workers. Nevertheless, Ferguson (2011) articulates that through this sense of security, children feel able to share their feelings, questions and worries with a social worker who can help them make sense of their concerns and 'hold on' to their feelings.. This requires the maintenance of professional boundaries, the use of ethical and value-based practice and a sensitive use of self (Ferguson, 2011).

Whilst recognising that the concept originates in a psychodynamic paradigm in relation to a parent-child relationship, Smith (2010a) uses the terms more broadly, to explain interaction in any interpersonal relationship. He suggests that individuals have the capacity to accept the strong emotive responses of others and can create relief and liberation of people in need by listening to their projections. He also relates this to practitioners working in frontline practice. Social workers in child protection teams are often subjected to projections of hostility and dependency and it remains a challenge to manage this (Smith, 2010b). Ruch (2005 and 2007) suggests the need for 'emotional', 'organisational' and 'epistemological' containment (this latter concept through team meetings, group supervision and debriefing) to hold on to the emotions, observations and uncertainties of staff in the same way in which social care expect, empower and sometimes teach parents to contain their children's raw and undeveloped feelings. Ruch (2010) provides the link between containment and attachment theories which is explored further by Shemmings (2015) promoting the importance of strong team management and having a supervisor who can engage in listening to reflections. This requires the supervisor to be emotionally available to the supervisee (Steckley, 2013). However Ruch's suggestion for epistemological containment highlights that collaborative, exploratory and communicative forums outside of supervision provide opportunities 'through thoughtful conversations and discussions, to transform the undigested material of practice encounters into holistically reflective responses' (2007: 676) and minimises the feeling of being overwhelmed. This was also exemplified by Scannapieco and Connell-Carrick (2007).

Bion (1962) and Miller-Pietroni (1999) explain that by failing to make the connections between our thoughts and feelings, we run the risk of losing sight of the people we are supporting. Frustrations regarding administrative processes, timescales and bureaucracy which hinder effective practice should also be contained by managers in order that the feelings do not cloud judgement, and that responsibilities are shared, without which, this can lead to a disempowered workforce (Ferguson 2011). This further supports the idea of organisational containment (Ruch 2007). which can lead to emotional exhaustion and 'compassion fatigue' (Conrad and Keller Guenthar 2006, Figley, 2002). This is a concept reinforced by Kapoulitsas and Corcoran (2014) and Bradbury-Jones (2013) who state that without active coping strategies to recognise and respond to these emotions, it leads to the depersonalisation of services and the deskilling of staff in traditional social work as well as clinical practice. Smith (2010b) and Toasland (2007) specifically relate resilience to supervision, which they suggest offers a primary opportunity for practitioner's containment and what Ruch (2007) describes as 'emotional listening'. Toasland (2007) develops Bion's (1977) ideas further in the relationship between the 'contained' who share their feelings and the 'container' who provides the listening ear and holds on to and manages these feelings. A 'parasitic' relationship is described as an unhealthy relationship in which understandings shared are received by the supervisor/container but are not sufficiently re-projected back to the worker in a supportive way to help them internally digest their responses. This creates dependency from the supervisee who uses the supervisor as a sounding board and only transfers anxiety. However, 'symbiotic' relationships are representative of healthier relationships in which the supervisee can rely on their supervisor for support and a positive regard of their work, their emotions and their capabilities, whilst sensitively having their feelings re-projected back to them in an objectively rationalised form. This both develops resilience to managing complex physical and psychological responses and also provides healthier dependencies. This means that supervisees feel able to ask for help and trust in being 'held', without feeling that their autonomy is compromised or their resilience doubted.

Ferguson (2011:205) speaks even more broadly of the use of containment and states that 'They (practitioners) can only really take risks if they feel they will be emotionally held and supported on returning to the office that their feelings and struggles will be listened to'. From a social constructionist perspective, Kapoulitsas and Corcoran (2014) criticised the historical view that anxiety is an indication of incompetence and that heightened emotional responses suggests a personal or professional deficiency. Instead, they explored resilience using practitioner's personal experience which evidenced young social worker's (aged 23-32) perspectives regarding how impromptu supervision allowed new insights through reflecting in a safe environment. Over time, this suggested that appropriate dependencies can allow for the development of resilience. Therefore, containment is a key aspect to the notion of 'self.'

The 'Use of Self'

Ward (2010b) and Banks (2012) suggest that social work is specifically complex because although broad moral and ethical guidelines are set out in professional codes, practice is performed at a very personal level. The concept of the 'Use of Self' is hard to define. Mandell (2008: 237) suggests that 'it is generally understood as being centred in a core, definable self-shaped by personal history and psychological and emotional experiences; in many instances it is understood to be operating outside of our consciousness'. This influences communication, willingness to make disclosures, ability to trust, biases and prejudices, empathy and the establishment and maintenance of boundaries, alongside the modelling of pro-social behaviours. However, the self is also influenced by social constructions such as the qualities and skills expected of social workers by the HCPC (2012a,b) and BASW (2012). It is also shaped by our political or religious beliefs and our voluntary and involuntary psychological and physical reactions (Edwards and Bess, 1998).

Sigmund Freud's key ideas on 'instinct theory' (1910) and the powerful drives of aggression and sex are questioned in modern interpretations of psychodynamic theory, for example by Guntrip (1977) who argued instinct is a control system which stands as only an element of our wider being. However, what is now widely accepted is the role our past experiences play on our formation of relationships. Anna Freud (1936) focused on the ego-defence reaction, a concept which she suggested is our signal to ourselves of the threat of imminent or perceived danger. Guntrip (1977) and Sigmund Freud (1910) suggested this needed to be contained by providing reliability and security in clinical environments in which to explore issues deemed unsafe. Yet, these were also early indications of the impact on professional wellbeing if not managed appropriately.

In order to address this, Guntrip (1977: 12) concentrated on the 'development of a stable core of selfhood'. Despite being written 38 years ago, this is still relevant in both clinical and non-clinical work and contemporary psychoanalytic theory. Due to the distance perpetuated by compulsory interventions, assessment and the stigma of child protection involvement, there is also an emphasis on social workers being seen not to power dress, and to use humour (Ferguson, 2011, Dewane, 1978), engage in direct work (Munro, 2011) and intervene transparently to reduce power imbalances. However, these measures alone do not equate to anti-oppressive practice and personality and the human nature of interactions are vital to effective relationship building (Sudbery, 2002). Ward (2010:52) refers to the self as 'our primary tool for practice', which is supported by Rossiter (2007), Heydt and Sherman (2005) and Dewane, (2006). This is relevant to containment due to the subjectivity of our understanding of our personal impact on service users, including the power dynamics which we create and the inconsistencies caused for families if we are not aware of what we bring to an interaction (Sudbery, 2002). This suggests that exploration provides learning regarding practice which is in line with social work values, alongside a constructive recognition of unhelpful values emerging which interfere with a non-judgemental approach. Therefore, this is also significant to the idea of accountability This can be best exemplified by Howe (2008: 37) who states that 'Emotionally speaking, in social relationships we are making constant adjustments. On the one hand we need to maintain good quality social interaction, whilst on the other to ensure our own needs and position are not lost'. In social work, it is widely recognised that hostile, defensive or apprehensive behaviour from social workers alienates families and creates a barrier to moving forwards, building trusting relationships and honesty (Smith, 2010b). Instead the type of relationship which harbours mutual respect, acceptance, understanding and both psychological and emotional availability leads to better outcomes for individuals and families. The recent shift towards more collaborative and restorative approaches to working with service user creates a 'holding environment' (Howe, 2008:182). This supports the notion of containment proposed by Bion (1962) and expounded by Toasland (2007). Therefore the 'use of the self' is important in developing mutually responsive and supportive relationships which was reinforced by Sheafor and Horejsi, (2003:69)

Transference and Countertransference

From a psychodynamic perspective, inexperienced social workers still develop their professional identities and therefore need to be nurtured to gain a greater awareness of the role their 'self' plays firstly in interpreting the information they are provided with and also in the messages they respond with, a concept which he describes as 'projection identification' (McTighe 2010). However, Munro (2011) and Rossiter (2007) suggest that this also applies to experienced staff who need continuous professional development throughout their career, to focus on recognising relational dynamics and the impact this has on case progression, congruence and cooperation.

The concept of 'Transference' (Freud (1910) is the projection of feelings onto another person, which can include love, sadness or rage. The concept of Countertransference' is 'a result of the patient's influence on his (the practitioner's) unconscious feelings' (Freud: 1910: 144) which is also seen as an emotional entanglement with the client. Although the process of transference and countertransference was deemed to be unhelpful and even dangerous in therapy, it is now seen as an interaction which occurs organically and often subliminally.

Thompson (1988) and Tauber (1988) encourage the recognition of what happens, why and how this occurs and suggest that instead of trying to ensure this does not influence the communication and outcomes of therapy or alternate interventions, we should identify ways in which these internal responses could be used as a valuable tool to advance practice. By taking a more open and transparent approach to reflecting on and admitting the presence of primitive and spontaneous responses, even when crossing professional boundaries, a less defensive stance can be taken. However, in relation to supervision this would require practitioners to feel that their supervisors are receptive to reflection rather than assessing professional competence, which in practice I have noted is a specific concern for interim staff whose jobs may be insecure due to the temporary nature of their contracts (Tauber 1988 & McTighe 2010). McTighe (2010) explains that clinical supervision encourages the learning that can be generated by the attention paid to both the conscious and unconscious communication which takes place in any interaction, a provision not adequately made in case-management style supervision. However, Ferguson (2011) highlights the need to do this, whether formally in supervision or using any other therapeutic space such as the car or office. This leads to the concept of reflexivity.

Reflexivity

Ruch defines reflection as 'attending to the thoughts and feelings aroused by events; reassessing the experience in light of its outcomes; and experimenting with new approaches in light of the reflection process' (Ruch, 2000:100). Horner (2004), Munro, (2011), and Constable (2013) suggest that reflection is a prerequisite for being an emotionally intelligent and effective social worker throughout one's career. They propose that this process enables the joining of analytic and intuitive reasoning to making sound judgements. In recent years, the assumption that conscious and logical thinking is preferable to the use of intuition and instinct has been partially overturned by the advances in neuroscience and neuropsychology. It is now widely accepted that the unconscious information which we both receive and deliver needs to be acknowledged in order to understand the impact of our automatic as well as reasoned reactions in diverse situations. Munro (2011) argues that despite the unconscious perceptions being unexplained, this does not eliminate the opportunity to seek to comprehend the impact that this has. Munro (2011), Howe (2008), and Fook and Gardner (2007) suggest that intuition is not merely an irrational feeling or instinct to be set aside, but practice experience, life histories, skills and knowledge are likely to feed into how we perceive things to be now.

Munro (2011:90) states that these feelings 'need not remain unconscious but can be articulated and this ability can be improved with guided practice and with explicit attention to eliciting the evidence that the unconscious was noting and interpreting'. Although she goes on to suggest the importance of this practice in both case consultation and supervision, this fails to explain how the two are differentiated. Throughout my statutory and voluntary sector placements as a social work student, I noted the tendency for the two to be seen in isolation. Although reflective supervision was deemed to be effective in informing practice and integrating theoretical principles with interventions, it was also considered to be the predominant environment in which reflections take place and a more factual, evidenced-based record of case progress was discussed in case supervision. Ruch (2000) discusses how the influences of increased bureaucracy and procedural based practice has led to depersonalised services failing to acknowledge the skills and vulnerabilities of practitioners and the individuality of service users.

From Ruch's analysis on reflection (Ruch, 2000) she outlines that contemporary material focuses on three dominant styles. 'Technical' reflection is the exploration of practice focusing on external sources of knowledge such as theoretical frameworks, and empirical research in decision making processes, with the aim of 'efficient, effective and measurable outcomes (Ruch, 2002: 204). 'Practical' reflection, is the evaluation of practice focusing on the analysis of professional performance, and the influences of both conscious and unconscious forces, and professional and personal assumptions, which is in line to Schon's 'Reflecting in action' (1983). Finally, 'Critical' reflection relates one's practice with both the conscious and unconscious mind, by encouraging assumptions to be challenged, and balancing ethical and moral dilemmas. It focuses on structural obstacles to social justice or desired outcomes and the power imbalances and oppression created during interactions and demonstrates a deeper level of learning (Ruch, 2000; Banks, 2012). However, it is now argued by psychodynamic and psychoanalytic theorists that transference and countertransference are so relevant in our current understanding of the work of frontline practitioners that a further model of reflection, defined by Ruch (2000) as 'process reflection' is required. This examines the practitioner's own thoughts and feelings in relation to the interaction with service users. Ruch (2000) suggests that when pulling together and recognising the value of these different strands of self-reflection, there is a greater chance of success of a holistic understanding, rather than only a relational appreciation of learning. Yet, the development of understanding can also intensify emotional responses because of the identification of influential occurrences in one's personal life, which again compounds the argument for an increased awareness of and structures for containment.

Yet, regardless of the positive working environment and improved morale created through effective team management and individual targeted support, what is undisputed is the pressure this places on supervisors to regularly set aside the time necessary to make any reflective opportunity meaningful and relevant in an outcome-focussed and task orientated work culture. The 'reflective process minimises blame, shame and doubt and identifies and applies creative and individual strategies in self-care and professional development to further strengthen their practice' (Marlowe et al, 2015: 70). I would argue that this is only possible where, as previously discussed, the 'container' or supervisor provides a secure and non-judgemental base. This came from a self-reported study and Ferguson (2013) and Davys and Beddoe (2009) provide the challenge that the success of reflexivity is objectively immeasurable and that effective practice is a fluid learning experience and as such cannot be quantified or validated.

I have often heard practitioners say that 'something just didn't feel right' and yet Marlowe et al study (2015) indicated that the physical senses experienced by social work students frequently either went unacknowledged or were not admitted, a concept which needs to be explored in itself due to the environment of fear and blame often cultivated in the social care sphere.

Analysis and recommendations for change

The research studies I have used are predominantly from the United States of America and Australia, due to the limited recent research available from the UK. Whilst I acknowledge that processes are different, the majority of social issues dealt with, resource limitations and societal perceptions are alike. Therefore they are still valid, due to the mainly qualitative data provided which give insight into practitioner's experiences and resonate with my own experiences both as a student and in discussion with long-serving colleagues in frontline child protection teams.

Containment has historically been an issue only identified in clinical services and yet the concept is being increasingly discussed in child protection literature, without being labelled as such. The literature commonly recognises that service-users in social care and clinical practice suffer from various stresses, and are supported through these adversities by social workers. Yet the social workers themselves often manage the distress of high numbers of service-users alongside organisational burdens. Howe suggests that 'stress on stress' can lead to burn out '(Howe, 2008:104 and Ruch (2000). In line with the political recommendations mentioned in the policy context, training and the use of creative and inclusive reflective meetings has provided valuable opportunities specifically for students and newly qualified staff (McTighe, 2011; Ferguson, 2013; Fook and Gardner 2007). However, very little by the way of increasing resilience across the experienced workforce has been evidenced and obstacles to openness and reflective practice have been repeatedly raised as a challenge to autonomous learning. I have deduced its importance and conclude that the greatest barrier remains the time commitment in busy environments which are not afforded to either staff or managers. The notions of containment, reflexivity and the use-of-self have been argued throughout the literature as more relevant to students and inexperienced staff who are still developing their professional identities and adapting to the multiple pressures of the job. However, the issue of burnout is more widely associated with longer serving workers.

The more recent research from Bradbury-Jones (2013), Smith (2010a) Ferguson (2011), McFadden et al (2014) and Higgins (2011) are beginning to acknowledge this. They look holistically at the need for reflective and exploratory style support even for experienced practitioners, who despite having a more developed sense of professional identity, struggle to make sense of interactions with families and are at risk of emotional exhaustion. Without adequate support frameworks, we need to consider that breaches of confidentiality are more likely when practitioners feel unable to withhold their anxieties and feel the need to off-load outside of the workplace. Even without inappropriately sharing confidential details, the literature has indicated that staff both physically and figuratively are unable to leave their work baggage at the office door.

The literature has unanimously verified the connection between self-understanding and emotional regulation by helping to hold, contain, explore and manage emotions and uncertainties which is most effectively done through the objective support of a secure container. The literature relating specifically to containment is limited, however, I have been surprised that this subject remains untaught and overlooked both in the social work education and in the reflective supervision in practice.

The psychodynamic perspective looks at the triggers of varying emotional responses, and the systemic approach focuses on exploring obstacles and adversities to 'unearth aspects of the situation that had not been explored' (Ruch, 2010:44). Although providing contrasting purposes for reflexivity, I have intentionally chosen to use an eclectic overview of varying theoretical perspectives due to the breadth of value that looking holistically at cause and effect provides. Demonstratively, both of these approaches seek to apply new meanings to interactions with a view to altering future behaviours, improving practice and positively affecting change by moving families forward in resolving problems. Marlowe et al (2015:60) conclude that the more reflective approaches taken in field practice 'represent an opportunity for students to cultivate both professional and personal skills by developing self-awareness, self-care, empathy, critical inquiry and an increased experience and understanding of power dynamics' supported further by Higgins (2011).

Scannapieco and Connell-Carrick (2007), Marlowe et al (2015) and Kapoulitsas and Corcoran (2014) suggest that opportunities for students and newly qualified staff have significantly supported their development of rational decision making skills, critical analysis and emotional containment, but fails to address how this can be done in a way which is not deemed to interfere with practice responsibilities. Although they acknowledge that time constraints challenge effective practice, the literature focuses on reflection that commonly mentions models for 1:1 or group supervision to build critical awareness skills. However, the literature on containment explains predominantly what can be done, why this is needed and who can do this, but does not provide examples or frameworks regarding how this could be followed.

Shemmings (2015) looked more generally at practitioner support, and advises that supervision does not necessarily suggest the need of a superior or senior colleague, but someone who can sit outside of the situation and remain more objective, allowing them to see the dilemma more clearly. Although this view suggests that peers can provide appropriate containment and promote critical awareness that reduces power imbalances and encourages openness and the admittance of self-doubt, this is contested by some of the literature that says reflection should take place as part of case management discussions rather than being a separate process. However, what is agreed and was expounded by Ferguson (2013) is that what works for one individual may not suit another, despite the consistent need for continuous professional development. Therefore requiring all staff to reflect, can create an unnecessary bureaucratic burden, which Munro (2011) advised against. Also, this would be of no benefit to staff or service users if its use is not valued and sufficient time and flexibility is not built in to increase meaningful participation. Hence, a working climate and culture shift is needed to create a more inclusive and supportive learning environment where emotions are deemed natural and honest, rather than indications of weakness. I would suggest that reflective opportunities are available for all staff, on a request based system by a practice consultant, but also encouraged through a more informal peer-buddy or mentoring system. Work time would therefore need to be allocated to allow the facilitation of this, as and when it is required. This would entail managers encouraging this during team meetings but also endorsing asking for manager support when emotional containment is ineffective. Previously this would have been hidden by practitioners. Ruch (2000) and Schofield (1998: 65) highlight that 'one of the most useful resources for containing anxiety is the capacity to make sense of what is going on', which ultimately also informs one's understanding of 'self'. This demonstrates the clear link between the concepts I have thematically explored and further reinforces my suggestion for increased reflective opportunities in which what practitioners think (their mind), what they feel (their emotion) and what they sense (physically in their body) is explored and rationalised

Despite Scannapieco and Connell-Carrick's study (2007) evidencing the key role that supervisors and co-workers had on retention, motivation and morale, there is inadequate empirical research to explore how containment and reflective supervision impacts on the career span and retention of social workers. There is also not enough research to understand whether the support was beneficial in the long term or only in the moment, or indeed to explore the change affected with families. Jacobson (2001) explains that despite the emotive and often very complex relationships built between social workers and service users, the same level of scrutiny and exploration is not given to how supportive or productive these relationships are or how they may be impacted by either the service user or practitioner, as this receives in other clinical professions. In counselling, substance misuse and mental health services, clinical practitioners are taught that reflecting on the nature of the relationship is vital in identifying the impact of the therapeutic relationship along with any transference or counter transference which may need to be addressed. However in non-clinical practice, this is dependent on practitioners creating their own opportunities to reflect, which is usually completed alone. Therefore, further research in the UK will need to be completed if the impact of emotional containment is to be understood across the career span of frontline social workers.

Although the use of self in social work is undeniable, as subconscious influences permeate our practice, the extent to which this is consciously used is unknown (Ward, 2010). Many practitioners cherish the less prescriptive standards found in social work and the autonomy this authorises, however, ultimately it leaves professionalism and professional boundaries open to interpretation, intuition and personal judgement. In contemporary practice social workers can be sanctioned or even struck off the register if things go wrong. This is also pertinent to the blame culture, with government plans threatening social workers for failing to recognise and protect children from sexual abuse (Stevenson, 2015), and the media holding social workers 'responsible' for child abuse, even deaths. This culture will only increase professional anxieties. Without adequate containment and reflection, this could lead to social workers rigidly following standardised procedures, therefore failing to utilise what has been evidenced as their primary resource in achieving individualised positive outcomes, their 'self'.

The literature irrefutably shows contradictions of social work values such as integrity, human dignity and worth, social justice and competence (BASW, 2012, HCPC, 2012a,b) in conflict with the realities of managerialism,. Stepney (2000:2) describes social care priorities as having shifted towards 'effectiveness, economy and efficiency' which the rise of managerialism has reinforced, yet Munro's suggestions (2011) have sought to address this. However, her research also demonstrates that the expectation that service-user's needs and organisational needs are put ahead of our own can be damaging.

I put forward a biased and undisputed case for increased and mandatory reflection opportunities within the workplace which includes the need for emotional and organisational containment. However, the overwhelming outcome from the literature shows that the current inadequate structures for social work lead to a disempowered, demotivated and burnt out workforce, and no counter argument against organisational support has been found.

Conclusion

I propose that instead of seeing opportunities for critical reflection as self-indulgent, a bureaucratic burden, or taking unjustified time away from direct work, they provide a positive impact on practice. In order to empower families and safeguard children, we need to fully incorporate a safe environment for staff that augments organisational containment through reflexivity which will produce better outcomes for workers and productivity for the organisation. 'Worker's state of mind and the quality of attention they can give children is directly related to the quality of support, care and attention they themselves receive from supervisors, managers and peers' (Ferguson, 2011: 205).

References

Anderson, D. G. (2000). 'Coping strategies and burnout among veteran child protection workers', *Child Abuse and Neglect*, 24, 6, 839-848

Banks, S. (2012). *Ethics and Values in Social Work*. 4th Edn. Basingstoke: Palgrave Macmillan

BASW. (2012). *The Code of Ethics for Social Work*. London: The British Association of Social Workers

Bion, W. (1962) *Learning from Experience*. London: Heinemann

Bradbury-Jones, C. (2013). 'Refocussing Child protection Supervision: An Innovative Approach to Supporting Practitioners'. *Child Care in Practice*. 19, 3, 253-266

Conrad, D., and Kellar-Guenthar, Y. (2006). 'Compassion fatigue, burnout, and compassion satisfaction among Colorado child protection workers'. *Child Abuse & Neglect*. 30, 10, 1071-1080

Constable, G. (2013) 'Reflection as a catalyst in the development of personal and professional effectiveness in C, Knott and T, Scragg (Eds) *Reflective Practice in Social Work*. London: Learning Matters. pp 53-69

Davys, A. M., and Beddoe, L. (2009). 'The reflective, 8, (8), 919–933

Department for Education (2014a) *Knowledge and Skills for Child and Family Social Work*. London: Department for Education. Available online at: https://s3-eu-west-1. amazonaws.com/rbi-communities/wp-content/uploads/sites/7/2014/07/Chief-Social-

Worker-Knowledge-and-Skills-Statement.pdf Last accessed 9/4/15

Department for Education (2014b) *Statistical First Release Children's Social Work Workforce: Key numbers as at September 2013*. London: Department for Education. Available online at: https://www.gov.uk/government/uploads/system/uploads/attachment_data/file/287259/Social_Work_Workforce_2012-13_SFR_v1.3.pdf Last accessed 4/3/15

Dewane, C. (1978). 'Use of humor in therapy'. *Social Work*, 23, 6, 508–510

Dewane, C. (2006), 'Use of Self: a primer revisited', *Clinical Social Work Journal*, 34, 4, 543-558

Douglas, H. (2007). *Containment and reciprocity: Integrating psychoanalytic theory and child development research for work with children*. Hove: Routledge

Edwards, J. and Bess, J. (1998). 'Developing effectiveness in the therapeutic use of self'. *Clinical Social Work Journal*, 26, 1, 89-105

Ferguson, H. (2011). *Child Protection Practice*. Palgrave Macmillan: Basingstoke

Ferguson, Y. (2013). 'Critical Reflection in Statutory Work' In Fook, J., and Gardner, F. (Eds.). (2013). '*Critical reflection in context: Applications in health and social care*'. New York: Routledge

Figley, C.R. (2002). 'Compassion Fatigue: Psychotherapists. Chronic Lack of Self Care. *Journal of Clinical Psychology*. 58, 11, 1433-1441

Fook, J. and Gardner, F. (2007). *Practising Critical Reflection: A Resource Handbook*. Maidenhead: Open University Press

Freud, A. (1936). *The Ego and Mechanisms of Defence* . London: The Hogarth Press. (Translated and reprinted in 1972)

Freud, S. (1910). *The Future Prospects of Psycho-Analytic Therapy. The Standard Edition of the Complete Psychological Works of Sigmund Freud, Volume XI (1910): Five Lectures on Psycho-Analysis, Leonardo da Vinci and Other Works*, 139-152

Guntrip, H. (1977). *Psychoanalytic Theory, Therapy and the Self*. USA: Basic Books

HCPC. (2012a). *Standards of Conduct, Performance and Ethics*. London: Health and Care and Professions Council

HCPC. (2012b). *Standards of Proficiency. Social Workers in England and Wales*. London: Health and Care Professions Council

Heydt, M.J. and Sherman N.E. (2005). 'Conscious Use of Self: Tuning the Instrument of Social Work Practice with Cultural Competence'. *The Journal of Baccalaureate Social Work* 10 (2). Pp25-40. Available online at http://mcnellie.com/525/readings/heydtsherman.pdf Last accessed 7/4/15

Higgins, D. (2011). 'Why reflect? Recognising the link between Learning and Reflection', *Reflective Practice: International and Multidisciplinary Perspectives*, 12, 5, 583-584

Horner, N. (2004). *What is Social Work? Context and Perspectives*. Exeter: Learning Matters

Howe, D. (2008). *The Emotionally Intelligent Social Worker*. Basingstoke: Palgrave Macmillan

Jacobson, W. B. (2001). 'Beyond therapy: Bringing social work back to human services reform'. *Social Work*, 46, 1, 51-62.

Kanter, J. (2004). *Face-to-Face with Children: The Life and Work of Clare Winnicott*. London: Karnac

Kapoulitsas, M and Corcoran, T. (2015). 'Compassion fatigue and resilience: A qualitative analysis of social work practice'. *Qualitative Social Work*. 14, 1, 86-101

Laming, Lord H. (2003). *The Victoria Climbie Inquiry*. London: The Stationary Office. Available online at: http://image.guardian.co.uk/sys-files/Society/documents/2003/01/28/climbiereport.pdf Last accessed 9/4/15

Mandell, D. (2008). 'Power, Care and Vulnerability: Considering Use of Self in Child Welfare Work'. *Journal Of Social Work Practice*, 22, 2, 235-248

Marlowe, J.M., Appleton,C., Chinnery, S-A and Van Stratum, S. (2015). 'The Integration of Personal and Professional Selves: Developing Students' Critical Awareness'. *Social Work Practice, Social Work Education*, 34, 1, 60-73

McFadden, P., Campbell, A and Taylor, B. (2014). 'Resilience and Burnout in Child Protection Social Work: Individual and Organisational Themes from a Systematic Literature Review' *British Journal of Social Work* (Advance Access published February 26 2014

McTighe, J. (2011) Teaching the Use of Self Through the Process of Clinical Supervision. *Clinical Social Work Journal*, 39, 3, 301-307,

Miller-Pietroni, M. (1999). 'Containment in theory and practice'. *Psychodynamics Counselling*. 5, 4, 207-427

Munro, E. (2011). *The Munro review of child protection: final report, a child-centred system.* London: The Stationery Office

Ofsted. (2010). *The voice of the child: learning lessons from serious case reviews. A thematic review of Ofsted's evaluation of serious case reviews from 1 April to 30 September 2010.* London: Ofsted

Rossiter, A. (2007). 'Self as subjectivity: toward a use of self as respectful relations of recognition'. In: D, Mandell (ed) *Revisiting the Use of Self: Questioning Professional Identities.* Toronto: Canadian Scholars Press. pp. 21–34

Ruch, G. (2000.) 'Self and social work: Towards an integrated model of learning'. *Journal of Social Work Practice: Psychotherapeutic Approaches in Health, Welfare and the Community*, 14, 2, 99-112

Ruch, G. (2005). 'Relationship–Based Practice and Reflective Practice: Holistic Approaches to contemporary child care social work'. *Child and Family Social Work*. 10, 2, 111-125

Ruch, G. (2007). 'Reflective Practice in Contemporary Child-care Social Work: The Role of Containment'. *British Journal of Social Work* 37,4. 659-680

Ruch, G. (2010). 'The contemporary Context of Relationship- Based Practice: Theoretical Frameworks Informing Relationship-Based Practice'. In. G, Ruch, D, Turney and A, Ward (eds). *Relationship-Based Practice.* London: Kingsley Publishers. pp13-45

Scannapieco,M. and Connell-Carrick, K. (2007). 'Child welfare workplace: The state of the workforce and strategies to improve retention', *Child Welfare*, 86, 6, 31- 52

Schofield , G. (1998). 'Inner and Outer Worlds: a psychosocial framework for child and family social work'. *Child and Family Social Work*, 3, 1, 57-67

Schon, D. (1983). *The Reflective Practitioner. How Professionals Think in Action*. London: Basic Books

Sheafor, B. W, and Horejsi, C. R. (2003). *Techniques and guidelines for social work Practice*. 6th ed. Boston, MA: Allyn and Bacon

Shemmings, D. (2015). Quick guide: How attachments affect your own practice. Community Care Inform. Available online at http://www.ccinform.co.uk/guides/quick-guide-attachment-practice/. Last accessed 26/3/15

Smith, M. (2010a). 'Containment and its Failure in an out of Hours Emergency Social Work Team'. *Journal of Social Work Practice*, 24, 1, 3-14

Smith, M. (2010b). 'Sustaining Relationships: Working with Strong Feelings. Anger, Aggression and Hostility'. In: G, Ruch., D, Turney and A, Ward. (eds) *Relationship-Based Practice*. London: Jessica Kingsley pp 102-117

Steckley, L. (2013). Therapeutic Containment and Holding Environments: Understanding and Reducing Physical Restraint in Residential Child Care. Scotland: Centre for Excellence for Looked After Children in Scotland. Available online at: http://www.celcis.org/media/resources/publications/PR_and_Containment_World_CYC.pdf Last accessed 9/4/15

Stepney, P. (2000). 'An overview of the wider policy context'. In P. Stepney and D. Ford (eds) *Social Work Models, Methods and Theories*. Lyme Regis: Russell House

Stevenson, L (2015) 'Social workers to face five years in prison for failing to protect children from sexual abuse, warns Cameron'. Community Care. Available online at http://www.communitycare.co.uk/2015/03/03/social-workers-face-five-years-prison-failing-protect-children-sexual-abuse-warns-cameron/. Last accessed 29/3/15

Sudbery, J. (2002) 'Key features of therapeutic social work: the use of relationship', *Journal of Social Work Practice*, 16, 2, 149-162

Tauber, E. S. (1988). 'Exploring the therapeutic use of countertransference data'. In: B. Wolstein (ed). *Essential papers on countertransference* pp 111-119. New York: New York University Press

TCSW. (2012). 'The Professional Capabilities Framework'. London: The College of Social Work

The Guardian/Paula McFadden (2013) 'Social workers must look after themselves and recognise their limits'. The Guardian. Published online 13th April 2013. Available at http://www.theguardian.com/social-care-network/2013/apr/23/child-protection-social-worker-burnout Last accessed 29/3/15

Thomas, J. (2013). 'Association of Personal Distress With Burnout. Compassion Fatigue and Compassion Satisfaction Amongst Clinical Social Workers'. *Journal of Social Service Research*. 39, 3, 365-379

Thompson, C. (1988) 'The role of the analyst's personality in therapy'. In B. Wolstein (ed). *Essential papers on countertransference*. pp 120-130. New York: New York University Press

Toasland, J. (2007. 'Containing the container: an exploration of the containing role of management in a social work context', *Journal Of Social Work Practice*, 21, 2, 197-202

Ward, A. (2010). 'The Use of Self in Relationship-Based Practice'. In: G, Ruch., D, Turney and A, Ward (eds). *Relationship-Based Practice*. London: Jessica Kingsley pp46-65

Winnicott, C. (1953). 'Transitional objects and transitional phenomena'. *International Journal of Psychoanalysis*. 34, 2, 88-98

5
A feminist analysis of mothers' involvement in child abuse

Alison Love

Introduction

Child abuse happens when an adult harms, or threaten to harm, a child under the age of 18, even if the harm is not deliberate (Gilbert et al, 2009). Child Sexual Abuse (CSA) is when a child is forced or persuaded to take part in sexual activities either directly or indirectly. CSA is a distressing area and can evoke powerful feelings for practitioners and research shows the long-term affect for survivors including mental health, attachment difficulties and social functioning. Research focuses on the mother's compliant involvement in abuse or failure to act to prevent CSA.

This chapter explore some of the existing research and literature with the aim to develop a different new way of understanding mothers of children who have been abused. I shall give a feminist analysis of CSA as it challenges the taken-for-granted assumptions about sexual abuse and femininity which restricts how women's experiences of sexual abuse are both understood and responded to. There is a particular focus on whether a personal history of CSA affects a mother's ability to safeguard her own children; this focus was born out of an understanding from professional experience that mothers are highly criticised in child protection proceedings and often are blamed, criminalised and persecuted thus replicating abuses of power for women.

Findings from evidence

Society has become more aware of childhood sexual abuse (CSA) and the possible effects of sexual abuse on children through the efforts of campaign groups (e.g. N.S.P.C.C). National data published in 2014 show 2,830 children in England were made subject to child protection plans in the year ending 31st March 2014 and over 23,000 sexual offences against children were recorded in the UK (Jütte et al, 2014). Exact statistics of the incidence of CSA are unknown. Excluding those aged 16 and 17 years, data is recorded by the police and therefore doesn't reflect the number of offences committed, only those reported. Data for offenders under-represent the scale of child abuse because not all cases come to the attention of the police and, even if they do, may decide it is not in the best interests of to investigate. Most sexual abuse is not detected, reported or prosecuted and one in three children do not tell anyone that they're being sexually abused (Radford, et al, 2011); it is an invisible crime only witnessed by the abuser and the victim. Although data does not reflect the total number of sexual offences committed against children it does provide an important picture of the amount of sexual abuse committed that the police record as an offence. Definitions of childhood is contentious although research in the UK showing below 16 years of age in line with the consensual age limit. The legal age of consent varies between countries.

Research shows CSA leads to poorer outcomes in later life and in particular greater parental challenges than mothers who have no personal history of CSA. There is an emotional dependence on children (Alexander, Teti & Anderson, 2000; Burkett 1991), parental aggression such as domestic violence (Capaldi & Clarke, 1998; Noll, Horowitz et al, 2003; Newcomb and Locke, 2001; Daigneault, Hebert & McDuff, 2009; DiLillo, Giuffre, Tremblay & Peterson, 2001; Flemming et al 1999; Bowen 2000, Faller 1989), anxieties around intimate aspects of parenting (Dougals, 2000; Grocke et al, 1995) and dysfunctional parenting attitudes (Rusico ,2001; Jaffe, Cranston & Shadlow, 2011; Cole, Woolger, Power & Smith, 1992; Dubowitz et al, 2001; DiLillo & Damashek, 2003). CSA survivors identify struggles in parenting as a result of their abuse (Courtois, 2010; Wright et al 2012; Allhaugh et al 2013) including lack of confidence as a parent (Banyard, 1997; Cole et al, 1992), and a lack of appropriate parenting strategies (Wright et al 2012; Voth and Tutty, 1999). It has been suggested some CSA survivors have difficulties bonding with their children (Schuetze & Das Eiden, 2005; Alexander 1992; Lyons-Ruth & Block, 1996; Leifer, Kilbane & Grossman, 2001). Furthermore, evidence shows that CSA is not a problematic risk factor, but a causal mechanism (Kendler et al 2000; Kim et al 2007). However, studies have highlighted how survivors demonstrate a high level of resilience and adaptive functioning (Cole et al, 1992; Poulsney & Follette, 1995; Fraser, Richman & Gallinsky, 1999; Mastern, Best & Garmezy, 1990). Liem et al (1997) reports 28% of those identifying CSA could be classified as resilient (Kim et al, 2007). Further studies show a negative focus on investigation and its hypothesis forms an explicit research aim rather than an unintended finding. CSA is widely written about and researched but the specific question of how a history of CSA impacts on a non-offending mothers ability to safeguard their children, has attracted little attention in research.

The following themes have been identified in current research – Intergenerational transmission, attachment difficulties, Emotional reactions and self-perceptions, parenting styles, interpersonal relating and sexuality, Social Functioning, and parental response to CSA disclosures.

Intergenerational transmission of CSA

Most studies support the cycle of maltreatment hypothesis; that is a history of maltreatment increases the likelihood of perpetrating abuse or of their children being abused. Various mechanisms for the intergenerational transmission of abuse have been posited. Social learning models hypothesise that children may learn to be abusive from parents who model abusive behaviour. The belief that abuse can be transmitted across generations, or that a cycle of abuse could be set up across generations was one of the earliest and most widely accepted theories of the causation of abuse (Egeland 1993). Whilst widely accepted for domestic violence, Finkelhor contented that sexual abuse can also be intergenerationally transmitted (Finkelhor, 1984); for instance Goddard and Hiller (1993).

Dixon et al (2005) suggest that only a minority of parents with a history of childhood abuse go on to abuse their own children. Individuals can have experiences that act as protective factors which can help break the intergenerational transmission of child abuse; such as emotional support, psychotherapy, stable environments and relationships (Egeland 1998, 1991). The number of adults who experienced CSA in their childhood do not go on to abuse their children is not determined in any study. Mothers who have experienced CSA in their childhood but break the intergenerational cycle are generally absent from research Future research would benefit from more widespread investigations to include these mothers.

This is supported by extensive research from DiLillo and Damashek (2003) who argue that whilst physical abuse is transmitted through direct perpetration by an adult to their children, the relative infrequency in which females perpetrate sexual abuse (Finkelhor 1979; Russell, 1983 in DiLillo & Damashek ibid p321) suggest intergenerational transmission of CSA would most often involve 'indirect processes' (p321) in which sexual abuse occurs at the hands of someone else. Although this supports the notions that children may be exposed to high risk situations it raises questions about what causes perpetrators of abuse. In this way arguments cannot be reduced to a simplistic notion that those who experienced CSA go on to perpetrate CSA.

Alaggia and Kirshenbaum (2005) show how, within intra-familiar abuse, family dynamics including violence, closed communication patterns and isolation can inhibit disclosure. On the other hand, it is widely believed that maternal support is an important factor in children's willingness to disclose (Gomes-Schwartz et al., 1990; Summit, 1983). Leiffer et al (2004) contend that maternal resilience acts as a protective factor to reduce the risk of continued intergenerational CSA.

A specific risk comes as some women maintain contact with their abuser because the family belief system denies the possibility that they will abuse again, leading parents to believe that their children are safe around a known perpetrator (Duncan, 2004). Uncritical acceptance of the intergenerational theory has led to anxiety among victims and biased assessments by social workers. Research questions the validity of intergenerational abuse in respect of CSA. Finkelhor et al (2005) observed that most sexual assaults are committed by someone the child knows. Their research found that 3% of sexual assaults were committed by family members, 12% were committed by strangers and 85% by friends and acquaintances of which, the vast majority of whom were also under the age of 18 years. Similarly, the NSPCC found that parents or guardians were the abusers in just 1.7% of sexual abuse cases (Radford et al, 2011).

Bowen (2000:198) speculates that the mothers past experiences of abuse has profound effects on later life, including living in an environment both within her immediate family and future relationships that put her children at risk for abuse.

Attachment difficulties

A growing body of research suggests an association between a [maternal] history of CSA and subsequent difficulties in relationships. Adult relationships may be problematic and unsatisfying (Beitchman, Zucker & Hood, 1992; Cole & Putman 1992, Flemming, Mullen Sibthorpe & Bammeo, 1999, Leifer, Kilbnane & Kalick, 2004) and exploitive or victimizing (Deblinger et al, 1993; Fleming et al, 1999). A study by Leifer, Kilbane and Grossman (2001 found that mothers of sexually abused children were more likely to have a history of disrupted early attachments than mothers of non-abused children.

Attachment theory ensures the bonding between infants and their caregivers enhances infants' ability to maintain proximity to their caregivers, thereby increasing their chances of survival (Bowlby, 1944-1991). Ainsworth et al (1978) identified three major patterns of infant-caregiver attachment, which they called secure, anxious (or insecure/ambivalent or insecure/resistant), and avoidant (or insecure/avoidant). In 1987, Hazan and Shaver proposed that attachment theory be extended to consider adolescent and adult romantic/sexual relationships. Notably, avoidant adults tend to be relatively uninterested in romantic relationships (Shaver & Brennan, 1992), have a higher breakup rate than secure adults (Hazan & Shaver, 1987; Kirkpatrick & Davis, 1994; Shaver & Brennan, 1992), and grieve less following a breakup (Simpson, 1990). Anxious adults tend to be obsessed with romantic partners and suffer from extreme jealousy (Carnelly, Pietromonoco, & Jaffe, 1991; Collins, 1996; Hazan & Shaver, 1987), which in the case of anxious men can lead to abusive behaviour (Dutton, Saunders, Starzomski, & Bartholomew, 1994). Like avoidance, anxious attachment is also related to a high breakup rate. Conversely secure adults tend to be highly invested in relationships and have long, stable ones characterized by trust, friendship, and frequent positive emotions (Collins & Read, 1990; Hazan & Shaver, 1987; Kirkpatrick & Davis, 1994; Simpson, 1990).

Alexander (1992) established that CSA frequently occurs in families where parent-child relationships are characterized by insecure attachments, regardless of whether abuse is intra-familial, extra-familial or both. Abused children become aware that their caregivers are their only source of comfort but are simultaneously threatened by their caregivers unpredictable and abusive actions; the caregiver then becomes a source of fear for the child while concurrently being their only attachment figure that can offer protection. (Alexander ibid). This violates the child's assumptions of social relationships and is thought to cause disorganised attachment behaviour and other traumatic effects (Birrell & Freyd, 2006; Kostolitz et al 2014) which play out in later relationships. Failure to form secure attachments early in life can have a negative impact on behaviour in later childhood and problems in parenting (Ricks, 1985) as well as disorganized attachments in later generations (Main & Hearse 1990).

Several studies support the idea that an insecure attachment relationship during childhood increases the probability of intergenerational transmission of abuse for parents who have experienced abuse as children (Egeland et al 1987; Main and Goldwyn, 1984; Zuravin et al 1996). Zuravin et al (ibid) found for those mothers who experienced CSA the risk of their own children being maltreated increased. However, traumatic experiences in adulthood may impact on attachment styles in later life since attachment is considered to be a lifelong approach; this is not addressed in research.

A criticism of the Attachment model is that it assumes that kind, honest, and respectful parents will have kind, honest, and respectful children and parents that are rude, aggressive, and abusive will have similar children. People are unpredictable and cannot be placed in such linear ideals. There are many other factors that influence an individual's character and aspirations including peers, experiences outside of the family and relationships.

Emotional reactions and self-perceptions

Emotional and behavioural problems, post-traumatic stress symptoms and depression are the common most likely consequences of CSA (Schuetze & Eiden, 2005), including, suicidal ideation and self-harm behaviours, anxiety, substance abuse, aggression, self-esteem issues, academic problems, and sexualized behaviour. Long-term effects of CSA indicate increased risk for individuals with a sexual abuse history (vs. non-abused individuals) of major depression, suicide, addictions, post-traumatic stress disorder, anxiety disorders (Briere & Elliott, 1994), antisocial personality disorder (Linehan, 1993), dissociation, increased sense of powerlessness (Finkelhor and Browne, 1985) and sexual dysfunction.

Parenting styles

Baumrind (1966) describes three categories of parenting: permissive, authoritarian and authoritative. Permissive parents demand little of their children and allow children to regulate themselves. Authoritarian parents however are very demanding on their children, do not explain demands and use punitive approaches to enforce their rules. Authoritative parents are said to demand much of their child but have clear expectations and a caring relationship with the child. However what is a family is a contested and complex debate. Baumrind's research on the concept of family is over 50 years old and probably less relevant in contemporary society.

Research in this area has not demonstrated consistent findings. Lyons-Ruth & Block's (1991) found where CSA had occurred, mothers decreased their involvement with infants and restricted maternal affect. Burkett's (1991) observations of mother-child interactions highlighted mothers who had a history of CSA may be more parent-child focused (as opposed to self-focused) compared to control groups. In contrast Oates et al (1998) found no difference in the perceptions of care and protection afforded to older children of mothers who had not experienced CSA when compared to mothers who had. Whilst Douglas (2000) reported anxiety and distress among CSA survivor mothers in relation to 'intimate' aspects of parenting however this study failed to account for other variables such as demographics and cultural background.

Interpersonal relations and sexuality

Davis and Petretic-Jackson (2000) found that many studies examining the long-term impact of CSA on adult functioning have primarily focused on the personal distress of survivors and have neglected the impact of CSA on interpersonal relationships. From their study in this area they reported that CSA survivors had difficulties with relationships, but that the specific nature and cause of the impact of CSA on interpersonal relationships are unclear, since survivors of CSA report considerable variability in both the range and severity of symptomatology.

It is unclear whether sexually aggressive men consciously select victims or whether a normal process of sexual attraction leads them to the women they ultimately sexually assault. It is possible that predatory rapists (those who assault strangers) may consciously choose their victims (Stevens, 1994, as cited in Marx et al., 2005) while acquaintance rapists may simply find themselves attracted to certain types of women (e.g., Kanin, 1984). Regardless, , a number of possible characteristics of CSA survivors have been posited to play a role in being targeted by sexual aggressors and hence are more at risk of becoming involved in abusive relationships. This has a negative effect on the environment children grow up in and places them at risk of either direct harm (physical abuse) or indirect harm (witnessing domestic violence). Smith and Saunders (1995) suggested that non-offending mothers tend to associate with partners who have similar personality traits, particularly anxiety. They concluded that anxiety traits may be one attribute in individuals who are targeted by perpetrators and ultimately place their children at risk of CSA.

In a study by Holmgreen (2014) on the impact of CSA on dating behaviours in adulthood, the results indicated that CSA relates to attachment anxiety but not to avoidance of the dating behaviours studied. While risky dating behaviours could be associated with increased rates of sexual assault, it was found that most of them were not predicted by attachment. Attachment avoidance, it was suggested, does relate to some key high-risk dating behaviour, and anxious attachment is associated with higher rates of sexual assault. Similarly, Tracey et al (2001) describe women with anxious attachment as more likely to become quickly involved in sexual encounters in order to feel close to their partners and to avoid being abandoned. Anxious attached adults can fall in love easily (Hazan & Shaver, 1987) and view sex as a means of expressing love similar to findings from Zayas and Shoda (2007). This would suggest that women may not be more attracted to sexually aggressive men, but find sexually aggressive behaviour more normal or acceptable and therefore are less likely to act to protect themselves or leave a relationship. In this way, love and violence become intertwined and it could be argued for perpetrators that violence is an acceptable way to solve problems and that love and violence go hand-in-hand (Stith et al., 2000). Consequently higher rates of parents with a childhood history of abuse (in both sexual and physical abuse cases) were reported in families where domestic violence was also present (Goddard and Hiller, 1993).

Revictimization is a consistent finding in CSA research (e.g. Messman-Moore et al, 2000; Neumann & Houskamp, 1996) in prospective as well as retrospective studies (e.g., Filipas & Ullman, 2006; Gidycz, Coble, Latham, & Layman, 1993; Livingston, Testa, & VanZile-Tamsen, 2007) and in community, clinical, and college samples (Filipas & Ullman; Jankowski, Leitenberg, Henning, & Coffey, 2002; Kearns & Calhoun, 2010; Livingston et al; Wyatt, Guthrie, & Notgrass, 1992). In a review of relevant research, it was estimated that sexual revictimization is experienced by anywhere from 32% to 82% of CSA survivors (Grauerholz, 2000).

Social functioning

According to Briere (1992) many adult abuse survivors utilize alcohol and other drugs compulsively to rid themselves or avoid painful memories, depression, and other difficulties associated with abuse. Research has linked parental substance misuse with a history of CSA (Dembo, Williams & LaVoie et al, 1989; Speiker et al, 1996; Ireland & Wisdom, 1994, Leiffer et al, 1993, Leiffer et al, 2004; Famularo et al, 1992; McClosky & Bailey, 2000). Although in Lieffer's study it is noted that the sample of urban African American Mothers in low income populations may not lead to transferable findings across populations and therefore may be less valid. Issues of race and culture and the impact of social ecology have not been examined in this study.

Parental response to child sexual abuse disclosures

Research has shown that mothers typically respond with belief and support when their child discloses sexual abuse (Bolen, 2002, Eliott &Cairns, 2001, Knott, 2008, Leifer et al, 2001). However, in instances where a mother struggles to accept a disclosure and seems to support her partner (abuser) rather than a child's account, the complexities of an already difficult situation become compounded.

Mothers whose children had been sexually abused have reported in many studies to experiencing serious psychological symptoms following disclosure of the abuse; this is reported to be heightened if mothers have experienced CSA. However, Goodwyn (1992) reported that non-offending Mothers with a history of CSA were able to provide a more responsive environment for children following disclosures of abuse if they retained detailed coherent memories of their experiences.

A feminist analysis of the literature

Most of the literature is contained within a patriarchal paradigm and for this reason using a feminist perspective will offer new insights. The Women's Liberation Movement (WLM), bought sex to the political forefront and in 1976 with the Sexual Offences (Amendment) Act and provided the first statutory definition of rape (prior to this rape was an offense at common law). The Criminal Law Revision Committee in their 1984 Report on Sexual Offences rejected the idea that the offence of rape should be extended to marital relations and it was not until 1991 the marital rape exemption was abolished in England and Wales after the case of R and R (R v R [1991] UKHL 12).

Post Structural feminists have looked at the deconstruction of power and argue that gender is culturally constructed with an emphasis on language, challenging traditional feminist certainties about lived experience, the nature of women's subordination and the use of the category 'woman'. Kristeva (1981) argued that the word 'woman' is socially constructed and exists only in opposition to the notion of man because feminist practice based on the notion of 'woman' is negative. The feminist perspective is a mode of analysis which focuses on the oppression of women in society, specifically of women's status and position in society.

Feminist views of CSA can be understood as on a continuum from liberal to radical. Liberal views tend to regard CSA as a gender-neutral assault on individual autonomy, likened to other forms of abuse, and focusing primarily on the harm that CSA does to individual victims. More radical views, in contrast, contend that rape and CSA must be recognized and understood as an important pillar of patriarchy. Patriarchy is a social system in which men disproportionately occupy positions of power and authority, central norms and values are associated with manhood and masculinity (Johnson 2005: 4-15). Radical feminists maintain CSA arises from patriarchal constructions of gender and sexuality within broader systems of male power, and emphasize the harm that CSA does to women and children as groups.

Feminists have consistently regarded child sexual abuse as a core feminist issue. One of the key factors is the imbalance of power between adult and child. That is not to say women cannot abuse power and trust or abuse children but studies suggests abuse of children is overwhelmingly perpetrated by men. Conflict theory argues that inequality in the family including dominance by a female partner, increases the probability of violence because the dominant partner will use violence to maintain power. Feminists have also argued that women use violence to maintain power which is a further consequence to a patriarchal society in which women traditionally have none. NSPCC research (2014) shows 91.8% of children and young people who reported being sexually abused by an adult did not live with them and said their abuser was male (Radford et al, 2011) and according to Bunting, women are responsible for up to 5% of sexual offences committed against children (2005).

Craig et al. (1989) argues that, although sexual abuse is seen as self-evidently wrong, revealing it results in resistance through denial and minimisation. It 'taps deeply into individual doubts and fears about sexuality and…challenges the abuse of male power in families' (Craig et al., 1989: 62). A social constructionist approach shows how professional and media debates about child sexual abuse draw on complex and contested discourses about childhood, the family, sexuality, gender, class and race (for example Parton and Parton, 1989).

Feminist writers have disputed family systems theorists around the responsibility of women for sexual abuse perpetrated by men (Birns and Myer, 1993; Elbow and Mayfield, 1991; Hooper and Humphreys, 1998; Joyce, 1997; Myer, 1985). Similar to an ecological approach, Family systems theory focuses primarily on the family and identify problems in the context of consequences in dysfunctional relationships among family members. If abuse occurs, the responsibility shifts to the mother, who is blamed for her failure to protect the child (Risley-Curtiss & Heffernan, 2003).

Theories such as cognitive dissonance, social learning theory and family dysfunction theories suggest the non-offending mothers have deliberately 'blocked out' (McLaren, 2013) the acts or her responsibility in it. This ignores the complex procedures taken to silence victims, to groom and deceive other family members. Non-offending Mothers risk being seen to break several social norms around motherhood and femininity.

Mother blaming is an issue. Being labelled as unable to protect your children as a result of the victimization they may have experienced as children and continue to face in current relationships not only serves to continue but also reinforces the victimization and becomes a self-fulfilling prophecy (Gelles, 1982). Fathers, whether perpetrators of abuse are often invisible in the records of children's services (Edelson, 1998), which is also a finding in Serious Case Reviews (see Peter Connolly, OFSTED 2014).

From a feminists perspective, the application of a 'failure to protect' ethos unfairly penalizes mothers who may have tried unsuccessfully to protect themselves and their children -sometimes at the risk of their own lives. This is evidence from the vast research cited already. There needs to be a shift in focus from personality disorders (diagnosed or deficit models) to attachment relationship and bonding which instigates a social-recovery model focusing on quality of relationships rather than individual pathology (Warner 2009).

Removing children from their families following disclosure affirms negative messages given to children during the grooming process and leads them to be blamed for the abuse and hold on to a personal sense of blame for which they have none. Practice which sees the male leave the home following disclosure aims to ensure that appropriate support can be provided to the child and non-offending mother to enable their recovery.

In discussions of power it is important to note the power given to Social Workers as agents of the state are in a position to make important life changing decisions. Radical social work critique argues that social workers use their authority as agents of social control, policing the potential deviance of marginalized social groups on behalf of state organizations that essentially reflected the interests of already privileged sections of society (Corrigan and Leonard, 1978). Social workers are mandated to develop relationships of co-operative power and collaboration wherever possible across many forms of social boundaries (eg families, agencies, communities) and in doing so are able to empower individuals. I would argue that you need to support families through disclosure and working in a collaborative manner. CSA stirs up powerful emotions for all those who become involved; it threatens ideals of childhood as a time and the family as a safe place which can lead to workers, (albeit unknowingly) perpetuating abuse to non-offending mothers and their children. In taking a punitive approach to addressing CSA this becomes part of the perpetrators continuation of abuse and denies closure to children. The combination of male control, and sanctions used to enforce gender stereotypes of motherhood combine to increase the entrapment and inequality from which CSA originates. Examinations of male power within the family show that abusers tend to see their wives and children as property which they can exploit including sexually. Incest is seen as an acceptable way of expressing 'normal' male/female relations in a patriarchal society. Statutory intervention transforms this to a gender neutral position of 'family violence. This serves to limit the responsibility of males in perpetrating CSA and other acts of violence to at best a shared blame discourse or a victim blaming ethos.

Research and social work practice do not take place in solidarity but are situated in a wider societal and political arena; they reflect the ways in which society constructs mothering, mothers, fathering, fathers, and families. The theory permeating Western beliefs is that the mothers directly affect the child's behaviour (Corcoran, 1998). The role definition of motherhood has passed through patriarchal systems for much of history and is reinforced in political, legal and practice frameworks where definitions and expectations on motherhood are constructed and reconstructed. Feminism attempts to reduce and eliminate ideas of ownership and imbalances of power, as well as hierarchical and dualistic thinking which have previously dominated the definition of motherhood. Allan (2003) reported that child and family workers blame mothers by drawing on discourses that suggest they should know what their children are doing, and who they are doing it with. Authoritative pressures therefore serve to obscure how the privilege of man and oppression of the women occurs (Butler 2004).

Sexual violence is not simply a gender issue and may be too simplistic to reduce to a natural patriarchy development. Instead CSA should be analysed along other multiple dimensions of power. It is difficult to understand how certain forms of CSA can be understood in terms of gender and power such as internet offending or child pornography. Gender bias has pervaded the treatment and prevention of child sexual abuse. Historically, the dominant explanation for incest was that girls seduced their fathers. It has been argued that mothers often used denial as a defence mechanism to resist recognizing familial abuse. Non-offending mothers are characterized as disordered and as silent colluders who are, at least partially, responsible for CSA (Gavey, Florence, Pezaro, & Tan, 1990). This ignores the complex circumstances in which mothers are deceived and prevented from knowing about the abuse.

A criticism of the feminist approach is that it could be described as collusive in establishing and maintaining imbalances between men and women by its focus on gender and ignores difficulties faced by powerless men by falsely representing men as always and only powerful and gaining privileges from their obedience to a patriarchal society. Patriarchal ideology focuses on simple binaries in explaining oppression (Harlow and Hearn, 1996; Healy, 2000). Alternatively by offering a feminist perspective it balances contemporary gender analysis of CSA.

Conclusions

There is considerable evidence that whilst for some women the long term impact of CSA is severe and enduring with complex and interrelated symptomology, for other survivors they are able to build positive relationships and protect and nurture their children.

The feminist approach to sexual abuse provides further insights than any other approach to understanding CSA. It places CSA in the context of understanding society and the social structure of power maintained by men over women. It also attributes responsibility to the abuser rather than the mother or the victim. However, the feminist perspective does have limitations. Although feminist theory emphasizes the survivors' feelings about the abuse giving consideration to psychological impacts, it is essentially a sociological approach and tends to focus on social structure and socialization. Tackling CSA will need an approach which can address the social, political and culture arena in which it occurs as well as an individual level.

A history of childhood abuse is a considerable risk factor in the aetiology of abuse to fundamentally safeguard children. This review does not suggest that previous research should be ignored or discounted but should be seen in the context of a wider debate of power and control in family dynamics. I have argued for a move away from discourses of blame in social work intervention to a more inclusive and empowering approach in understanding the mother's role. Instead of assuming non-offending mothers are compliant in abuse but rather, be seen within a multi-faceted aspect of family dysfunction within a complex issue of power that is under researched.

References

Alaggia, R., & Kirshenbaum, S. (2005) Speaking the unspeakable: Exploring the impact of family dynamics on child sexual abuse disclosures. *Families in Society.*, 86, 2, 227-234

Alaggia R., (2009) *An Ecological Analysis of Child Sexual Abuse Disclosure: Considerations for Child and Adolescent Mental Health*

Alexander, P.C. (1993) The differential effects of abuse characteristics and attachment in the prediction of long-term effects of sexual abuse. *Journal of Interpersonal Violence*, 8, 346-362

Bartholomew, K., Henderson, A., & Dutton, D. (2005) Insecure Attachment and Abusive Intimate Relationships In Clulow, C. (Ed.), *Adult Attachment and Couple Psychotherapy. The 'secure base' in practise and research* (pp. 43-61) London: Routledge

Bowlby, J. (1958) The Nature of the Child's Tie to His Mother. *International Journal of Psychoanalysis*, 39, 350-371

Cloitre, M., Scarvalone, P., & Difede, J. (1997) Posttraumatic stress disorder; self- and interpersonal dysfunction among sexually retraumatized women. *Journal of Traumatic Stress*, 10, 437-452

Duncan, K.A., (2004) *Healing from the Trauma of Childhood Sexual Abuse*. Westport : Praeger

Finkelhor, D. (1979) *Sexually Victimized Children*. New York: Free Press

Finkelhor, D. (1984), *Child Sexual Abuse: New Theory and Research*, The Free Press, New York

Finkelhor, D. (1994) Current information on the scope and nature of child sexual abuse. *The Future of Children*, 4, 2, 31- 53

Finkelhor, D., & Browne, A. (1985) The traumatic impact of child sexual abuse: A conceptualization. *American Journal of Orthopsychiatry*, 55, 530-541

Gold, S.R., Sinclair, B.B., & Balge, K.A. (1999) Risk of sexual revictimization: A theoretical model. *Aggression and Violent Behaviour*, 4, 457-470

Goddard, C.R. and Hiller, P.C. (1993), 'Child sexual abuse: assault in a violent context', *Australian Journal of Social Issues*, 28, 1, 20-33

Harris, J. R. (1998) *The nurture assumption: Why children turn out the way they do.* New York: Free Press

Hazan, C., & Shaver, P. R. (1987) Romantic love conceptualized as an attachment process. *Journal of Personality and Social Psychology,* 52, 511-524

Henderson, A., Bartholomew, K., Trinke, S., & Kwong, M. J. (2005) When Loving Means Hurting: An Exploration of Attachment and intimate Abuse in the Community Sample. *Journal of Family Violence,* 20, 4, 219-230

Hill, A (2007) *Sexual abuse child protection.* Research. Community Care Inform [online]

Holmgreen, L. (2014) 'Child Sexual Abuse, Attachment, Dating Behaviors, And Sexual Assault' Dissertations (2009 -) Paper 347

Ireland, T.O., & Wisdom, C.S. (1994) Childhood victimization and risk for alcohol and drug arrests; *International Journal of the Addictions,* 29, 235 -274

Kanin, E.J. (1984) Date rape: Unofficial criminals and victims; *Victimology,* 9, 95-108

Leifer, M., Kilbane, T., and Grossman, G. (2001) A Three-generational study comparing the families of supportive and unsupportive mothers of sexually abused children. *Child Maltreatment,* 6, 4, 353-364

Lyons-Ruth, K & Block, D. (1996) The disturbed caregiving system: Relations among childhood trauma, maternal caregiving and infant affect and attachment. *Infant Mental Health Journal,* 17, 257-275

Marx, B.P., Heidt, J.M., & Gold, S.D. (2005) Perceived uncontrollability and unpredictability, self-regulation, and sexual revictimization.; *Review of General Psychology,* 9, 67-90

Noll, J.G., & Grych, J.H. (2011) Read-React-Respond: An integrative model for understanding sexual revictimization. *Psychology of Violence,* 1, 202-215

Ruche, D., Runtz, M., Hunter, M., (1999) Adult Attachment: A Mediator Between Child Sexual Abuse and Later Psychological Adjustment. *Journal of Interpersonal Violence,* 14,184-207,

Sable, P. (2008) What Is Adult Attachment? *Clinical Social Work Journal,* 36, 21-30

Smith, D.W., and Saunders, B.E., (1995) Personality Characteristics of Father Perpetrators and nonoffending Mothers in incest dyadic analysis; *Child Abuse & Neglect,* 19, 5, 607-617

Speiker, S.J., Bensley, L., McMahon, R.J., Fung, H., & Ossiander, E., (1996) *Sexual abuse as a factor in child maltreatment by adolescent mothers of pre-school aged children. Developmental and Psychopathology,* 8 497-509

Tracy, J.L., Shaver, P.R., Albino, A.W., and Cooper, M.L., (2001) Attachment styles and adolescent sexuality. In P. Florsheim (Ed.), *Adolescent romantic relations and sexual behavior: Theory, research, and practical implications* (pp. 137-159). Mahwah, NJ: Lawrence Erlbaum

Zayas, V., & Shoda, Y. (2007) Predicting preferences for dating partners from past experiences of psychological abuse: Identifying the psychological ingredients of situations. *Personality and Social Psychology Bulletin,* 33, 123-138

Zeanah, C.H. and Zeanah, P.D. (1989) Intergenerational transmission of maltreatment: insights from attachment theory and research. *Psychiatry,* 5, 177-196

6
Key issues arising from practice under section 17 of the Children Act 1989

James McCullough

Introduction

The purpose of this chapter is to explore key issues that arise from practice under section 17 of the Children Act 1989, in particular the extent to which social workers involve parents to inform their own decisions by being transparent in assessment. This chapter will analyse relevant literature, theory and policy alongside the experiences that I gained from a practice placement within a children and families statutory social work setting.

Background

As a concept social work is perpetually difficult to encapsulate, given its central location within social welfare systems that are in turn shaped by various governmental policies and are affected by a diverse range of dynamic cultural and economic contexts, (Banks, 2012: 1 and Bamford 2015). However, consistency can be found in the promotion of what are commonly regarded as *modern social work values*, which have been evident within many western societies since the 1970's and have been influenced by the emergence of various social movements, such as feminism, anti-racism and disability rights, (Lishman, Yuill, Brannan and Gibson, 2014: 8).

With specific reference to the United Kingdom, the Health and Care Professions Council (HCPC) revised its *'Standards of conduct, performance and ethics'* in August 2012, which outlines the statutory duties and expectations placed on registered health and care professionals, (HCPC, 2012). This is supported by *'The Code of Ethics for Social Work'*; last reviewed by The British Association of Social Workers (BASW) in January 2012, which enshrines the values and ethical principles that endorse social justice, empowerment and non-judgementality, (Dominelli, 2009: 17). These include: *respecting the right to self-determination, being trustworthy* and *providing information*, (BASW, 2012), which should be intrinsic elements of everyday social work practice. In this chapter I focus on the implementation and compliance with such guidance in order to explore some of the issues that arise from social work practice under section 17 of the Children Act 1989.

The introduction of the Children Act 1989 is widely regarded as a significant development in English law as it replaced numerous pieces of complex and inconsistent legislation with a single framework to facilitate decision-making processes that are concerned with furthering the best interests of children (Allen, 2005: 1).

The Human Rights Act 1998 is another vital piece of legislation that strengthens the rights of individuals, which is based on the European Convention on Human Rights. During my statutory children and families social work placement I was primarily required to fulfill two roles under section 17 of the Children Act 1989: firstly, the assessment of children and families in response to concern for the welfare of children (under the guidance outlined in the *Framework for the Assessment of Children in Need and their Families*, (Department of Health, Department for Education and Employment, and Home Office, 2000)); and secondly, working with children and families who were subject to Child(ren) in Need (CIN) Plans (non-compulsory interventions that are ultimately designed to safeguard and promote the welfare of children), Westwood (2014: 31).

Under section 17 of the Children Act 1989 parental consent is required in order for a local authority to assess the welfare risks to children. This also requires parental consent for the local authority to share relevant information with other agencies, such as education, health and police (as promoted by *Working Together to Safeguard Children*, (Department for Education, 2013)) which is widely considered as crucial to the process of effectively safeguarding and promoting the welfare of children, (Horwath, 2009: 104). Therefore, as statutory social work assessment and intervention with children and families under section 17 of the Children Act 1989 requires informed parental consent, it suggests parents could decline local authority help if they wish.

Review and analysis of literature

As outlined there are ethical issues and principles I wish to explore. The first of which is the complex concept of self-determination, which is the ideology of freedom and autonomy. Self-determination is constructed on a set of values and ideas that were formed outside of social work, although they are often imported in to practice. Spicker (1990: 221) suggests that by virtue of the nature of self-determination it carries little relevance to social work practice as clients are subject to intrinsic pressure and are part of a relationship that is constructed within the context of power and authority. Spicker (1990: 222) digressed to argue that individuals can only experience true freedom and autonomy from the constraints and coercion of others, such as social workers, if they are able to make their own choices.

I share this perspective and would also argue that whilst the concept of self-determination appears to fit with the ideological values inherent within social work there is a significant limit to its applicability, especially in the child protection arena, as ultimately a local authority's statutory power is used where there is conflict between care and control issues (Spicker, 1990: 225). In the context of my experience in statutory practice with children and families, I would suggest that there is little capacity to demonstrate a commitment to implementing self-determination with parents, as they are not always explicitly informed of their rights. In contrast, Munro (2008: 83) suggests that although the child protection system in England is to some extent justifiably limited by respect for a family's qualified right to privacy (Article 8 of the Human Rights Act 1998), the use of coercion by a social care practitioner is often required in order to create an opportunity to assess a child's welfare. Munro (2008: 83) stressed the importance of the way in which coercion is exercised by practitioners, as the insensitive use of coercive power may affect the extent to which an effective and long-term social work relationship can be built between the worker and the parent. Furthermore, Munro (2008: 83) highlights the importance of drawing on evidence from a range of professional sources when assessing the welfare of a child under section 17 of the Children Act 1989.

I would argue that coercion may be necessary to protect children, and as supported by Ferguson (2011: 51), despite the fact that it appears to negate the ethical principle of self-determination, as suggested by Ferguson (2011: 51). In the context of my experience in statutory practice, I have previously been advised by management and colleagues to firmly assert my authority as a representative of children's services in order to gain consent to share information with other agencies from resistant parents to share information with other agencies to enable an holistic assessment of a child's welfare, (Holland, 2011: 150). Therefore, whilst ideological concepts such as self-determination, autonomy and freedom are essential to ethical social work, the extent to which they are woven into practice, is in reality significantly limited (Spicker, 1990: 221).

The Children Act 1989 stipulates that the relationship between the family and the local authority should (where possible) be based on the notions of partnership and participation, which require practitioners to empower children and families, provide open information and promote the active involvement of families within the decision-making processes that concern their welfare, (Ryan, 1999: 3). In an article that considers the presence of both partnership and paternalism in the domain of child protection, Calder (1995: 754) suggests that most professionals prefer their partnership to be on a voluntary basis, whereby there is a mutual perception of welfare issues and how these can be addressed. He argues that partnerships between parents and social care practitioners are more likely to succeed if they are underpinned by shared power.

However, whilst I understand the nature of partnership in social work and the necessity to implement it within practice, I would argue that there is no such thing as a voluntary partnership between a parent and the local authority in the context of child protection, (supported by Spicker, 1990 p. 228), and that whilst the idea of shared power between such parties may seem ideal, it does not exist in reality because of the conflict of control in a local authority fulfilling its protection function. Therefore, I suggest that it is apparent that if a parent declined involvement from a child protection service, it may prompt the local authority to exercise the legal power available to it in order to establish the welfare of a child, thus the nature of the relationship would not be voluntary, (Herring, 2013: 583).

This is why I do not consider there to be any degree of shared power between a parent and a child protection service, as ultimately the parent fulfils the less powerful position of having their parenting capacity scrutinised by a local authority whilst the service adopts the role of control, (Calder, 1995: 751). In this respect, I would agree with the work of Beckett (2010: 53), who suggested that even when a social worker's role is not supported by explicit legal power from the outset, such as practice under section 17 of the Children Act 1989, a parent may still feel empowered to comply with the request and expectations of a service by virtue of their vulnerable position and uncertainty over what may action otherwise be taken, (Beckett, 2010: 53).

Rooney (in Beckett 2010) talks of the concept of involuntary clients in social work, whereby people feel compelled to accept a service because of their apprehension over the consequences of not doing so (such as parents having children removed from their care). Beckett (2010: 53) suggests that in spite of the degree of emancipatory rhetoric and emphasis on the concept of partnership throughout social work discourse, social workers are still agents of control in child protection and it is not always recognised that the relationship between a parent and a practitioner is primarily based on an imbalance of power, as opposed to a mutual sharing of power.

My experience in statutory social work practice, has shown how children and families that have been subject to CIN Plans who have strongly disputed the assessed welfare risks, chose to go along with the plan for fear of the consequences if they do not cooperate (Beckett, 2010: 53). The extent to which social workers are clear with parents regarding their rights under section 17 of the Children Act 1989 and (namely) the options available to them in any given set of circumstances regarding issues of child welfare is not always known; therefore this suggests a clear breach of what the legislation intended.

This is primarily due to a lack of social work confidence in understanding and ability to apply relevant legislation to their practice, such as the theoretical non-compulsory nature of assessment and intervention under section 17 of the Children Act 1989. Universities need to teach legislation alongside practice to ensure newly qualified social workers understand the full ramifications of this provision.

In this particular social work placement I observed families being maintained on CIN Plans that may have otherwise been closed to the service if they were openly informed that they could rightfully withdraw consent for the local authority to continue an assessment or intervention. This is morally and ethically unjust as it asserts coercive influence to seek compliance against their wishes. The families in such positions were not assessed to pose a risk of significant harm to the children and so a child protection investigation (under section 47 of the Children Act 1989) was not likely to have been instigated. In his work on paternalism and partnership in child protection, Calder (1995: 751) identified that one particular form of paternalism is exemplified by workers misleading parents by withholding certain information, which would mirror the suggestion of Beckett (2010:62) and support the observations that I made during my placement within a statutory children and families social work team.

In his work examining the use of authority by social workers, Ferguson (2011: 164) suggests that practitioners should promote and empower resistant parents to become more open and honest with their expression of feelings of a child protection intervention. He argues that parents should be given the opportunity and freedom to convey their thoughts regarding the child welfare issues at play and on the necessity of a local authority response to such concerns, which would allow for the facilitation of positive engagement and trust between the two parties. Ferguson (2011: 164) highlights that the greater degree of sincere empathy a social worker demonstrates to a parent, the more they will feel empowered to express their feelings.

However, whilst I share the understanding that a skilled social worker would facilitate the engagement of parents by empowering them to share their views), I do not feel that parents would often trust a child protection service enough to be open due to their fear of the consequences of such honesty, (Cleaver, Cawson, Gorin and Walker, 2008: 56). I suggest that due to the public's knowledge of the powers that can be enforced by a statutory child protection agency a parent would be particularly apprehensive about being honest with a social worker regarding the concerns for their child's welfare, (Phillips, 2004: 171).

I feel that this explicitly reflects the extent of the inherent power imbalance between a local authority and a family, especially in the context of child protection, (Hill, 2010: 17). Therefore, considering that parents will be aware of such powers, I do not feel that we can expect them to be as honest as suggested by Ferguson (2011: 164).

A theme alluded to earlier in this chapter is the presence of risk aversion in statutory child protection social work. I feel that this concept is significantly linked to the reasons why a service may be more inclined to become involved with a family (or indeed *remain* involved with a family). A local authority could remain in a position of assessment for a prolonged period of time, as a precautionary response to potential child welfare concerns rather than a proportionate interventionist approach (Calder, 1995: 750).

Beckett (2010: 60) argued that social workers are placed under increasing pressure by external sources (such as the mass media, the general public and other professionals) to intervene with families at risk of experiencing welfare issues, but are not necessarily meeting the threshold for a child protection investigation (under section 47 of the Children Act 1989). Families considered to be in need of some form of social support are often overwhelmed by the involvement of various services and agencies that tend to have little clear rationale for their work, other than an urgency to initiate and sustain their involvement with a family.

In considering these suggestions I have been able to observe such practice in my own experience of working in a statutory social work setting, whereby the service has initiated contact with a family following the expression of child welfare concerns and assessed that the family requires intervention without explicitly outlining the reasons for it. This is a primary example of how a service misuses its authority (Calder, 1995: 752). In a discipline that is so profoundly built on the notions of a plethora of ethical principles and the ideologies of anti-oppressive practice, I would suggest that the extent to which these are applied in child protection practice is worrying (Clifford and Burke, 2008: 9).

I was required to complete an assessment of whether a mother was sufficiently meeting her child's welfare needs, following the expression of concern by another practitioner. In assessing the family using the *Framework for the Assessment of Children in Need and their Families*, (Department of Health, Department for Education and Employment, and Home Office, 2000) I was able to establish that the concerns were not significant enough to warrant further statutory involvement with children's services. My recommendation was authorised by management however, because the mother provided care for another child who was involved with a separate department within the service, it was agreed that the family would continue to receive statutory intervention and were made subject to a CIN Plan. The mother expressed strong disapproval; however, she was not informed by the service that this intervention was voluntary. As well as being an example of unethical practice, it is a reflection of the current risk-averse nature of contemporary child protection practice in England, influenced by the considerable number of high-profile serious case reviews and deaths of children over recent years.

Following the tragic death of Baby Peter in August 2007, there was a significant rise (60%) in the number of child protection investigations into alleged child abuse in England (under section 47 of the Children Act 1989) between 2009 and 2014. This is a trend that can also be seen across other areas of the child protection system over this period, such as the rise in the number of children made subject to child protection plans (50%) and the overwhelming increase in the number of Care Order applications made by the local authority

(104%), (Jones, 2015). I believe that such statistics re an indication of how the child protection system in England has become over-responsive to the concerns for child welfare as opposed to evidence, compared to a time when perhaps a more measured service-level response to such issues would have been taken and the rights of parents would at times carry more weight, (Bainham et al., 1999: 92).

Bainham et al., (1999: 89) completed a socio-legal analysis of the concept of being a parent and how this stands within our society. It was suggested that despite the dominance of the welfare principle that's set out in the Children Act 1989, the law does in fact place a degree of emphasis on the rights and interests of parents in a variety of ways. Namely, it was argued that the state is only entitled to intervene if a child has or is likely to suffer significant harm under the supervision of their parents. Bainham et al., (1999: 92) propose that in the absence of evidence of harm, the state should refrain from imposing an intervention. This is supported by Watson (1980: 103) in his view on self-determination in social work (as cited in Spicker, 1990: 222).

However, whilst I would agree that this approach would perhaps be a truer demonstration of self-determination and parent autonomy in child protection practice, I do not believe that such a non-interventionist stance would ultimately promote and safeguard the welfare of children, as proposed by Schur (1973: 155) regarding responses to delinquency among young people in America. Instead, I feel that a greater level of transparency should be delivered when working with families under section 17 of the Children Act 1989, which would essentially empower them to make more informed decisions on the basis of the information that they provide.

In looking at how a local authority may intervene with a family following the expression of concern for the welfare of a child, it's important to consider the four perspectives outlined by Fox Harding (Herring, 2013: 581) regarding the tripartite relationship between the parent, the child and the state. The *laissez-faire and patriarchy* approach, which promotes that local authority intervention with families should be kept to a minimum and that parents' privacy should be respected (as outlined in Article 8 of the Human Rights Act 1998). Somewhat oppositional to this is the *state paternalism and child protection* approach, which promotes local authority intervention with families to whatever extent is necessary in order to ensure the safety of children (which can be linked to Article 3 of the Human Rights Act 1998). Thirdly, the *defence of the birth family and parents' rights* advocates the importance of optimal contact between parents and children, which should be integrated in to state intervention where possible. Finally, Fox Harding outlines *children's rights and child liberation* as an approach adopted by the state when responding to child welfare concerns, which places significant emphasis on the views of the child (Herring 2013:581).

I would contend that there are elements of each of these approaches within the Children Act 1989; however, to varying extents, (Herring, 2013: 581).

Although the introduction of this fundamental piece of legislation promoted the importance of the views of the child and the provision of care for children by their birth families, it is vastly outweighed by the necessity to protect children from harm, (Holt, 2014: 9). The welfare principle is seen to be the aspect that underpins most of the act and therefore it would correspond that the default approach to intervening with children and families appears is that of *state paternalism and child protection*. A local authority's most common approach to responding to child welfare concerns is to intervene with a family (initially by completing an assessment) and by imposing whatever on-going intervention is considered necessary (if any), which would often supersede the rights and autonomy of parents, and potentially infringe Article 8 of the Human Rights Act 1998.

I would propose that whilst the *laissez-faire and patriarchy* approach would not necessarily be an effective way of ensuring the absolute safety of children, there are elements to the approach that could be balanced to take account of child protection issues. An area of practice in social work that I feel could be promoted when working with children and families is the concept of participation. The ideologies of participatory practice have since gone on to be supported throughout national and local policies, and are now woven in to literature on empowerment in modern day social work, (Payne, 2014: 306). In this context, the idea of participation refers to the involvement of individuals with the decision-making processes of the services which they receive, whereby they have a degree of choice and are able to exercise a certain extent of power, (Adams, 2008: 31).

Ultimately, practice within a child protection system involves decision-making processes that are designed to ensure the safety of every child that may be at risk of harm, and it is quite clear that within this there will be parents that do not share the local authority's perceptions of risk. However, I do believe that there is significant value in promoting the participation of parents within the decisions that are made around the welfare of children and securing their best outcomes, (Flynn and Starns, 2004: 81). Healy (1998) suggests that the issue of power remains a central tension between the concept of participation and child protection practice, and that an authority's repressive use of power in such contexts should be embraced and subject to constant reflection, rather than be denounced by those within practice contexts.

Healy (1998: 907) alludes to the work of Foucault (1978) in his analysis of power and suggests that not only can his approach facilitate the understanding of the use of repressive power, it can also be applied to acknowledging the productive use of statutory power within the context of child protection practice (given the extent to which it can be utilised to safeguard the most vulnerable members of society, such as abused children). Healy (1998: 909) uses the foundations of post-structural theory to consider how the notion of professional judgment (historically critiqued by those that promote the concept of service user participation) can be effectively incorporated in to a participatory approach to child protection practice.

The very nature of the risk assessment process is fundamentally based on the exercise of professional judgment, which is central to practice in the child protection system, (Horwath, 2009: 85). However, the concept of judgment is somewhat oppositional to the ideals inscribed within modern social work values, hence why this notion provides the basis for critique and informs participatory practice. Criticism of professional judgment can create tension when they're applied to practice in the child protection system. In this respect, it's proposed that whilst social workers should be sensitive to the position of service users, an ethos of participation that refutes the notion of judgment is ultimately not applicable to the necessary assessment of abuse and neglect in child protection practice. Healy (1998: 911) also suggests that the critique of professional judgment is often formed on the ideals of mutuality between social workers and service users; a concept that is particularly difficult to secure in the child protection arena, given the statutory power that is often exercised by a local authority to safeguard the welfare of children.

Healy (1998: 911) concludes that participatory practice in the field of child protection should not retreat from the necessity of judgement, but should promote transparency with parents and ascertain their views of the assessed risks to a child. I would agree with the work of Healy (1998), as whilst promoting the active participation of parents in the child protection system should be a fundamental aspect of practice, it should not be at the expense of assessing whether a child is at risk of harm, which is a statutory duty for all local authorities, (Hill, 2010: 12). The suggestion that social workers should practise a greater degree of openness and clarity with parents is a theme that has been consistently raised throughout this chapter and is an issue that I believe needs to be considered further. Although the safeguarding of a child's welfare should be the ultimate priority in statutory social work practice, I believe that the position of parents is crucial to the development of children and that parental rights and responsibilities should hold a central role in practice with children and families (as set out in section 3(1) of the Children Act 1989), (Abbott and Langston (2006).

Conclusion

As outlined in the introduction to this chapter, there has been limited research into this area due to a lack of empirical evidence. The concept of self-determination is an area that is significantly linked to social work practice, given its close association with freedom and autonomy, Spicker (1990: 221). However, the extent to which it is utilised in the child protection arena is limited, despite its apparent links to the core values and ethics inherent within social work. As an ideology, self-determination implies that an individual has the freedom and power to make their own decisions. However, due to the nature of child protection, it is often necessary for a local authority to prevent a parent from exercising complete autonomy by imposing a degree of statutory power in order to safeguard a child from harm, (Hill, 2010: 46). Therefore, a difficult balance needs to be struck between empowering parents to promote their parental rights and responsibilities within section 3(1) of the Children Act 1989, and the role of the state to intervene with families where there may be child welfare concerns, (Davies, 2012: 105).

Whilst I agree that it is imperative to safeguard children from harm, I feel that it's also important to consider the ways in which parents are forced in to working in partnership with a local authority and by acknowledging the power imbalances that ensures ethical practice. Calder (1995: 754) indicates that the introduction of the partnership principle has promoted a shift towards the involvement of parents in the child protection system and that their relationships with local authorities can be formed on a voluntary basis, but could be a reflection of parents' reluctance to decline the intervention of statutory services through fear of the consequences were they not to co-operate. Ferguson (2011: 164) stresses the value of empowering resistant parents to express their thoughts on the involvement of child protection services in facilitating the development of positive engagement (and ultimately the safeguarding of children's welfare).

I believe that the apparent tendency for a local authority to withhold information is evident within child protection practice as it allows a service to remain in a position whereby it is able to measure and control the welfare of children, despite the guidance set out in the *Framework for the Assessment of Children in Need and their Families* (Department of Health, Department for Education and Employment, and Home Office, 2000), which specifies that assessments under section 17 of the Children Act 1989 should not be unnecessarily intrusive or continued without a clear purpose. A culture of interventionism has emerged as a key theme in the child protection system due to the increase in pressure on local authorities to intervene when there is evidence to get it right. This is best exemplified by local authorities bringing children into voluntary care when parental agreement is required under section 20 of the Children Act 1989, where the President of the Family Court, Lord Mumby, criticized the local authority for not seeking consent in a clear and transparent way (Mumby, 2015). Such pressure appears to have been exacerbated by the publication of high-profile serious case reviews and inquiries in to child deaths over recent years, many of which have highlighted the failures of child protection services and fellow agencies in exercising their duties to safeguard children from harm, (*The Victoria Climbié Inquiry*), (Laming, 2003).

Therefore, I believe that, as a result of societal pressure, local authorities withhold information from parents regarding their right to withdraw consent for statutory assessment and intervention. I have formed this belief from the observations that I made during my placement in a statutory child protection setting and from the literature reviewed. In particular, the principles that I consider to be most disregarded in practice are a social worker's responsibility to be trustworthy and to provide information to parents.

Therefore, it is essential that parents should be informed from the outset of any voluntary intervention with a local authority that requires their informed consent, that it can be withdrawn at any given time because such involvement is not compulsory. I also believe that a greater emphasis should be placed on outlining all available options to a parent that's subject to such assessment or intervention (including that their refusal to accept such local authority involvement may, or may not, result in a child protection investigation under section 47 of the Children Act 1989). Local authorities should avoid the risk-adverse culture that has been dominating practice over recent years (Corby, Shemmings and Wilkins 2012 p.58) and embrace risk as part of managing change.

The benefits of such a shift in the statutory response to child welfare concerns are threefold. Firstly, it would enable families to exercise a greater degree of control over the way in which they choose to function in the privacy of their own environments, which would perhaps be a truer reflection of the values and ethics that are said to be central within modern social work practice, (Cleaver, Cawson, Gorin and Walker, 2009: 55). Secondly, such a shift might also reduce the rate of re-referrals to the service as the closure of statutory social care interventions for low-risk children and families may empower them to maintain the changes that they achieved during the period in which they were receiving support, (Hill, Head, Lockyer, Reid and Taylor, 2012: 336). Thirdly, I would suggest that a move away from a risk-averse approach would enable an increase in the resource capacity of local authorities and allow for children and families most at risk to receive a more focused and effective service. Ultimately, I believe that this shift would lead to an increased sense of autonomy for low-risk children and families and a more effective protection of children in need and at risk of harm by the local authority.

References

Abbott, L. and Langston, A. (2007) *Parents Matter: Supporting the Birth to Three Matters Framework*. Maidenhead: Open University Press

Adams, R. V. (2008) *Social Work and Empowerment*. 4th ed. Aldershot: Palgrave Macmillan

Allen, N. (2005) *Making Sense of the Children Act: And Related Legislation for the Social and*

Welfare Services. Fourth edition.. Chichester: John Wiley

Bainham, A., Day-Sclater, S. and Richards, M. (1999) *What is a Parent? A Socio-legal Analysis*. Portland, OR: Hart

Bainham, A. and Gilmore, S. (2013) *Children: The Modern Law*. 4th ed. Bristol: Jordan

Banks, S. (2012) *Ethics and Values in Social Work*. 4th ed. New York: Palgrave Macmillan

Beckett, C. (2010) *Assessment and Intervention in Social Work: Preparing for Practice*. London: Sage

Calder, M. C. (1995) Child Protection: Balancing Paternalism and Partnership. *British Journal of Social Work*, 25, 749-766

Cleaver, H., Cawson, P., Gorin. S., and Walker, S. (2009) *Safeguarding Children: A Shared Responsibility*. Chichester: Wiley-Blackwell

Clifford, D., Burke, B. and Burke, B. (2008) *Anti-oppressive Ethics and Values in Social Work: Past Caring?* 4th ed. Basingstoke: Palgrave Macmillan

Corby, B., Shemmings, D., and Wilkins, D. (2012) Child Abuse: An Evidence Base for Confident Practice. 4th ed. Croydon: Open University Press/McGraw-Hill

Davies, M. (2012) *Social Work with Children and Families*. Basingstoke: Palgrave Macmillan

Department for Education. (2013) *Working Together to Safeguard Children: A Guide to Inter-agency Working to Safeguard and Promote the Welfare of Children*. London: HM Government. Available online at: https://www.gov.uk/government/uploads/system/uploads/attachment_data/file/ 417669/Archived-Working_together_to_safeguard_children.pdf [Accessed 6th April 2015]

Department of Health, Department for Education and Employment and Home Office. (2000) *Framework for the Assessment of Children in Need and their Families*. London: The Stationery Office. Available online at: http://webarchive.nationalarchives.gov.uk/20130401151715/https://www.education.gov.uk/publications/eOrderingDownload/Framework%20for%20the%20assessment%20of%20children%20in%20need%20and%20their%20families.pdf [Accessed 6th April 2015]

Dominelli, L. (2009) *Introducing Social Work*. Bristol: Polity Press

Ferguson, H. (2011) *Child Protection Practice*. Basingstoke: Palgrave Macmillan

Flynn, H. and Starns, B. (2004) *Protecting Children: Working Together to Keep Children Safe*. London: Heinemann

Fook, J. (2002) *Social Work: Critical Theory and Practice*. London: Sage

Gray, M. and Webb, S. A. (2013) *The New Politics of Social Work*. Basingstoke: Palgrave Macmillan

Health and Care Professions Council. (2012) *Standards of conduct, performance and ethics*. London: Health and Care Professions Council

Healy, K. (1998) Participation and Child Protection: The Importance of Context. *British Journal of Social Work*, 28, 897-914

Herring, J. (2014) *Family Law: A Very Short Introduction*. Oxford: Oxford University Press

Herring, J. (2013) *Family law*. 6th ed. London: Pearson

Hill, A. (2010) *Working in Statutory Contexts*. Cambridge: Polity Press

Hill, M., Head, G., Lockyer, A., Reid, B., and Taylor, R. (2012) *Children's Services: Working*

Together. Gosport: Pearson

Holland, S. (2011) *Child and Family Assessment in Social Work Practice*. 2nd ed. London: Sage

Holt, K. (2014) *Child Protection*. Basingstoke: Palgrave Macmillan.

Horwath, J. (2009) *The Child's World: The Comprehensive Guide to Assessing Children in Need.* 2nd ed. London: Jessica Kingsley

Hughes, L. and Owen, H. (2009) *Good Practice in Safeguarding Children: Working Effectively in Child Protection*. London: Jessica Kingsley

Kay, J. (2003) Protecting Children: A Practical Guide. 2nd ed. London: Continuum

Jones, R. (2015) *The Story of Baby P: Setting the Record Straight.* Slides from a presentation by Ray Jones (Professor in Social Work at Kingston University London and St. Georges, University of London) at Solent University in March 2015

Laming, Lord H. (2003) *The Victoria Climbié Inquiry*. London: The Stationery Office. Available online at: https://www.gov.uk/government/publications/the-victoria-climbie-inquiry-report-of-an-inquiry-by-lord-laming [Accessed on 6th April 2015]

Lishman, J., Yuill, C., Brannan, J. and Gibson, A. (2014) *Social work: An Introduction.* London: Sage

Milner, J. and O'Byrne, P. (2009) *Assessment in Social Work*. 3rd ed.. Basingstoke: Palgrave Macmillan

Munro, E. (2008) *Effective Child Protection*. 2nd ed. London: Sage

Phillips, R. (2004) *Children Exposed to Parental Substance Misuse: Implications for Family Placement*. London: British Association for Fostering and Adoption

Rooney, R. H. (1992) *Strategies for Work with Involuntary Clients*. New York,: Columbia University Press

Ryan, M. (1998) *The Children Act 1989: Putting it into Practice*. Aldershot: Ashgate

Schur, E. M. (1973) *Radical Non-intervention: Rethinking the Delinquency Problem*. Englewood Cliffs, NJ: Prentice-Hall

Spicker, P. (1990) Social Work and Self-determination. *British Journal of Social Work*, 20, 221-236

Stanley, J. and Goddard, C. (2002) *In the Firing Line: Violence and Power in Child Protection Work*. 1st ed.. Chichester: John Wiley

The Policy, Ethics and Human Rights Committee (2012) *The Code of Ethics for Social Work: Statement of Principles*. Birmingham: The British Association of Social Workers

Watson, D. (1980) *Caring for Strangers*. London: Routledge

Westwood, J. (2014) *Children in Need of Support*. Basingstoke: Palgrave Macmillan

7
Key issues in the involvement of fathers in child protection

Jacqueline Pilgrim

This chapter will focus on fathers' involvement in child protection social work. The literature on 'fathers and social work' is wide ranging (Ryan 2000, 2006; Sonenstein et al, 2002; Daniel & Taylor, 2001; Featherstone, 2009; Ferguson, 2011). The term 'father' is specific to males only. Whilst acknowledging the legal importance of 'Parental Responsibility' the project focuses on father-figures inclusively who are involved in parenting and caring of children, which can be multifaceted due to dynamic family relationships and family structures as children could have multiple father-figures (Bellamy, 2009). However, it is the individual perceptions of the fluid concept of 'fatherhood' and how the child or father-figure identify with the role of 'father.'

From my own practice placement I observed some outstanding work with fathers. I also observed some fathers being overlooked or ignored by a diverse range of professionals and mothers. Furthermore, children being placed at risk of harm via various modes of circumstances or situations, which is not gender specific, as women and mothers can also harm children too.

Are fathers 'pushed' away from engaging in child protection?

Children come to the attention of Children Services due to concerns of need, abuse and neglect. The issue of fathers, risk and Child Protection Social Work Practice (CPSWP) is a continuous challenge, which for a number of decades has dominated policy makers, professionals and communities in the UK as well Internationally (Munro, 2004, 2008, 2010, 2011a, 2011b). Yet it is predominantly mothers who are the focus of engagement and involvement when, safeguarding children (Scourfield, 2003, 2006; Featherstone, 2003, 2006, 2010; Lee et al, 2009; Lewis, 2000).

The UK legislative framework and recent policy developments can be confusing and contradictory in regards fathers engagement. The Children Act 1989 and 2004 specifies engagement with fathers including those without parental responsibility. The Child Care Act 2006 stipulates engagement with fathers particularly those from excluded or minority groups. The Working Together (2013) policy document highlights inter-professional's legal obligations to promote welfare, protect and safeguard children as everybody's responsibility (Dugdale, 2014). However, despite these changes, children are still being placed at significant risk of harm. Gammell, (2008) reports that on average three children die each week in the UK. Failure to engage with fathers has been evidenced in Serious Case Reviews (SCR) for decades. Indeed, high profile child death inquiries, such as Victoria Climbié and Peter Connelly, have frequently found social workers and other practitioners failing to share information. Fundamentally, there has been a lack of attention regarding abusive men to identify, involve or engage fathers in matters relating to children and families (Brandon et al, 2006; 2009; Sinclair and Bullock, 2002; Laming, 2009). In a recent SCR published by Southampton Local Safeguarding Children's Board in to the death of Child K, it was stated: 'Professionals may have been intimidated by Mr X, a violent man. His refusal to engage with any professional was not challenged'. Similar, issues were identified following the review of Child Q on the Isle of Wight, as a result social workers and other professionals were too afraid to act (Bedford, 2015; Harrington, 2015: 62). Brandon et al (2009: 52) in their research of SCR between April 2005 and March 2007 found that professionals often adopted what they term 'rigid or fixed thinking'. Fathers were both labelled and polarised as 'all good or all bad' (ibid). This fixed approach has led to attributions around fathers reliability and trustworthiness, whereby workers have excluded fathers and ignored their expressed views because they have been labelled as a bad father (Sinclair and Bullock, 2002).

Current changes have lacked gender analysis, or consideration of the diversity of fathers and other social divisions. Similarly, there is limited literature on Black and Ethnic Minority fathers, gay fathers, fathers with disabilities, single-fathers and fathers of children with imprisoned mothers. These dimensions are important as not all fathers and masculinities are equal; nor is fathering stereotypical traditionally patriarchal, but is an exceptionally diverse and complex concept so often ignored (Featherstone, 2003; Featherstone et al, 2007: 15; Flynn, 2012; Connell, 2005).

Child protection, neglect and abuse is still considered to be the mothers' domain as the central homemaker of families. Despite social structural and economic changes following the rise of feminism and postmodern ideologies, this view is socially constructed, and manifests due to cultural norms and gendered divisions of labour (Featherstone, 2001, 2003, 2004). As a result of these attitudes and assumptions about mothers, as the primary care giver, there are greater expectations, unfair burdens and inequalities placed on mothers by Children Services to safeguard, protect and bring about change (Ferguson and Hogan, 2004 & Ryan 2000). Scourfield (2003), demonstrated that fathers were too often ignored even when they were putting the children and mother at risk of harm. Mothers are gatekeepers and can maintain father's invisibility due to implacable hostility and parental alienation; as a result little is known about their backgrounds, vulnerabilities, including genetic, medical or hereditary conditions, and their strengths as potential care givers. Brown et al (2009) suggest this approach is deeply rooted in culture, society and social work. The mother's gatekeeping behaviour remains constructed, controlled and unquestioned, and serves a purpose. For some mothers, they view children as their territory and not the father, particularly in some cultures (Ferguson and Hogan, 2004). It is further reinforced as 'men are not considered the business of child protection workers' (Scourfield, 2006: 441).

In the UK the issue of general exclusion could be perpetuated by changes in Parental Responsibility, Family Law, non-residency and non-biological status of father-figures (Ewart-Boyle et al, 2013). Research in the USA of 1,958 cases demonstrated that only one third of mothers identified the father when asked (Malm et al, 2006). The majority of childcare professionals generally and in particular frontline social work practice are female and it is still viewed as a woman's job (Ferguson, 2011). According to the General Social Care Council (GSCC 2010), during 2009-10, 77% of registered social workers were female, while 23% were male. However, the recruitment of male workers had increased by 17% from previous years (Parker and Crabtree, 2014). Velazquez and Vincent (2009: 9) suggest that when a male case worker is interacting with a father there is less inclination for defensiveness and less pre-occupation with perceived negativity or unfair treatment. However should the gender of the worker really matter? However, Featherstone's (2004) research suggests that it is not necessarily about the workers gender, what is important is the attitude, cultural views, and expectations of men, fatherhood and masculinity. Lewis (2000) argues fatherhood is a multifaceted construction and as such studies cannot examine the true nature of fatherhood in its entirety. It is the professional relationship and working alliance between the fathers and professionals which is pivotal for successful engagement (Featherstone 2004).

In a USA study, 44% of workers attitudes revealed that it was easier to work with mothers than fathers (Malm et al, 2006) which Goff (2012) concurs with. However, the current social work climate continues to battle with issues around not having enough time to engage more effectively with families (Munro 2004 & 2011b). Featherstone (2010) further suggests that fathers are viewed practically as 'feckless and irresponsible.' Rivett (2010) suggests that rather than adopting a binary approach, fathers are 'simultaneously harmful and vulnerable' this reduces the risk of one dimensional thinking and descriptions. Whether fathers are considered a risk, vulnerable or a resource, one thing is for sure, that positive outcomes for mothers and children are difficult to achieve without engaging the father, because paternal information is paramount for the health and wellbeing of the child. Likewise, the research evidence supports the involvement of fathers as being positive for children's future outcomes (Ferguson and Hogan, 2004).

Fathers are described as present but not involved (Brown et al's 2009 p. 26) and as manufactured 'ghost' fathers. This is because 'in order to see a ghost, one must first believe in their existence and relevance'. Despite historical and socio-economic developments, social work and other disciplines including Health and Education are still viewed as women's business despite the different manifestations of fathering and the changing shape of family life (Scourfield, 2006: 445). However, the concept of family has remained relatively unchanged, despite new developments, increasing diverse family structures, including, same-sex families, single-parent families, multiple step-families (Smart and Neale, 1999; Featherstone, 2009).

Social Work language is a complicated issue. Language can have different meanings and understandings, which can be powerful and oppressive to individuals and groups, impeding fatherhood identity. From observations fathers may not be involved due to his individual personal needs or work commitments. Unfortunately current CPSWP does not operate flexible hours, interventions or provisions to enable engagement with fathers outside of core business hours.

There is evidence of why fathers resist being involved in child protection and engaging in the process. Fathers may be resistant of entering a predominant female domain as this can be intimidating, evoking negative feelings, discomfort and self-consciousness (Clapton, 2013; Scourfield et al, 2013). It is reported that some fathers are reluctant due to previous childhood and adult experiences and resistant behaviour could be associated with their paternal authority being threatened. Fathers who present as resistant could be viewed with suspicion resulting in punitive approaches being adopted and the management of risk being heightened (Ewart-Boyle et al, 2013). However, generally the lack of engagement is accepted without question or exploration echoed within the literature (Ferguson and Hogan, 2004). Social workers may 'communicate aggressively and confrontational' provoking further resistance (Forrester et al, 2008: 23) and inadvertently reinforcing gendered parenting roles, through language, or through the use of punitive, authoritarian and compulsion approaches to secure engagement. This also raises questions of the dilemmas for meaningful and purposeful engagement due to feigned or disguised compliance. Furthermore, compulsory approaches can be disempowering and oppressive, which conflicts with social work values. Forrester at al (2008) suggests that balancing care and control with children's rights can create ethical dilemmas around Human Rights.

In O'Donnell et al's (2005) Focus Group Study supported by other studies (Berlyn et al 2008), fathers provided explanation for their resistant behaviours. Fathers were fearful they will be exposed as having poor parenting skills and therefore labelled as a poor father. Fathers may fear other professions, being in a 'double bind' between the mother and child, fearing losing custody or child contact (Featherstone et al, 2010: 11). The general perception is that CPSWP is not there to support and help them 'emotionally or physically' resulting in feeling like 'cardboard cut outs' rather than genuine involvement (Cameron et al, 2014: 15).

Ferguson and Hogan (2004:15) suggest that what can affect father's engagement in Child Protection, are pre-judgements driven by media amplification or stories told within social work practice. They suggest that such messages of 'dangerousness' can 'float around the system' heightening concerns in gendered occupations. As a consequence fathers are either labelled as non-nurturers or dangerous. If there are reports that the father has been intoxicated or abusive towards the social worker, this can reduce the likelihood of engagement with him, thus, creating a ricochet effect amongst team members of gendered occupational discourse, labelling fathers as non-nurturers and dangerous, especially if the father is intoxicated or abusive towards the social worker (O'Donnell et al, 2005). Fathers are harshly screened as either absent, irrelevant, threatening or no good, or mothers and fathers are deemed both as bad as each other (Scourfield 2003). Ferguson and Hogan (2004) in their Ireland case study utilising 24 'vulnerable' fathers, 12 mothers, 12 children and 20 professionals - 'vulnerable' father is defined as a man who is known to be struggling to be a good enough parent due to having involvement with social services and family support agencies (p.24). They identified that constructs of dangerousness were as a result of the feelings and emotions from family members narratives. This in turn, prevented the social worker from having direct contact with the fathers, failing to hear the fathers voice and which should form part of their assessment that is often unreported (Maxwell et al, 2012).

Baynes and Holland (2012) screened 40 child protection cases and found a third of fathers had no contact with a social worker before the Initial Child Protection Case Conference. Social workers need to proactively assess and engage with all significant men in a child's life, understanding that some may pose risks, some may be an asset or resource whilst others incorporate aspects of both. Furthermore, the level of perceived risk or fear 'versus' the actual likelihood of violence needs due care and creative consideration to promote engagement and inclusion of fathers (Smith, 2005). Social work physical assaults are often perpetrated by female clients but male workers are most likely to be targeted (Scourfield 2003).

Similarly, workers avoidant or ambivalent behaviour should be explored and supported in reflective supervision. Supervision is paramount to ensure practice is safe and where anxieties, feelings and emotions are managed appropriately and objective decisions can be collectively made (Howe, 2008). This is an issue of moral panic that fuels a blame culture in child protection is acute when actually very little is known about fathers because the information about fathers is not known. The labelling and demonization of men without rigorous assessment and analysis goes against social work values and ethics and reinforces oppressive and discriminatory practice. Ferguson (2012) suggests that 'what is required is a sea change in attitude, culture and approach' towards fathers.

Are fathers 'pulled' in, to engage with CPSWP?

Positive attitudes and the emotional intelligence of workers is fundamental to building relationships, effective communication and engagement (Howe, 2008). This was the findings from Family Rights Group where 162 parent support professionals found that it was the manner in which fathers were approached and communicated that ensured successful engagement (Ashley et al, 2006). A local authority Children-in-Need Social worker promoted a positive attitude for change in practice by increasing father's engagement within 18 months amongst a team of 12 social workers (Cooper, 2012). The outcomes resulted in a change in process as the names and telephone numbers of fathers were captured at the Initial Assessment stage. Furthermore, fathers were seen in person and invited to attend the Child Protection Conference. If the father was unreachable social workers recorded their attempts of engagement. The results showed significant improvement and father involvement increased from 8% to 20%. Clapton (2013: 28) suggests 'workers should not conclude that a non-resident father has written himself out of the child's life;' he concurs with gaining and recording all personal details of fathers at the initial stage of the process.

Identification and community based initiatives and programmes (e.g. Sure Start) assist with father's engagement, which has proven successful for some young fathers (Barnardos, 2012). Ghate et al (2000) suggest that offering services that better sit with the concept of traditional masculine qualities, to include physical activities, making service provision specific for males only could be seen as an incentive for higher levels of engagement. Likewise, those professionals who were able to encourage fathers earlier on in the process, promoting their paternal role and in the interest of their children, had the most success in sustaining and 'holding' their engagement (Ferguson and Hogan, 2004 p13). Also as evidenced in the USA (English et al, 2009: 233). Research by Malm et al (2006) on non-resident fathers found that the identification, location and contacting of fathers within 30 days of the case opening has proven to be successful in fathers engagement. Interagency working provides effective learning for how other professions can engage with fathers together. Ferguson and Gates (2015) experienced similarities in their Health Study with Family Nurse Partnership. Their research was centred on how health practitioners made links with fathers and through the adoption of relational, holistic and therapeutic methods enabled positive father engagement. The health practitioners made an early assumption prior to father engagement. Contextually, they viewed all fathers to be vulnerable, which promoted the caring element of the Health occupation. The rationale for this, was linked to the psychosocial perspective, supporting and nurturing fathers.

Social workers work with fathers that are often unreachable, defensive, hostile, resistant, reluctant, ambivalence, or absent. Fathers involvement remains low and is viewed as 'absent', without challenging such perception or understanding of why?

Debate

The literature highlights two research questions:

1. In the context of CPSWP – Are fathers 'pushed' away from social work engagement?
2. Are fathers 'pulled' into engagement with CPSWP?

I use the metaphor of 'push' and 'pull' to describe this conundrum. Contextually, If a father is viewed as a risk, vulnerable, absent, non-resident or reluctant, it appears some can be 'pushed' away from engaging. If a father is identified as safe or a commodity they can be 'pulled' into engaging.

Raising awareness, training and education on gender inequalities could develop practice knowledge and a better understanding of the 'push' and 'pull' factors. Facilitation could provide an opportunity, whereby the 'push' factors, reverse into 'pull' factors, promoting a learning culture, rather than a blame culture. In turn, improving fathers engagement is also in the best interest of the child and family as a whole. Critically, the evidence base of what works best is limited. The risks of not engaging effectively with fathers is well known and widely reported (Ofsted, 2011). Critically if children are coming to the attention of Children Services due to concerns of risk, neglect and abuse, it is the responsibility of the social work profession along with other statutory and voluntary professions to work together identifying and engaging with fathers for the purpose of child protection (pull) because it is everybody's responsibility and paramount for the welfare and safety of the child.

From my own experience, I did not always consider fathers in this context, especially when they are not living with their child. I now understand this was due to a lack of knowledge of the 'push' and 'pull' issue as a key facet of their relationships within the complex family ecological system. On reflection, this unintentionally reinforces an anti-father culture, of marginalisation, oppression, and gender inequality. Cameron et al's (2014: 14) research suggest that men's lack of involvement is not necessarily due to their absence or difficulties in engaging but from a strong tendency amongst child welfare workers to overlook fathers involvement with their families. The inclusion of fathers need to be viewed as a priority, whereby they are 'pulled' into practice so that Social Workers and other professionals more holistically monitor, assess, manage the risk through observing parenting capacity as part of their duality role. This, enables seeing, hearing and feeling the world of the child, preserving the whole family approach.

Language can be powerful barrier within a feminist perspective reducing fathers' rights. Is it more appropriate to refer to fathers as a hard to reach group that are marginalised? Munro and Hubbard argue they are (2011). The dynamics identified in the 'push' factors, along with exclusion, could be viewed as institutional weakness, because fathers, children and families are failed by the system.

Effective communication and building relationships are at the heart of social work practice, but it is not straight forward, as human interaction is multi-layered and culturally complex. What is required is transparency, honesty and a respectful authoritative dialogue (Ruch, 2010; Woodcock-Ross, 2011; Olivers and Charles, 2015); and these methods could 'pull' fathers towards engagement with child protection. Likewise, Munro (2011b) wants social workers to be more relational in practice, spending time with children and families. However, despite the Munro Review practice has not made sufficient change (DFE, 2014). Social workers generally work independently, in their dual role between family welfare and child protection. However, whilst work is generally overseen by management from a distance; this is consumed with assessing and monitoring as opposed to intervening, supporting and empowering (pull). I have observed outstanding practice with fathers, but this is not always recognised. I had many opportunities to put 'myself' in a fathers' shoes, undertaking 'strengths based' and empowering work with fathers. However, as a student I recognise I had the time to prepare and 'pull' them in, make an early connection, build the relationship, it helps one tune-in, providing motivation, empathy, acceptance, and hope as well as providing practical support. Critically, you only get one chance at the initial stage of engagement because beginnings are essential. Forrester et al (2008) suggests that empathic practice promotes effective practice (pull); whilst Lavallette (2011) identifies that the current systemic social worker processes in contrast undermine the quality and skills of child protection work (push).

It is important to be curious and challenging when engaging with fathers. Asking the right questions, at the right time, in order to provoke and engage a response (Woodcock-Ross, 2011). Likewise, asking the 'self' questions: What are his family values? What is really going on in this fathers world? What is his reality like? What does this father want and need? How does he view his children? What does being a father mean in today's society? Is he child focused? It is all about doing the simple things properly' (Laming's (2003p. 105).

The use of 'self' as a tool in social work is essential for effective communication and building professional relationships (Ruch, 2010; 2010a). I have observed fathers being nervous, anxious, and erratic and avoiding eye contact. Their sometimes erratic reactions could be associated with self-protection, self-regulation or underlying feelings of guilt, shame, loss and grief (Kroll, 2010). The reality is that without engaging and making the effort to build rapport, early assumptions, labelling and judgements are made in error. Several fathers spoke openly about their feelings of shame and loss. The grief was due to not having regular child contact, as a result of the risks, or from biased reports from the mother's perspective.

Conclusion

There are many conflicting and competing theories and ideas which arguably contribute to the 'push' and 'pull' factors of fathers engagement with child protection. Research is complex due to the diverse nature of social work practice. However, the knowledge base provides insight of causality between family relationship and the dynamics within the ecological system. I therefore, recommend further research be undertaken.

Fathers are generally excluded from child protection conferences but must be given greater involvement so that practice can truly become more child focused. The need to 'pull' and engage with fathers is paramount as evidenced from serious case reviews yet we still fail them. The engagement of fathers in the CPSWP is an issue and children will continue to be placed at significant risk of harm unless fathers are at an early point identified and included. I would advocate a systemic-relationship-based approaches for effective engagement when 'pulling' fathers into CPSWP. Father engagement must start early, giving equal access of opportunity and an informed choice to improve safety and outcomes for children, mothers and families. Promoting a father's needs and involvement in the assessment process, up holds the values of social work, and is a moral and legal matter because fathers are 'significant' in the child's life. That said, father's engagement must be safe, flexible, meaningful, helpful, and purposeful and not a mere bolt-on addition but an integrated, inclusive approach. Finally, I want to advocate and promote father-inclusivity within all social work as an essential element of good and effective practice. The patriarchy view of mothers as the dominant care giver compounds the 'Push' factors for fathers being excluded. We must change the mind set of social workers and rethink the way they view father's engagement in the reunification of care.

References

Ashley, C., Featherstone, B., Roskill, C., Ryan, M. and White, S. (2006) *Fathers Matter: Research findings on fathers and their involvement with social care services*, London. Family Rights Group.

Asmussen, K. and Weizel, K. (2010) *Evaluating the evidence: Fathers, Families and Children*, London: National Academy for Parenting Research, Kings College.

Barnardos (2012) Are we nearly there yet Dad? Supporting young Dads journeys through fatherhood. [Accessed 1 February 2015]. Online: http://www.barnardos.org.uk/are_we_nearly_there_yet_dad.pdf

BASW. (2002) *The Code of Ethics for Social Work*. Birmingham: BASW.

Baynes, P. and Holland, S. (2012) Social Work with Violent Men: A child protection file study in an English Local Authority. *Child Abuse Review*. Vol. 21. No.1. 53-65.

Bedford, A. (2015) *Serious Case Review Relating to the Q family*. [Accessed 28 March 2015]. Online: http://www.iowscb.org.uk/serious_case_reviews

Bellamy, J. (2009) A national Study of Male Involvement among families in contact with the child welfare system. *Child Maltreatment*. Volume 14. No.3 pp.255-262.

Berlyn, C., Wise, S. and Soriano, G. (2008) *Engaging fathers in child and family services. Participation, perceptions and good practice*. National Evaluation Consortium. [Accessed 01 February 2015] Online: https://www.dss.gov.au/sites/default/files/documents/op22.pdf

Brandon, M., Howe,. A., Dagley, V., Salter., C. and Warren. C. (2006) What Appears to be helping or hindering practitioners in Implementing the Common Assessment Framework and Lead Professional Working? *Child Abuse Review*. Vol. 15. pp. 396-413.

Brandon, M., Bailey, S. Belderson, P., Gardner, R., Sidebottom, P., Dodsworth, J., Warren, J. and Black, J. (2009) *Understanding SCR and their impact: A Biennial Analysis of SCR 2005-7*, Research Report DCSF-RR129, London, DCFS.

Brown, L., Callahan, M., Strega, S., Walmsley, C and Dominelli, L. (2009) Manufacturing Ghost Fathers: The paradox of father presence and absence in child welfare. *Child and Family Social Work*. Vol.14. No.1. pp.25-34.

Burgess, A. and Osborn, M. (2013) *Engaging with Men in Social Care: A good practice guide*. Wiltshire, Fatherhood Institute.

Cameron, G., Coady, N. and Hoy, S. (2014) Perspectives on being a father from being involved with child welfare services. *Child and Family Social Work*. Vol. 19. pp.14-23.

Clapton, G. (2009) How and why social work fails fathers: Redressing an Imbalance, social works role and responsibility. *Practice Social Work in Action*. Vol. 21. No.1.p p.17-34.

Clapton, G. (2013) *Social Work with Fathers Positive Practice*. London. Dunedin Academic Press Ltd.

Coady, N., Hoy, S.L. and Cameron, G. (2013) Fathers experiences with child welfare services. *Child and Family Social Work*. Vol. 18 pp.275-284.

Coakley, T.M., Shears, J.K., and Randolph, S.D. (2014) Understanding Key Barriers to Fathers' Involvement in their Children's Lives. *Children and Youth Services*. Vol.34. No.4. p.343-364.

Connell, R. W. (2005) *Masculinities*, 2nd eds, Cambridge, Polity.

Cooper, J. (2012) Engaging Fathers: Why Social Workers need to know more about Gender and Masculinity. [Accessed 11 February 2015]. Online: http://www.communitycare.co.uk/engaging-fathers/

Daniel, B., and Taylor, J. (2001) *Engaging with Fathers: Practice Issues for Health and Social Care*. London: Jessica Kingsley Publishers.

DFE (2014) *Rethinking Children's Social Work: Department for Education Children's Social Care Innovation Programme*. [Accessed 15 February 2015]. Online: https://www.gov.uk/government/uploads/system/uploads/attachment_data/file/342053/Rethinking_children_s_social_work.pdf

DoH (2000) *Assessing Children in Need and their Families: Practice Guidance*. Norwich. The Stationary Office.

Dugdale, D (2014) *Guide to hidden men: The Challenge of engaging men in child protection*. [Accessed 27 February 2015 Online: www.ccinform.co.uk/guides/guide-hidden-men/]

English, D.J., Brummel, S. and Martens, P. (2009) Fatherhood in the child welfare system:

Evaluation of a pilot project to improve father involvement. *Journal of Public Child Welfare.* Vol. 3 No.3 pp.213-234.

Ewart-Boyle, S., Manktelow, R., and McColgan, M. (2013) Social Work and the Shadow Father: Lessons for engaging fathers in Northern Ireland. *Child and Family Social Work.* doi: 10.1111/cfs.12096.

Fatherwork (2015) *Generative Fathering Defined.* [Accessed 15 February 2015] Online: http://fatherwork.byu.edu/generativeDefined.htm

Featherstone, B. (2001) Putting Fathers on the Child Welfare Agenda; A research review. *Child and Family Social Work.* Vol.6, No.2. pp.179-186.

Featherstone, B. (2003) Taking Fathers Seriously. *British Journal of Social Work,* Vol. 33, no.2. p.239-254.

Featherstone, B. (2004) *Family Life and Family Support: A Feminist Analysis.* Basingstoke: Palgrave Macmillan.

Featherstone, B. (2006) Why Gender matters in child welfare and protection. *Critical Social Policy.* Vol.26, No.2. pp.294-314.

Featherstone, B. (2009) *Contemporary Fathering: Theory, Policy and Practice.* Bristol, Policy Press.

Featherstone, B. (2010) Writing fathers in but mothers out!!! *Critical Social Policy.* Vol.30. No.2. p.208-224.

Featherstone, B., Rivett, M. and Scourfield, J. (2007) *Working with men in Health and Social Care.* London: Sage.

Ferguson, H. (2011) *Child Protection Practice.* Basingstoke. Palgrave Macmillan.

Ferguson, H. (2012) Fathers Child Abuse and Child Protection. *Child Abuse Review.* Vol.21. pp.231-236.

Ferguson, H. and Gates, P. (2015) Early Intervention and Holistic, Relationship-Based Practice with Fathers: Evidence from the work of the family Nurse Partnership. *Child and Family Social Work.* Vol.20. pp.96-105.

Ferguson, H. and Hogan, F. (2004) Strengthening Families through Fathers: Developing Policy and Practice in relation to Vulnerable Fathers and their Families. Waterford. The Centre for Social and Family Research.

Flynn, C. (2012) Caring for Children of Imprisoned Mothers: Exploring the Role of Fathers. *Child Abuse Review.* Vol.21. No.4. pp.285-298.

Forrester, D., McCambridge, J., Waissbein, C., Emlyn-Jones, R. and Rollnick, S. (2008). Child risk and parental resistance: Can Motivational Interviewing improve the practice of child and family social workers in working with parental alcohol misuse? *British Journal of Social Work.* Vol.38.p p.1302-1319.

Forrester, D., Westlake, D., McCann, M., Thurnham, A., Shefer, G., Glynn, G. and Killian, M. (2013) *Reclaiming Social Work? An Evaluation of Systemic Units as an approach to Delivering Children Services.* [Accessed 03 March 2015]. Online: http://cdn.basw.co.uk/upload/basw_11812-8.pdf

Gammell, C. (2008) *Three children die from abuse every week.* [Accessed 01 March 2015] Online: http://www.telegraph.co.uk/news/uknews/baby-p/3703059/Three-children-die-from-abuse-every-week-Ofsted-chief-Christine-Gilbert-reveals.html Ghate, D., Shaw, C. and

Hazel, N. (2000) *Engaging fathers in preventive services: Fathers and family centres.* Joseph Rowntree Foundation.

Goff, S. (2012) The participation of Fathers in Child Protection Conferences: A Practitioner's Perspective. *Child Abuse Review.* Vol. 21. pp.275-284.

Harrington, K. (2015) *A Serious Case Review: Child K.* [Accessed: 01 March 2015]. Online: http://southamptonlscb.co.uk/wp-content/uploads/2012/10/Child-K-Overview-Report.pdf

Heubner. R.A., Werner, M., Hartwig, S. and Shewa, D (2008) Engaging Fathers: Needs and Satisfaction in Child Protection Services. *Administration in Social Work.* Vol.32. No.2. pp.87-103.

HM Government (2013) *Working Together to Safeguard Children: a guide to inter agency working to safeguard and promote the welfare of children.* [Accessed: 02 March 2015]. Online: https://www.gov.uk/government/publications/working-together-to-safeguard-children

Houston, S. (2003) Moral Consciousness and Decision Making in child and family social work. *British Adoption and Fostering.* Vol. 27. pp.61-69

Howe, D. (2008) *The Emotional Intelligent Social Worker.* Basingstoke. Palgrave Macmillan.

Ixer, G. (2000) Assessing Reflective Practice: New Research Findings. *Journal of Practice Teaching in Health and Social Work.* Vol.23. No.3. pp.19-27.

Jones, R. (2014) *The Story of Baby P: Setting the Record Straight.* Bristol. Policy Press.

Kroll, B. (2010) 'Only Connect…Building Relationships with Hard to Reach People Establishing rapport drug with Drug Misusing Parents and their children'. In Ruch, G. and Turney, D. and Ward, A. (eds) *Relationship-Based Social Work: Getting to the heart of Practice.* London: Jessica Kingsley Publishers.

Laming, H. (2003) *The Victoria Climbie Inquiry,* London: TSO.

Laming, H. (2009) *The Protection of Children in England: A Progress Report.* London: Stationary Office.

Lavalette, M. (2011) *Radical Social Work Today – Social Work at the Cross Roads.* Bristol: The Policy Press.

Lee, S.J, Bellamy, J.L and Guterman, N.B (2009) Fathers, physical child abuse and neglect: Advancing the knowledge base. *Child Maltreatment.* Vol.14. No.3. pp.227-231.

Lewis, C. and Lamb, M.E (2007) *Understanding Fatherhood: A review of recent research.* Joseph Rowntree Foundation, York.

Lewis, C. (2000) *A man's place in the home: Fathers and families in the UK.* Joseph Rowntree Foundation. Online: http://www.jrf.org.uk/sites/files/jrf/440.pdf [Accessed 01 March 2015].

Malm, K., Murray, J. and Green, R. (2006) *What about the dads? Child welfare agencies' efforts to identify, locate and involve non-resident fathers.* Washington, DC: U.S. Department of Health and Human Services. [Accessed 12 February 2015] Online: http://aspe.hhs.gov/hsp/06/CW-involve-dads/index.htm.

Maxwell, N., Scourfield, J., Featherstone, B., Holland, S. and Tolman, R. (2012) Engaging Fathers in children welfare services: a narrative review of recent research evidence. *Children and Family Social Work.* Vol. 17. pp.160-169.

McConnell, N., Barnard, M., Holdsworth, T., and Taylor, J. (2014) *Caring Dads Safer Children:*

Interim Evaluation Report. London. NSPCC.
Munro, E. (2004) The impact of audit on social work practice, *British Journal of Social Work*. Vol 34, No.4. pp.1075-95.
Munro, E. (2008) *Effective Child Protection*. Sage. London.
Munro, E. (2010) Learning to reduce risk in child protection, *British Journal of Social Work*. Vol.40 No.4. p.1135-51.
Munro, E. (2011a) *The Munro review of child protection: Interim report. A child's journey*, London: Department for Education.
Munro, E. (2011b) *The Munro Review of Child Protection: Final Report A Child Centred System*: London: HMSO.
Munro, E. and Hubbard, A. (2011) A Systems Approach to Evaluating Organisational Change in Children's Social Care, *British Journal of Social Work*, Vol. 41 No. 4. pp.726-743.
O'Donnell, J.M., Johnson, W.E., D'Aunno, L.E. and Thornton, H.L. (2005). Fathers in child welfare: caseworkers' perspectives. *Child Welfare*, Vol.84. No.3. pp.387-414.
Ofsted (2011) The Voice of the Child: Learning Lessons from SCR. [Accessed 15 January 2015]. Online: http://www.ofsted.gov.uk/resources/learning-lessons-serious-case–review
Olivers, C. and Charles, G. (2015) Enacting Firm, Fair and Friendly Practice: A Model for Strengths-Based Child Protection Relationships. *British Journal of Social Work*. 1-15 doi: 10.1093/bjsw/bcv0f5
Osborn, M. (2014) Working with fathers to safeguard children. *Child Abuse & Neglect* 38: pp.993-1001.
Palm, G. (2014) Attachment Theory and Fathers: Moving from 'Being there' to 'being with'. *Journal of Family Theory and Review*. Vol. 6. pp.282-297.
Parent, C., Saint-Jacques, M.C., Beaudry, M. and Robitalle, C. (2007) Stepfather involvement in social interventions made by youth protection services in stepfamilies. *Child & Family Social Work* Vol.12 No.3. pp.229-238.
Parker, J. and Crabtree, S.A. (2014) Fish Need Bicycles: An Exploration of the Perceptions of Male Social Work Students on a Qualifying Course. *British Journal of Social Work*. Vol.44 No.2.p p.310–327.
Payne, M. (2014) *Modern Social Work Theory*. 4th ed. Basingstoke. Palgrave Macmillan.
Rivett, M. (2010) Working with violent male carers (fathers and stepfathers). In Featherstone, B., Hooper, C.A., Scourfield, J and Taylor , J (eds) *Gender and Child Welfare in Society*. West Sussex, Wiley.
Rogers, E. (2015) 'Social Workers learn how to work with Fathers'. [Accessed 28 February 2015]. Online: http://www.cypnow.co.uk/cyp/case-study/1149200/social-workers-learn-fathers
Roskill., C. Featherstone., B. Ashley, C. and Haresnape, S. (2008) Fathers Matter Volume 2: Further findings on fathers and their involvement with Social Care Services. London: Family Rights Group.
Roskill, C. (2011) Research in three children's services authorities. In Ashley, C. *Working with risky fathers: Fathers Matter Volume 3: Research Findings on working with domestically abusive fathers and their involvement with children's social care services*, London, Family Rights Group.
Ryan, M. (2000) *Working with fathers*. Oxford: Radcliffe Medical.

Ryan, M. (2006) The experiences of fathers involved with social services departments. A literature review. In Ashley, C., Featherstone, B., Roskill, C., Ryan, M. and White, S. (eds) *Fathers Matter 1 – Research findings on fathers and their involvement with social care services*. Family Rights Group: London, pp.13-24.

Ruch, G. (2010) 'Setting out the Terrain', In Ruch, G. and Turney, D. and Ward, A. (eds) *Relationship-Based Social Work: Getting to the heart of Practice*. London: Jessica Kingsley Publishers.

Ruch, G. (2010a) 'Theoretical Frameworks Informing Relationship-Based Practice', In Ruch, G. and Turney, D. and Ward, A. (eds) *Relationship-Based Social Work: Getting to the heart of Practice*. London: Jessica Kingsley Publishers.

Scott, K.S. and Crooks, C.V. (2004) Effecting change in maltreating fathers: Critical principles for intervention planning. *Clinical Psychology: Science and Practice*. Vol.10. p.95–111.

Scourfield, J. (2003) *Gender and Child Protection*, London. Palgrave Macmillan.

Scourfield, J. (2006) The Challenge of engaging fathers in the child protection process. *Critical Social Policy*, Vol. 26, No.2. pp.440-449.

Scourfield, J., Maxwell, N., Holland, S., Tolman, R., Sloan., L., Featherstone, B., and Bullock, A. (2013) *Improving the engagement of fathers in Child Protection*. National Institute for Social Care and Health Research. Cardiff.

Scourfield, J., Cheung S. Y., and Macdonald, G. (2014) Working with fathers to improve children's wellbeing: Results of a survey exploring service provision and intervention approach in the UK. *Children and Youth Services Review*. Vol. 43.p p. 40-50.

Sinclair, R. and Bullock, R. (2002) *Learning from past experiences – A review of SCR*. [Accessed 27 February 2015]. Online: http://lx.iriss.org.uk/sites/default

Smart, C. and Neale, B. (1999) *Family Fragments?* Cambridge. Polity.

Smith, M. (2005) *Surviving Fears in Health and Social Care: The Terrors of the Night and the Arrows of Day*. London. Jessica Kingsley Publishers.

Somer, M. (1994) The Narrative Constitution of Identity. A Relational and Network Approach. *Theory and Society*. Vol.23. pp.605-649.

Sonenstein, F., Malm, K. and Billing, A. (2002) *Study of fathers involvement in Permanency, planning and child welfare casework*. U.S Department of Health and Human Services.

Stepney, P. (2009) *Radical Social Work in Practice: Making a difference*. Bristol: The Policy Press.

Strega, S., Fleet, C., Brown, L., Dominelli, L., Callahan, M. and Walmsley, C. (2008) Connecting father absence and mother blame in child welfare policies and practice. *Children and Youth Services Review*. Vol. 30. No.7. pp.705-716.

Taylor, C. and White, S. (2006) Knowledge and Reasoning in Social Work: Educating for Humane Judgement. *British Journal of Social Work*. 36: pp.937-954.

Velazquez, S. and Vincent, S. (2009) Strengthening Relationships between non-resident fathers and their children. *Fostering Father Involvement*. Vol.19. No.1. pp.8-10.

Woodcock-Ross, J. (2011) *Specialist Communication Skills for Social Workers: Focusing on Service User's Needs*. Basingstoke: Palgrave Macmillan.

8
The issue of physical touch with children and young people

Joanna Genter

Introduction

Human interaction sits at the core of social work practice, underpinning professional intervention with service-users. As one of the five senses, physical touch is a key attribute to human functioning, but the subject of touch does not explicitly feature on taught social work programmes, unlike other aspects of social worker/service-user interaction (Koprowska, 2012), despite senior social work academics recommending an open debate on the subject (Powell, 2001). However many other disciplines contribute to touch-based knowledge including neuroscience, psychology, cultural anthropology, sociology, theology and education. This chapter will look at the literature around touch and physical contact with children to develop the discussion and make key recommendations to practitioners and policy makers.

Ferguson (2011:104) asserts that, in contemporary child protection forums, 'of all the contentious issues… none provokes more heated feelings, argument and debate than touch'. Social work practice with children and young people is largely underpinned by the Children's Act 1989, where the welfare of the child is paramount (HM Government, 1989). It is therefore important to establish whether or not touch features in this remit. Whilst touch has qualities to potentially enhance professional practice, its lack of prominence in social work training and policy in practice settings leaves social workers operating in the dark (Ferguson, 2010; Green and Day, 2013). This is in contrast to social workers' understanding of the need to establish and maintain professional boundaries with service-users, which is identified as a key requirement for ethical practice (HCPC, 2012).

The word 'touch' is ambiguous. Useable as a noun and a verb, it possesses various meanings and connotations. For the purpose of this project, I have defined touch as non-sexual, non-violent physical contact between people. The recent well-publicised scandals of child abuse in Rotherham (Jay, 2014) and Oxfordshire (Oxfordshire Safeguarding Children Board, 2015) provides evidence of how individuals use abusive touch to harm children. This leads to fear because of heightened anxiety about the need to improve child protection but at the same time reinforces barriers to dialogue about the appropriate use of touch by professionals.

We live in a society where we are suspicious of those around us, and we are fearful to trust well-meaning individuals, including ourselves. Some have heralded this as a 'moral panic', where the undermining of our sense of trust has threatened what we are all about as individuals and caregivers (Johnson, 2000). The prominence of concerns over child abuse and child sexual exploitation in our professional and social worlds means that physical touch in social work is 'an area fraught with anxieties, assumptions and defensive practice' (Kelly, 2014, p.395). Additionally, the sense of risk associated with 'getting it wrong' has never been higher. In February 2015, the UK Prime Minister announced that social workers deemed to have failed in their duty to protect children and young people may face arrest and jail (BBC, 2015a).

Inherent in this discussion is risk aversion, where the growth of neo-liberal managerialism in social work seeks to identify and contain risk. Where risks cannot be negated, they are managed, documented, and subject to ongoing monitoring. Webb (2006) acknowledges that today's world is saturated with and preoccupied by risk. He asserts that the impact of risk is dramatically changing the contribution of social work to society; from a political viewpoint, 'risk…is a form of governmentality that undermines traditional practices of value and relationship building' (p.47). The UK media plays an influential role in society, using power to influence the thinking of its audience. Cohen (2002) writes about how the media can trigger a societal reaction to an event, to the extent that 'it not only increases the deviant's chance of acting…, it also provides him with his lines and stage directions' (p.137). The notion that the media can operate with such force to galvanise public reaction and steer events impacts how organisations respond to and manage situations. There is an ever present awareness that the media has its own agenda, driven by the need to captivate public imagination and sell news. Cohen (2002) considers media reporting of social workers in the mid-1980s following highly-publicised child deaths. Whilst trying to rescue situations, social workers ended up being blamed, doomed to negative media portrayals in whatever light they were presented.

Discussion

In order to explore the subject of touch in social work, it is necessary to outline the context in which it sits in modern day society. The continued development of global modernisation means that people are more mobile, as Thompson asserts (2007). Furedi (2005) writes about the prominence of a 'politics of fear' in modern society, which serves to manipulate the public, to the extent that 'fear has become the common currency of claims in general' (p.130). Events such as the attacks on the World Trade Centre in 2001, the conviction of serial killer Doctor Harold Shipman in 2000, and the outbreak of Ebola in Africa in 2014 are examples of how local and world events have led personhood to be recast as 'the vulnerable subject' (Furedi, 2005, p.132). Therefore it is not just a 'politics of fear' that impacts on society but also the nature of how one sees oneself in the world.

Furedi and Bristow (2010) highlight how government responses are often triggered by prominent local and global events in a reactive sense. Following the death of Victoria Climbié in 2000, and the murders of Jessica Chapman and Holly Wells in 2002, a raft of safeguarding measures were introduced to 'learn the lessons' and better protect children from abuse. This included the development of a national vetting scheme and the publication of the government green paper, 'Every Child Matters'. These developments hugely influence the day-to-day practices of those working with children and young people. Furedi and Bristow (2010) recognise that child protection policy development 'does not limit itself to scrutinising *who* works with children…; it increasingly legislates for *how* adults should interact with children in their care' (pp.30-31). This observation prompts consideration of what is written about the use of physical touch as a form of interaction.

Touch is not mentioned in the Standards of Conduct, Performance and Ethics issued by Health and Care Professions Council (HCPC, 2012). The Standards highlight that social workers, acting in the best interests of service-users, 'must not abuse the relationship... (but be) responsible for professional conduct' (2012, p.8). The British Association of Social Work (BASW) Code of Ethics does not allude to whether social workers should or should not use touch in practice (BASW, 2012). It reiterates the focus of social work as meeting human need, by using professional integrity to 'maintain professional boundaries… and not abuse their position for personal benefit, financial gain or sexual exploitation' (p.10). In contrast, the American National Association of Social Work (NASW) Code of Ethics makes explicit reference to the use of touch by social workers (NASW, 2008, Standard 1.10).

Local Authorities (LAs) have issued guidance to support the use of touch between professionals and children and young people but this inconsistent, which leads to anomalies in how children experience touch, for example, when being restrained (National Children's Bureau, 2004). Whilst some LAs provide policy guidance on the physical handling of children, guidance within the document may not be consistently explicit. A short paragraph describing touch through 'positive handling', for example, first aid or helping a child hold a paintbrush, may be followed by several pages on the use of restrictive physical intervention (Hampshire County Council, 2012). Additionally, statements encouraging the use of touch to demonstrate care are often followed by an explicit caution regarding innocent actions being misconstrued (Surrey County Council, 2010).

Literature on touch presents something of a disparate picture, where touch practices in social work are rarely researched and opinion about the use of touch by professionals is divided. Empirical data specifically focused on social workers' use of touch in practice with children and young people is sparse; consequently this review also draws on literature exploring the use of touch by other professionals working with children to develop a more considered view.

The Argument for touch

Smith et al. (2013), in writing about the nurture of children in residential care, describe physical touch as 'one of the most obvious and powerful ways to express care' (p.44). Whilst the majority of children's social workers are not based in residential settings, this point is amplified elsewhere. Ferguson (2011) refers to touch by social workers as 'humane and nurturing... expressing care and promoting healing for children, as part of ethical good practice' (p.102). This concept of touch as an expression of care can be associated with the start of life where care-giving touch experienced in the womb, and as a newborn baby, is essential for growth and development (Field, 2010). Montagu (1986) cites work by Harlow (1958) who experimented with baby monkeys to reveal the powerful, innate need for touch. Terming this 'comfort contact', Harlow demonstrated this was vital for healthy emotional development, finding infant monkeys valued tactile stimulation more than nourishment. Gallace and Spence (2010) conducted an overview of the science of interpersonal touch, highlighting various experiments where interactive touch resulted in a perceived more positive experience by the person who was touched. They acknowledge the lack of understanding as to why interpersonal touch has such a dramatic effect on people and recommend further research.

In the Republic of Ireland, it is identified that social workers' use of touch with children predominantly occurred as a result of a practical need, for example, keeping a child safe when crossing the road (Lynch and Garrett, 2010). Whilst this was the case, participants expressed recognising the multiple benefits of touch, highlighting its ability to convey empathy, provide healing, support communication, and reassure and comfort children. In discussing the notion of touch, respondents highlight 'appropriate' and 'inappropriate' touch, where examples of appropriate touch included it being child-initiated, practical, providing safety, and being play-focused. But such definitions are contested.

The use of touch to keep children safe is endorsed by Ferguson (2009, 2010, 2011), who asserts the 'troubling absence of touch in child protection today' (2011, p.99). He describes 'professional touch' as something different to a medical or health examination. Ferguson (2011) emphasises how greeting a child or a social interaction with a child by a social worker could include picking them up, hand holding or walking together. Drawing attention to the cases of Peter Connolly and Jasmine Beckford, children known to Children's Services who died at the hands of their carers, Ferguson highlights how children can become 'untouchable' to professionals, describing the discouragement of touch as deeply regrettable. Ferguson underlines the value of touch as being able to reveal harm in a less forensic way than a medical examination, and that, for social workers, 'initiating tactile involvement with a child must always be on the agenda' (p.107). The author reflects on a practice experience where playful ruffling of a child's hair revealed an otherwise hidden bruise, which better informed the social worker about the child's well-being.

A study conducted in the US explored how, when, why, and with whom clinical social workers used touch in therapy with child and adult clients (Strozier et al., 2003). Subscribing to a definition of touch as 'any non-sexual contact with the client's person, including a touch on the arm or shoulder, or shaking hands' (p.49), the authors used a snowball sampling method to gain data via questionnaires from 91 social workers. Almost all respondents reported the use of touch in practice with their service users, with over half hugging their service-users and almost a third holding hands with their service-users. Therapeutic reasons prompted the use of touch; to demonstrate empathy, to model healthy touch, to communicate acceptance and to re-parent. More than 40% of respondents viewed touch as healing. It is acknowledged that, as a US-based study, the notion of a social worker in a therapeutic setting is quite different to that of a UK social worker in a children's setting. Additionally, the snowball sampling technique has been criticised for providing data to fit the authors' hypothesis (Polgar and Thomas, 2008). It is noted that whilst termed an 'exploratory study' (p.52), the research did prove the one hypothesis set out by the authors regarding social workers' use of touch and practice training.

Children and young people have expressed positive views where they have experienced touch by professionals. A research study by Sudberry et al. (2010) explored the use of 'holding' techniques as an intervention for children with severe attachment difficulties in a specialist residential care setting. 'Holding' is a physical response to the behaviour displayed by a young person, which may involve them being held across the laps of two therapists, making eye contact and then talking about their lives. The researchers undertook interviews with twenty-three current and thirty-two former residents, using semi-structured interviews and focus groups. Fifteen employees from a total of ninety were interviewed, and surveys were distributed to parents and social work purchasers of residential packages. The research revealed that, overall, the young people valued what they experienced in the setting; they repeatedly expressed their sense of safety, and how restraint was important for keeping them, other residents and adults safe.

Sudberry et al. (2010) reported that young people sometimes express ambiguous feelings in relation to the holding technique; 'it does feel good (but) it's hard' (p.1543). A similar sentiment was expressed in a study undertaken to explore the views and experiences of children and young people and staff regarding physical restraint in residential child care settings in Scotland. Steckley (2012) undertook seventy-eight in-depth interviews, involving thirty-seven young people and forty-one residential staff members, across twenty establishments. In their responses, some young people discussed orchestrating a situation that resulted in them being restrained driven by a 'need to be held to comfort' (p.550). Almost a third of the staff perceived that young people had sought restraint in order to meet touch-related needs.

Doyle (2006) draws on her experience of working with abused children, deploying therapeutic interventions to help children address misconceptions and negative emotions associated with past ill-treatment (p.86). She describes establishing a 'no uncomfortable touching' rule at the outset of her work with a child so that inappropriate sexual behaviour can be managed consistently and sensitively. Doyle also acknowledges that children can feel so defiled by abuse that they consider themselves 'untouchable'. Doyle expresses how physical comfort needs to be carefully considered as it can benefit some but can distress or confuse others.

Where a child has experienced harmful and inappropriate touch in the past, an experience of healthy touch can help remodel the child's understanding. In a study of 10 foster families in South Wales, Rees and Pithouse (2008) explored the fostering experience for the foster child and the foster family. Whilst some foster carers avoided touch for fear of an allegation, the majority offered physical comfort and hugged children. This was seen as a 'value-driven commitment by carers that stems from the humanistic mission in fostering' (p.345).

In Lynch and Garrett's (2010) study, over half the respondents identified that their perception of touch as a positive intervention was linked to their own family experiences of touch. This illustrates how 'the self' impacts on the way a practitioner undertakes their professional role.

The argument against touch

Even when social workers recognise the benefits of touch in practice with children and young people, they rarely use it (Lynch and Garrett, 2010). Reasons given by participants for not using touch included 'the risks of misinterpretation, allegations, causing harm and its potential to amount to something more sinister' (p.396). There was a consensus of fear of touch among the participants, and a 'real fear of the act of touch being open to misinterpretation, both from children and other people' (p.393).

The fear generated by the prospect of using touch with children and young people acts as a barrier to this aspect of professional practice. A study conducted by Ruch (2014) involved social workers using reflective case discussions to explore their experiences of working with children, and the obstacles and opportunities for child-centred communication. Practitioners were 'keenly aware of how empathy, if conveyed through physical touch, heightened their professional vulnerability to allegations of misconduct' (p. 2156). This illustrates what Ruch describes as the 'uncomfortable' nature of communicating with children. Pemberton (2010) reports the case of a children's residential care worker who was falsely accused of sexual assault following an occasion when he put his arm around a young person. The damage caused to the worker had a life changing effect. The young person later admitted fabricating the story, believing 'social workers were never meant to touch children'.

Confusion about whether professionals are 'allowed' to touch children is not just experienced by young people, but also by professionals. A UK-based study researched the use of touch between professionals and children of all ages and in a range of settings (Piper et al., 2006a). Data was gained through direct observations of interactions between adults and young people, semi-structured interviews with young people and appropriate adults, and interviews with parents. Additionally, staff members were invited to discuss any 'critical incidents' to illustrate the culture of practice. One of the findings from the study was that many respondents wrongly assumed that touch between adults and children and young people was prohibited by legislation.

The study also revealed the complexity of professionals using touch with children and young people in a manner that was seen to be 'child-led'. The study uncovered examples of adults legitimising unasked-for touch by, for example, giving a child a hug when they were crying, and portraying the child as 'asking for it' even though they had not expressed wanting to be touched (Piper et al., 2006a, p.7). Whilst this was not viewed to be sinister by the adults reporting it, it alludes to adults seeking to portray touch as being child-initiated to avoid it being misinterpreted as representing their desire to touch. Piper et al. acknowledge how the language of 'asking for it' relates to paedophilic discourse and therefore does not serve to fully protect the adult, resulting in endless double-binds.

The US based study of the use of touch by social workers in a therapeutic setting highlighted that 82% of respondents used touch despite reporting that they were not educated or trained for this element of practice (Strozier et al, 2003). Additionally, although touch is an intervention endorsed by these professionals, they were not able to provide a clear consensus for the reasons to use or not use touch. Respondents referred to using touch, based not on education or theory, but on intuition. There appears to be a prevailing disagreement about the requirement for guidance to support practitioners in their use of touch with service users. Piper et al. (2006a) reported that whilst some of their respondents thought more guidelines would be helpful, a significant minority rejected the suggestion, regarding them as an imposition. A respondent provided an example of how she was challenged by an Ofsted Inspector as her actions, whilst meeting the needs of a behaviour modification programme for a child, did not adhere to her organisation's practice guidelines. A degree of inflexibility meant she was open to criticism for not adhering to the rules, despite meeting the agreed needs of the child.

Culture is perceived to impact on readiness to use touch in practice. Lynch and Garrett (2010) were prompted to explore the subject of touch following time in the Republic of South Africa and observing that 'hugs of reassurance…were freely given… physical touch was very much a part of daily interactions as a social worker with children in South Africa' (p.389). Contrast in the use of touch by people of different cultures was highlighted by Jourard in the 1960s when he observed conversations between friends in café settings. During conversations lasting for the same amount of time, friends in England did not touch at all, whilst in the US, they touched twice per hour. In contrast, friends in a French cafe touched 110 times per hour and in Puerto Rico, 180 times per hour. This appears to indicate how geographical location links to culture, which in turn influences the use of touch. However, the growth of mobility since the 1960s means cities are now far more multi-cultural, making it less simple to deduce direct correlations between people, place and culture.

Concern has arisen that the growth of technology has resulted in people touching less (BBC, 2015b). Steckley (2012) highlights that staff's personal histories and establishment culture impact how the complexities of touch are understood. A social worker may have negative past experiences of touch resulting in an avoidance of this aspect of practice. Smith et al. (2013) highlight that where touch is used by carers who are tentative or self-conscious, 'children can pick up on the adult's discomfort and potentially misinterpret it' (p.45).

The use of touch in a child protection capacity is seen by some to be going beyond the social work remit. Lynch and Garrett (2010) found the majority of respondents considered that Fergusons' promotion of 'professional touch' risked confusing medical and social work staff remits.

The infrequency of social worker contact with children was cited as a reason for practitioner reluctance to use touch (Lynch and Garrett, 2010). Respondents' views included the notion that touch needed to come from someone closer to the child than a social worker, for example, a foster carer. This raises the importance of touch occurring in a relationship where trust has been established to underpin the interaction. The idea expressed is that the social worker relationship is not the right context for touch to be used with the child. Steckley (2012) identified that the use of touch can serve to escalate rather than defuse heightened emotions. Where a social worker might only visit a child or young person for a short period, the use of touch could provoke a response that was difficult to manage.

It is also acknowledged that a relationship in with touch occurs requires a deeper level of engagement between the practitioner and the service-user, and is likely to be more emotionally demanding for the professional. Steckley (2012) highlights how touch can support therapeutic containment for a young person, where a carer hears and absorbs a young persons' emotions, and 'gives back' the emotions in a more manageable form.

Analysis of evidence

The literature reveals touch to be a highly complex area of practice encompassing many ethical and practical dilemmas. Notions of touch as 'taboo' and 'ambiguous' prevailed, supporting the author's experience in practice settings. The empirical data specifically focused on UK-based social workers' use of touch in practice with children and young people amounted to only one paper (Lynch and Garrett, 2010), reinforcing the need to better understand what happens when social workers meet with children (Ruch, 2014). Whilst touch is a generic part of our existence and functioning, its use in professional settings with children and young people generates endless questions.

The need to talk about touch

The literature indicates that professionals do not readily or easily talk about touch as a method of intervention in practice. Studies included examples of respondents being initially reticent to engage in research given the subject matter (Lynch and Garrett, 2010; Piper et al., 2006a). Some feared that the sensitivities around touch made even talking about it a threatening prospect (Strozier et al. 2003). The word touch is so heavily laden with multiple and negative meanings that it has come to represent something that people do not want to be associated with. Powell (2001) acknowledges that in becoming synonymous with abuse, touch is demonised as part of a child abuse discourse. The power of discourse to create barriers to good practice can silence the debate about the use of touch between professionals and service-users (Maidment, 2006). In not talking about touch, its absence from the social work agenda is legitimised. To raise the subject of touch would risk one's actions appearing questionable and potentially suspicious.

The literature revealed the view that not talking about touch was deemed safer than 'opening up a can of worms' (Piper et al., 2006a). Links can be made to present day society, where the exposure of historical child sexual abuse offenses has shocked and appalled, including the case of Jimmy Saville in 2012. A UK government independent inquiry followed into concerns that public bodies had failed to protect children, and the scale of establishment links hindered the appointment of a lead investigator. The idea of paedophiles in powerful places and establishment cover-ups is alarming and hugely damaging to public confidence (BBC, 2015c). The concept that popular public figures, who loomed large in UK households were actually child abusers, robbed people of their trust. Where knowledge of such scales of abuse laid dormant for years, the 'opening up a can of worms' reveals information which feeds the child sexual abuse discourse. No child is safe and no adult is trust-worthy; society comes to comprise of those who are in danger, and those who are dangerous (Foucault, 1988).

In response to the lack of dialogue on the subject of touch, social workers voiced wanting more discussion (Lynch and Garrett, 2010). Whilst the literature highlights positive underlying views of the role for touch, the lack of open and honest discussion hinders it being embraced as a constructive element of professional practice. This creates a situation where 'professionals have unwittingly colluded in their own disempowerment' (Piper et al., 2006b, p.163). Lack of discussion on this subject has generated an unspoken 'not-knowing' about touch. Consequently practitioners are left questioning what is best practice, what is appropriate, what is safe? Whilst social workers are expected to embrace uncertainty in their role, dialogue on touch would improve knowing, including knowing what is unknown. One questions the source of this predicament. Does the lack of an evidence base lead to disengaged professionals and academics? Without firm subject knowledge, do students, practitioners and educators lack authority to embrace discussion and training? In the quest for absolute knowledge, is the subject of touch simply too 'messy' as to generate sufficient truths to justify the effort? Or, does the association of paedophilia reign so great as to silence all quarters?

Meeting the child's needs

Whilst social workers are comfortable using touch to fulfil a practical requirement, they are less at ease using touch in other ways, (Lynch and Garrett, 2010). This can be seen to illustrate a fear-induced practice approach, where professionals use touch in a way that is easy to defend and carries minimal risk of being misconstrued. This outcome reflects a society of adults who perceive touch for reasons of safety as appropriate, and touch to provide comfort as potential abuse. The continued unease with breastfeeding mothers in public illustrates the degree of confusion more broadly within society concerning touch. It is almost incomprehensible to think that an act of touch, which so clearly meets a child's needs and is supported by legislation in the Equality Act, 2010, is questioned (HM Government, 2010). Yet it is, resulting in political comment, national media hype and public demonstrations (The Guardian, 2014). For social work, the impact of fear around touch results in a constrained and disingenuous practice; whilst practitioners assert that their lack of touch protects the child, the child's potential need for touch as comfort, assurance or in communication is neglected.

When the child protection agenda was advocated as justification *for* the use of touch by professionals, social workers displayed ambivalence (Lynch and Garrett, 2010; Ferguson, 2011). They maintained this use of touch was not their role, attributing it to other agencies. One queries the impact of interagency working and it being linked to child death inquiries (NSPCC, 2014). It is feasible that changes to practice and policy, including through the statutory guidance document Working Together to Safeguard Children (HM Government, 2013), have served to reinforce agency divides. As a result, whilst agencies might work collectively, certain jobs are seen to be the responsibility of certain agencies.

Children and young people expressed how the use of touch demonstrated care, and was something that they valued (Steckley, 2012, Lynch and Garrett, 2010; Rees and Pithouse, 2008). However, several factors encouraged professionals to avoid touch including the pressure of time, and the risk of burn out (Ferguson, 2011; Lynch and Garrett, 2010; Strozier et al., 2003). Workload pressure results in little time to nurture relationships with service-users that enable the development of trust to support the use of touch. This is despite the relationship being identified as the enabling element to progress social work procedures (Broadhurst et al., 2010). It can be observed that efforts are being made to address this and re-establish the importance of relationships and effective direct work with children and families (DfE, 2014). Such initiatives attempt to re-address organisational culture, where the development of task-centred social work to cope with time pressure has negatively impacted on social work relationships.

Responding to risk

The risk of getting touch wrong was perceived as grave, with potentially damaging consequences for the child, the social worker and the profession. Practitioners were presented as managing the gargantuan fears associated with false allegations, either through malice or misinterpretation (Green and Day, 2013). Subsequently, professionals displayed an enhanced awareness of their use of touch (Lynch and Garrett, 2010; Strozier, 2003; Piper et al., 2006b), and in order to manage risks, some professionals avoided touch all together. The existence of 'no touch' policies in some child care settings justified this approach illustrating how the *possibility* of wrongdoing becomes the focus, rather than the *doing* of wrongdoing (Piper et al., 2006b).

The literature suggests risk management is prioritised over quality social work, negatively impacting social workers' (Webb, 2006 & Broadhurst et al., 2010, p.1060). The Report of Inspection of Rotherham Metropolitan Borough Council asserted 'Rotherham has at times taken more care of its reputation than it has of its most needy' (Casey, 2015).

Risk is something that needs better managing by professionals through critical, reflective supervision. (Fook, 2002). The opportunity to 'reflect in action' as situations potentially involving touch arise, and to 'reflect on action' after the event (Schon, 1983) is a necessity for practitioners dealing in the unexpected environmental, relational and emotional dynamics of practice (Ruch, 2014). Such discipline would better equip practitioners with a deeper insight into their practice, enabling them to own their use of touch, conscious of how their response addresses the needs of the child. The sense of self runs deep in social work, linked to individual narratives and identity (Wiles, 2013). This can be observed in most elements of social work practice, and touch is no exception.

Conclusion

Touch is an intrinsic part of our human functioning. Whilst complex, its considered use offers a wealth of ways in which to enhance social work practice with children and young people. For too long social workers' use of touch has been influenced by knowledge of damaging and abusive touch, which has powerfully altered mind-sets and negatively impacted practice. The absence of touch in work-based discussions and in social worker training has come to reinforce the notion that touch is off the social work agenda. Importantly, this is not the result of research or a thorough practice review, but is a consequence of the dominance of fear around the use of touch.

Social workers cannot operate in a vacuum of fear and children should not lose out as a result of defensive practice. An ethical and theoretical approach that enables effective engagement in complex situations is required, facilitated by open dialogue on the subject of touch. Such an approach will generate opportunities to improve service-users' experiences of social work, and social workers' experience of practice.

Recommendations

The use of touch in social work practice to feature on social work education syllabuses.

- Training in touch to be delivered to social workers, particularly those working with children and young people in a child protection setting.
- Touch to be an open discussion with children, young people and their families so that everyone is clear on what might be expected from the social worker
- Use of Reflective Supervision to monitor how workers can better manage risk
- Further research to be undertaken to gain a more comprehensive picture of the use of touch by social workers

References

British Association of Social Workers (BASW) (2012) *The Code of Ethics for Social Work*. Birmingham: BASW

BBC (2015a) 'Child Sexual Exploitation 'A National Threat' – Cameron', Available at: http://m.bbc.co.uk/news/uk-31720979 (Accessed: 8 March 2015)

BBC (2015b) 'A Point of View: Does Technology Make People Touch Each Other Less?' Available at: http://www.bbc.co.uk/news/magazine-31026410 (Accessed: 4 April 2015)

BBC (2015c) 'The Historical Child Abuse Inquiries and What Happens Next', Available at: www.bbc.co.uk/news/uk-politics-28189858 (Accessed: 4 April 2015)

Broadhurst, K., Hall, C., Wastall, D. White, S. and Pithouse, A.(2010) 'Risk, Instrumentalism and the Humane Project in Social Work: Identifying the Informal Logics of Risk Management in Children's Statutory Services', *British Journal of Social Work*, 40, pp1046-1064

Casey, L. (2015) 'Report of Inspection of Rotherham Metropolitan Borough Council', [Online]

Available at: www.gov.uk/government/uploads/system/uploads/attachment_data/file/401125/46966_Report_of_Inspection_of_Rotherham_WEB.pdf (Accessed: 8 April 2015)

Cohen, S. (2002) *Folk Devils and Moral Panics* (3rd Edn). Abingdon: Routledge

Department for Education (DfE) (2014) 'Consultation on knowledge and skills for child and family social work'. [Online]. Available at: www.gov.uk/government/uploads/system/uploads/attachement_data/file/379033/Consultation_on_knowledge_and_skills_for_child_and_family_social_work_-_government_response_pdf(Accessed: 26 March 2015)

Doyle, C. (2006) *Working with Abused Children*. 3rd edn. Basingstoke: Palgrave Macmillan

Easterbrook, P., Berline, J., Gopalan, R., and Matthew, D. (1991) Publication bias in clinical research, *The Lancet* 337,(8746). [Online]. Available at: www.jameslindlibrary.org/wp-data/uploads/2014/07/Easterbrook_PJ_1991.pdf (Accessed: 8 April 2015)

Foucault, M. (1988) 'Sexuality, Morality and the Law', in Kritzman, L. D. (ed) *Michel Foucault: politics, philosophy and culture. Interviews and other writings 1977-1984*. New York: Routledge

Ferguson, H. (2009) 'Performing child protection: home visiting, movement and the struggle to reach the abused child', *Child and Family Social Work*, 14, pp.471-480

Ferguson, H. (2010) 'Walks, Home Visits and Atmospheres: Risk and the Everyday Practices and Motilities of Social Work and Child Protection', *British Journal of Social Work*, 40, pp.1100-1117

Ferguson, H. (2011) *Child Protection Practice*. Basingstoke: Palgrave Macmillan

Field, T. (2010) 'Touch for socioemotional and physical well-being: A review', *Developmental Review*, 20, pp.367-383

Fook, J. (2002) *Social Work Critical Theory and Practice*. London: Sage

Furedi, F. (2005) *Politics of Fear*. London: Continuum International Publishing Group.

Furedi, F. and Bristow, J. (2010) *Licensed to Hug*. London: Civitas

Gallace, A. and Spence, C. (2010) 'The Science of Interpersonal Touch', *Neuroscience and Biobehavioral Reviews*, 34, pp.246-259

Green, L. and Day, R. (2013) 'To Touch or Not to Touch? Exploring the Dilemmas and Ambiguities Associated with Touch in Social Work and Social Care Settings', in Carey, M. and Green, L. (eds) *Practical Social Work Ethics: Complex Dilemmas within Applied Social Care*. Surrey: Ashgate

Guardian, The (2014) Sit in the corner: Nigel Farage's tips for mothers breastfeeding in public. [Online]. Available at: www.theguardian.com/lifestyle/2014/dec/05/sit-in-corner-nigel-farage-tips-for-mothers-breastfeeding-in-public (Accessed: 10 April 2015)

Hampshire County Council (HCC) (2012) Physical handling guidance for early years settings. [Online]. Available at: www.hants.gov.uk (Accessed: 17 February 2015)

Health and Care Professions Council (HCPC) (2012) Standards of Conduct, Performance and Ethics. London: HCPC

HM Government (1989) Children Act. [Online]. Available at: www.legislation.gov.uk/ukpga/41/contents. (Accessed: 15 January 2015)

HM Government (2010) Equality Act. [Online]. Available at: www.legilsation.gov.uk/ukpga/2010/15/introduction (Accessed: 1 April 2015)

HM Government (2013) Working Together to Safeguard Children: A guide to inter-agency working to safeguard and promote the welfare of children. [Online]. Available at: www.gov.uk/government/publications/working-together-to-safeguard-children (Accessed: 30 September 2015)

Jay, A. (2014) Independent Inquiry into Child Sexual Exploitation in Rotherham. [Online]. Available at: https://www.rotherham.gov.uk/download/id/1407/independent_inquiry_cse_in_rotherham (Accessed: 8 April 2015)

Johnson, R. (2000) *Hands Off! The Disappearance of Touch in the Care of Children.* New York: Peter Lang

Jourard, S (1966) 'An exploratory study of body accessibility', *British Journal of Social and Clinical Psychology*, 5, 221-231

Kelly, A. (2014) 'Review of Practical Social Work Ethics: Complex dilemmas within applied social care', *Adoption and Fostering*, 38(4) pp395-397

Lynch, R. and Garrett, P. (2010) "More than Words': touch practices in child and family social work', *Child and Family Social Work*, 15, pp389-398

Koprowska, J. (2012) 'Curriculum Guide – Communication Skills'. [Online]. Available at: www.tcsw.org.uk/Curriculum-Guides/ (Accessed: 8 April 2015)

Maidment, J. (2006) 'The Quiet Remedy', *Families in Society*, 87, 1, pp.115-121

Montagu, A. (1986) *The Human Significance of the Skin.* (3rd edn). New York: Harper and Row

National Association of Social Workers (NASW) (2008) Code of Ethics. [Online]. Available at: www.socialworkers.org/pubs/code/default.asp (Accessed: 17 February 2015)

National Children's Bureau (2004) 'Report on the use of Physical Intervention across Children's Services', [Online]. Available at: www.ncb.org.uk/resources/res_detail.asp?id=597 (Accessed: 17 February 2015)

National Society for the Protection of Children from Cruelty (NSCPP) (2014) Voluntary Agencies: Learning from Serious Case Reviews, [Online]. Available at: www.nspcc.org.uk/preventing-abuse/child-protection-system/case-reviews/learning/voluntary-agencies/ (Accessed: 8 April 2015)

Oxfordshire Safeguarding Children Board (2015) Serious Case Review into Child Sexual Exploitation in Oxfordshire: from the experiences of Children A, B, C, D, E, and F. [Online]. Available at: www.oscb.org.uk/wp-content/uploads/SCR-into-CSE-in-Oxfordshire-FINAL-FOR-WEBSITE.pdf (Accessed: 8 April 2015)

Parton, N. (2008) 'Changes in the Form of Knowledge in Social Work: From the 'Social' to the 'Informational'?', *British Journal of Social Work*, 38, pp.253-269

Pemberton, C. (2010) 'Should children's social work be a touch-free zone?' [Online]. Available at: http://www.communitycare.co.uk/2010/08/20/should-childrens-social-work-be-a-touch-free-zone/ (Accessed: 15 December 2014)

Piper, H., Stronach, I. and MacLure, M (2006a) 'Touchlines: The Problematics of Touching Between Children and Professionals'. (European and Social Research Council (ESCR) funded project - RS-000-22-081). [Online]. Available at: https://www.esrc.ac.uk/my.../7e5e0fa8-a9bf-4f94-9a6d-65f77d449c87 (Accessed: 6 February 2015)

Piper, H. Powell, J and Smith, H. (2006b) 'Parents, Professional and Paranoia – The Touching of Children in a Culture of Fear', *Journal of Social Work*, 6(2), pp.151-167

Polgar, S. and Thomas, S. (2008) *Introduction to Research in the Health Sciences*. Philadelphia: Elsevier.

Powell, J. (2001) 'Sometimes when we touch'. [Online]. Available at: http://www.communitycare.co.uk/2001/07/19/sometimes-when-we-touch/ (Accessed: 17 February 2015)

Rees, A. and Pithouse, A. (2008) 'The intimate world of strangers – embodying the child in foster care', *Child and Family Social Work*, 13, pp338-347

Ruch, G. (2014) "Helping Children is a Human Process': Researching the Challenges Social Workers Face in Communicating with Children', *British Journal of Social Work*, 44, pp.2145-2162

Schon, D. (1983) *The Reflective Practitioner*. New York: Jossey Bass

Smith, M., Fulcher, L. and Doran, P. (2013) *Residential child care in practice – Making a difference*. Bristol: Policy Press

Steckley, L. (2102) 'Touch, Physical Restraint and Therapeutic Containment in Residential Child Care', *British Journal of Social Work*, 42, 537-555

Strozier, A. Krizek, C. and Sale, K. (2003) 'Touch: its use in psychotherapy', *Journal of Social Work Practice*, 17, 1, pp.49-62

Sudberry et al (2010) 'To have and to Hold: Questions about a Therapeutic Service for Children', *British Journal of Social Work*, 40, pp.1534-1552

Surrey County Council (2010) 'Touch and the use of restrictive physical intervention when working with children and young people'. [Online] Available at: www.south-farnham.surrey.sch.uk/attachments/download.asp?file=196&type=pdf (Accessed: 3 February 2015)

Swade, T., Bayne, R. and Horton, I. (2006) 'Touch me never', *Therapy Today*, 17, 9, pp.41-42

Thompson, J. (2007) *Ideology and Modern Culture*. Cambridge: Polity Press

Webb, S. (2006) *Social Work in a Risk Society*. Basingstoke: Palgrave Macmillan

Wills, F. (2013) "Not Easily Put Into a Box': Constructing Professional Identity', *Social Work Education*, 32, 7, pp854-866

9
The re-victimisation of women in domestic violence

Samantha Belbin

Introduction

This chapter aims to explore whether Child Protection Services blame and re-victimise female victims of domestic abuse. It will explore the impact of domestic violence on mothering, the extent to which traditional feminist theory can help to contextualise the position of women in society, the role of child protection in domestic abuse and whether this leads to further victimisation. Relevant research, theory and policy will be viewed to understand this issue, and help analyse and underpin findings and future recommendations.

Context

During a social work placement at a women's refuge, my interest in domestic abuse with women increased. Accounts from these women portrayed the difficulties and horrors they faced. Moving into front line social work and assessing families where domestic abuse was present, I found the timescales, duties and thresholds of child protection, would leave social workers feeling frustrated. I questioned whether we expected too much from these mothers, whether professionals had given enough, or whether these women really should be held accountable for not protecting their children? . Women are reported to be the victims in 87% of reported incidents, where men are deemed to be the perpetrators (Cleaver et al, 2011), and it is felt that women are more likely to experience increased fear and anxiety than men in these circumstances (Harne & Radford, 2008).

Domestic abuse is rarely confined to physical abuse; it is a mixture of physical and psychological violence (Cleaver et al, 2011). The government offers a clear definition that states 'any incident or pattern of incidents of controlling, coercive, threatening behaviour, violence or abuse between those aged 16 or over who are, or have been, intimate partners or family members regardless of gender of sexuality.' (Home Office, 2013) This encompasses psychological, physical, sexual, financial and emotional abuse (Home Office, 2013). I therefore will be referring to domestic violence as abuse, as I feel this appropriately covers the subject area considering violence is not the only aspect of abuse.

It is very difficult to define the prevalence of domestic abuse to date, due to victims being reluctant to reveal their experiences. Women's Aid (2003) states that violence against women is the most common form of physical interpersonal crime, with 1 in 4 women being exposed to this. The Office for National Statistics found that between 2012 – 2013, 1.2 million women were reported to be suffering from domestic abuse and a further 330,000 women had been sexually assaulted (Home Office, 2014).

Child protection, defined by *Working together to safeguard children'* guidance (2013), is about protecting children from harm and enhancing their well-being It is the complex system of overlapping services to promote and safeguard children from maltreatment, to ensure that they grow up in a safe environment. The Children Act (1989) enables Children's Services to be able to intervene to protect children when they are at risk of, or are suffering 'significant harm', under section 47 of the Children Act (1989) or under section 17 if assessed as a Child in Need (HM Government, 1989)

Following government statistics of the characteristics of Children in Need between 2013- 2014, it emerged that out of the 175,000 continuous assessments being completed, 145,700 (83.1%) of these found domestic abuse was the most common factor (DofE, 2014). Three quarters of children on the 'at risk register', live in households where domestic abuse occurs (Women's Aid, 2003). These findings are alarming and highlights the prevalence of domestic abuse, as well as the impact this has on social work. A serious case review (SCR) held in 2012 for Daniel Pelka, found that there were 27 incidents of domestic abuse that were not adequately addressed.

Evidence and research

Why do women stay in violent relationships? Female victims of domestic abuse tend to be targeted by perpetrators who are skilled at coercion, and engage in a perpetual cycle of forming sequential relationships where violent behaviour is repeated (Keeling & Fisher, 2012). This can be likened to the term 'grooming', whereby a perpetrator seeks out a vulnerable victim and offers the notion of security and love, but seeks to control. This may for some women appear as protective but changes quickly into domination (DAIP, 2011).

Women who try to leave abusive relationships face the risk of being re-abused; violence escalates at this point as the perpetrator starts to feel they have lost control Bell et al (2009). Therefore professionals need to be mindful that ending a relationship does not guarantee safety; it is the way in which a woman ends the relationships that will have a significant impact on their subsequent experiences (Bell et al, 2009). Women face further threats to themselves or their children. Fear is instilled in them over time through intimidation - such as destruction of their possessions, increased physical or sexual violence, constant surveillance or imprisonment (Harne & Radford, 2008). Male perpetrators have also been known to threaten the woman with having full custody of children, which results in the mother staying for fear of losing their (Kaufman Kantor & Little, 2003). Contrary to this, a study completed in 2004 of 20 women who had attempted to stop the violence from their abuser, found that the children's interests became secondary to those of their mother's, as they did not see the need to protect their child from harm. (Buchbinder & Eisikovits, 2004). However battered mothers can get trapped in a psychological process caused by their abuser that will contribute to their difficulties in protecting their children from harm (Kaufman Kantor & Little, 2003). A mother may prioritise her abusers needs over her children, in order to avoid further violence (Cleaver et al, 2011). It is very easy to agree that women should be blamed for their inability to protect their children, but often very little time is spent gaining the view point of the mother to gain an understanding of the difficulties they have faced in doing so.

Kaufman Kantor & Little (2003) found that mothers tend to remain with their abusive partner because he is the children's father and they love him; these women feel that by staying with the abuser, they are doing the right thing for the sake of their children. As a result of prolonged domestic abuse and effects their parenting. Mother's tend to fail to provide nurture that the children require for their emotional development (Kaufman Kantor & Little, 2003). In some cases women blame their children for having similar characteristics to the perpetrator and often children become violent towards their own mother (Kaufman Kantor & Little, 2003),. Men belittle or insult a woman in front of her children, as this undermines and limits respect that children might hold. This kind of behaviour means that a mother loses her authority to be able to parent confidently (Cleaver et al, 2011).

Abused mothers go on to abuse their own children (Kaufman Kantor & Little, 2003) (Damant et al, 2009). This is a clear form of child abuse and child protection services cannot condone or excuse this; explanations may be provided for this behaviour such as the mothers childhood experiences or as a corollary to the ongoing abuse they have suffered from their partner (Kaufman Kantor & Little, 2003). This may provide a reasonable explanation, but it cannot be used as an excuse. A study completed by Damant et al (2009) explored the relationship of women's victimization and abuse of their children. Out of 27 participants in the study, 11 had admitted to the abuse of their own children.

Domestic abuse towards women highlights their place as secondary to men. In order to explore this further in terms of societal views of women, it is essential to explore feminist theory, as they have the view that power wielded by men is the underpinning basis for their violence against women (Milner & Myers, 2007). Yollo & Bograd (1998) suggest society is structured along the dimension of gender and power within patriarchal society, and is largely in the hands of men. It is the threat of violence that reminds women of their subordinate place (Milner & Myers, 2007). Radical feminism locates men's violence to women 'within the context of structural inequalities, the key mechanism of which the heteropatriarchal exercise of power and control over women.' (Milner & Myers, 2007, p. 86) It could be argued that 'subjection and submission were sanctioned by the church and state' (Mullender, 1996, p. 29) and therefore women experiencing abuse at the hands of their partners is embedded in social history. Landes (1998) argues that biological determination is one way of explaining the universal devaluation of women, as we are all assumed to have an interest in personal survival and therefore society/culture has its own interest in this continuity and survival. Landes suggests that women are classed within 'nature' and men within 'culture'. This is because a woman's body and their functions class them within the nature context, and it is the social roles and their place in society that view them as lower value. Changes to this can only occur if a different cultural view point is grown out of social actuality (Landes, 1998).

First wave feminist thinkers in 19th and early 20th century considered the bureaucratic state, capitalism and the patriarchal family to be the three sides of the triangle for women's oppression (Landes, 1998). By the 1970's, feminists went onto explore relations between capitalism and patriarchy, housework and labour, motherhood and oppression - which lead into the family environment being deemed as appearing to reproduce capitalism within the home and subsequently oppress women on a daily basis (Landes, 1998). Does the addition of child protection social work in the context of the triangle for women's oppression, add another dimension of oppression? Even in contemporary family life in the 1990's, there were the same struggles with roles and power, rape within marriage was not made illegal until 1992 (House of Commons, 1992) highlighting the roles constructed by our society. Women not being allowed to control their own lives is based on the marginalization of women, doubly as mothers, in society (Jenney, 2011).

Women invite violence into their lives. By professionals and society blaming women (the victim) for the abuse, it implicates them as partially responsible for their own suffering, whilst allowing sympathy for the abusers (Mullender, 1996). A woman remaining with her abusive partner allows for the implicit assumption that she is tolerating abuse. This narrow view point can lead to professionals failing to recognise structural, material or cultural barriers to their leaving. Instead an individualist approach is required to view the social, political and economic context (Burman & Chantler, 2005). Because the way society views mothers being responsible for their children, they become blamed for not protecting them. This allows for the focus to shift away from men violence onto the woman's 'deficiencies' as a mother (Damant et al, 2009).

Social work is historically dominated by women and born out of the actions of women, however in the need to professionalise the profession, Jenney (2011) argues that it has parallels in the abuse of women. The profession has been characterised by male privilege and power, and influenced by gender inequalities; and largely reflected in the senior management structure as male dominated.

The changes the suffragettes and feminist movements made has seen greater equality for women. With women's growing economic independence, women have more choice in leaving their unsatisfying relationships (Sernau, 2014). However women with children tend to be left as sole custodians of their children, limiting their earning potential and support system, making them at risk of 'feminization of poverty' (Sernau, 2014, p. 153). It could be argued that women's violence towards their children, arises from their victimization and oppression within society as mothers (Damant et al, 2009).

Epstein (1999) felt that women are valued and judged by three maternal stereotypes, which are 'the all-sacrificing mother', 'the all-knowing mother' and 'the nurturing mother/breadwinning father.' (Epstein, 1999, cited in Johnson & Sullivan, 2008, p. 243) Epstein argues that the all-sacrificing mother will be able to overcome any obstacle given to protect her young. The all-knowing mother will be intuitive to her children's needs and know everything about them, in turn, they are held to a higher standard of blame than their male partner, who is accepting of the fact that society views males as ignorant to their children. With the nurturing mother and breadwinning father, it is expected that the mother's sole responsibility is to raise her children, whilst the father provides the resources to sustain the family. It is because of these stereotype images that women are held to a higher standard of care-giving responsibility than their male partners (Epstein, 1999). Is motherhood a social construction of which a mother's instinct falls into this category? Research into this is limited. Media and society would appear to like us believe that all mothers are autonomous and efficacious (Collett, 2011) however in relation to women suffering domestic abuse, this would be dependent on their ability to be autonomous in their situation. As a society we appear to have moved from a notion of remaining with your husband for the sake of your children, to being required to leave your husband for the sake of the children.

Child protection struggles to provide systematic help to battered mothers because of the constraints of their responsibilities (Edleson, 1999) and be able to best support mothers, Munro's (2012) ecological approach should be used when assessing a child's needs. Munro called for the revision of 'The Framework for Assessment of Children in Need and their families (2000)' that underpins the 10 principles, which included the need for assessments to be ecological. This was based on the development of the 'Framework for Assessment (2000)' as it found that professionals were becoming too focused on investigating alleged abuse, rather than paying attention to the quality of care they were receiving. Taking an holistic view allows for the mothers account and experiences to be taken into consideration in order to assess the social, emotional and physical impact of living with a particular household. Yet Munro's recommendations were made 3 years ago and little change has been seen in terms of assessing domestic abuse. Damant et al (2009) suggests that there is a need to be attentive to the complex power dynamics and interactions present in families, and therefore a need for social workers to intervene simultaneously on these different problems.

Men's roles as parents appear to be changing and more are becoming 'hands on fathers'. Sure Start (2010) in particular has made services available to the education of parenting to fathers, recognising the importance of their role. It is noted though that in cases of assaults against children, this tends to be from males – yet not enough attention is paid to their parenting roles and therefore it would appear that society does not accept a father's role in parenting and instead there is a continued underlying bias that women are the primary parents (Kaufman Kantor & Little, 2003). Within social work, if a woman is absent from a child protection visit this is noted and questioned, yet if a father is absent it is accepted - as is the notion of 'invisible fathers'. This is mainly due to a father's lack of availability and traditional attitudes (Horwath, 2010). Because of these societal expectations, mothers are not treated as individuals and her problems are only considered when it has an impact on the children (Mullender, 1996).

Analysis of evidence

It can be challenging for a profession to ensure a child's safety and maternal safety when Child Protection is traditionally child centred in its mission and approach to interventions (Jenney, 2011). Within the Children Act (1989), there is no mention of domestic abuse, despite its prevalence within child protection. This could be explained by the age of the act and therefore changes made in society post 1989? It would appear that further legislation has addressed this, as the Adoption and Children Act (2002) has an extended the definition of the meaning of harm, to include harm is suffered by seeing or hearing ill treatment of others, especially within the home. This has an impact on social work and their duty to assess domestic abuse within the home. Children Act (2004) also does not make specific mention of domestic abuse, but it provides the legislative basis for developing effective and accessible services that are focussed on the needs of the children. The Working Together guidance (2013) provides direction for all professionals to ensure that domestic abuse is addressed early and support is provided. A new offence has been achieved within the Serious Crime Bill in March 2015. In relation to controlling or coercive behaviour in intimate or family relationships, could be argued as an example of feminist movement and power coming through, or as an expression of male oppression in that it has taken several years for this bill to be passed.

One of the difficulties of working within child protection is the frustration that domestic abuse can cause. For example, to professionals it can seem a simple task to request a woman to ask her perpetrator partner to leave the home, without exploring the potential danger. Additional complications arise if a victim is faced with the perceived or real threat of losing her children because of her relationship; these victims may start to omit or change information about their situation, which creates difficulties for workers to make accurate assessments on the family (Jenney, 2011). Social workers and the profession can bring an element of fear that prevents victims from seeking help. Social care interventions can create fear in clients, and hostility or defensiveness. When discrepancies occur between professional and client, workers can engage in mother blaming because of their different levels of understanding; which can lead into mothers being portrayed as minimizing the severity of the situation or classed as denial (Krane & Davies, 2000). This highlights the need for relationship based practice and a better understanding for practitioners of the difficulties of living with a perpetrator. Relationship based social work refers to an approach that focuses on building rapport to further positive engagement (Murphy et al, 2012). Relationship based practice has been fully embedded into contemporary social work despite the evidence of potential benefits. Therefore there is a strong rationale for non-intervention in domestic abuse cases, especially if it is thought that nothing will change regardless of an intervention (Burman & Chantler, 2005). In terms of social work ethics, workers not intervening does not follow a consequentialist ethical stance and therefore is not following best practice (Parrot, 2010). Mullender (1996) also feels that workers not providing women with information needed to leave their situation. Abuse can create short term cognitive dysfunction, which can affect a victims risk assessment abilities and information retention. Abuse can cause serious health and psychological problems, as well as stress and anxiety which leads to forgetfulness and experiencing difficulties concentrating (Du Toit, 2009)(NHS, 2014). There needs to be a solid support structure for the victim, that provides 'security'.

Feminists have argued that battered women are survivors of 'harrowing, life-threatening experiences' (Yllo & Bograd, 1988, p. 15) who therefore have many adaptable qualities and strengths, that are developed in intense anxiety based situations that protect their children. Is it fair to call women 'bad mothers' in light of this? The role of child protection incorporates the need to increase the safety of women and their children and end the man's violence and support women whilst challenging men (Burton et al, 1989).

Women are less likely to reach out for support in a culture of victim blaming. Damant et al (2009) states that women are more likely to seek support for their parenting, over their experiences of domestic abuse. Therefore it would seem logical that intervention strategies need to be aware of factors contributing to their poor parenting.

A study completed in Canada by Lapierre & Cote (2011) involved looking at local and national child protection policies and interviewing front line workers and their managers on domestic violence. It was noted that there was a general agreement that there was a need to work with these families, but their aim was to ensure the safety of the child and not to address the parents' issues. One participant stated that 'in child protection work, we're not there to put an end to domestic violence. We're there to protect the child...Our interventions do not directly address domestic violence. (Lapierre & Cote, 2011, p. 317). The participants tended to position women as responsible for their child's safety and development, and found it easier to work with these women on this, rather than with male partners, therefore shifting the blame away from their violence (Lapierre & Cote, 2011).

Are social workers, who are predominantly female, influenced by the patriarchal influences of male dominance and control? Do they consciously unconsciously avoid direct confrontation due to fearful paralysis? There is also the possibility that social workers fear asking questions into parental relationships, as this may open up a 'Pandora's box' and the worker feel unequipped to respond (Horwath, 2010). It is a balancing act for workers to be relational in their approach, whilst having no option but to robustly intervene and intrusively to protect the child. This may mean that workers need to be ready to discriminate against one parent if an intervention is to be successful.

Child protection systems focus on ensuring child safety and well-being, but who insures the mother's safety and well-being? Social workers responsibility is to practice within the legal and ethical boundaries of their profession; meaning they must 'understand the need to protect, safeguard and promote the wellbeing of children, young people and vulnerable adults.' (HCPC, 2012, p. 7) The definition of a vulnerable adult states an adult 'who is or may be unable to take care of him or herself, or unable to protect him or herself against significant harm or exploitation' (DOH, 2015, p.9). These definitions are compartmentalised into different sections of the social care system, i.e. one for children, the other for adult. This results in a lack of joined up thinking. Could it be argued that a woman suffering from domestic abuse is classified as a vulnerable adult? A social worker's responsibility would therefore be to aid their protection with the safety of the child in mind. Recognising these women as victims and not their inactions, would potentially allow for professionals to acknowledge and therefore act upon the need for protection and support.

Internationally countries are beginning to treat a child's exposure to domestic abuse as a form of maltreatment (Johnson & Sullivan, 2008). Campbell also reports a mother was given a longer sentence than the man who raped her daughter. The prosecution wanted to send a stern lesson to mothers and place blame on them for staying with their abuser. In many USA CPS policies, it has stated that women should choose to end the abuse being perpetrated against them (Johnson & Sullivan, 2008). Therefore it would seem an effective form of intervention would be for the role of prosecutors, judges and the court system to be re-thought (Epstein, 1999). Although the study was American, the Domestic violence, Crime and Victims Act (2004) in the UK has created a new offence in the respect of child deaths. A person can be made guilty of such an offence if the child or vulnerable adult dies as a result of an unlawful act, and the defendant was aware of the risk, yet did not take reasonable steps to prevent this from happening. This means that all members of a household are liable for this and in the case of domestic violence; it could be aimed at mothers. However a victim is classed as 'at risk' because of a history of violence and serious physical harm therefore, it could be argued that a mother is also a victim. It is inconceivable to think that parents would be held accountable for children exposed to violence at school or on the street, and no child abuse or neglect charge is made in these situations, due to the level of danger being perceived to be out of their control (Johnson & Sullivan, 2008). It is accepted that these parents are unable to escape the economic entrapment of this situation, but is this different from domestic abuse? Although I would argue not.

Such women feel punished for something that their perpetrators had done, and a sense of injustice. However to counter-balance this, there was some positive experiences reported of involvement from social services. Some of the mothers reported that having a case worker refrain from placing blame on them, gave them a sense of relief. The women felt supported and believed . Being kept informed and workers intervening on their behalf was another common theme that made these women feel grateful, as well as knowing that their abusers were being confronted about their responsibility for the situation. Johnson & Sullivan's recommendations stated we cannot assume that women are the enemy in these scenarios. It is essential for workers to show empathy and not falling into labelling women as 'bad mothers'. This study has highlighted the voice of the mother and the oppression they felt, but it has also failed to highlight the voice of the child in domestic abuse and as victims as well. Although this study was completed in the USA it has similarities to the UK's child protection system. The study had a small sample size, which does not reflect the large proportion of domestic abuse sufferers. Lapierre (2008) argues that mothers viewed as 'failing' is exacerbated by the idea that exposure to domestic abuse is an automatic form of child abuse, implying that all children are affected by their exposure to domestic abuse.

To what extent are women influenced by micro influences and if they are encouraged to believe the macro influences of ingrained societal oppression of victim blaming messages? I would argue that Children Services is as dominating as a perpetrator of abuse? Societal has false expectations of women that lead to the oppression of the child. Not only does a woman have to endure a dominant and controlling male, they are 'forced' to turn to a service that exposes them to being further victimised. Keeling & Wormer (2011) found in their study of 7 women who had had involvement with social workers following domestic abuse, they had told them what to do, rather than use a strengths or motivational based approach to help empower women to make their own decisions. Through instructing women enforces control and surveillance on them, that results in professional behaviour becoming aligned to that of male perpetrators - which becomes a paradox for both the social worker and victim (Keeling & Wormer, 2011). There needs to be a balance within child protection work that allows mothers to feel empowered, whilst ensuring the safety and protection of the child. Social workers hold authority over women, in that they can use and abuse of their power. Women may perceive this to be a 'punishment' if they do not comply with the demands of the social worker and it becomes a perceived threat of 'either he must go, or the children do' (Keeling & Wormer, 2011).

Although Child protection requires a level of state monitoring when a child is at risk of significant harm greater understanding of the complex power relationships in the family is needed to avoid blaming the mother, This also has an impact on the child in that they are expected to leave behind familiar surroundings, friends and family which can cause a strong sense of anxiety. I also argue that if workers have little understanding of domestic abuse, children will be wrongly removed from their mother - adding to further harm.

Conclusion

I have explored the impact domestic abuse has on women the implications on parenting ability to protect their child. Society blames women for child protection risk. I would agree that women are re-victimised s w by child protection and that the overall argument is that of care vs. control. Social work with mothers needs to be relational and their views and experiences to be taken into account, but this is somewhat prevented by the legal framework, the need to 'control' mothers to avoid risk. It is about balancing the legal parameters of this. The human rights of the mother must be balanced with those of the child – and within a child centred structure this can be difficult to achieve. Article 8 of the Humans Right Act (1998) states a right to a private family life, but will need to be balanced against its impact upon the human rights of others.

Research has highlighted women are targeted by perpetrators. If practitioners were to understand and take into account women's experiences and fears, then intervention is more likely to be focused on empowerment. Keeling and Fisher (2012) suggest that interventions need to focus on the empowerment of women to better understand the 'grooming' process. This would enable them to identify the perpetrator's deviant tactics. It is important that women, who are unable to recognise such tactics, are not held responsible for the violence they suffer. A domestic abuse victim cannot be held responsible for the abuse they have suffered, in the same way that a victim cannot be held responsible for their home being burgled. Although it could be argued that by leaving a door open it makes the burglary easier and therefore morally to blame.

Assumptions should not be made that once a perpetrator has left the home, the family is safer. The victim is vulnerable to further abuse from the perpetrator or a new perpetrator if the pattern is not broken. The literature findings have established the difficultly in ending abusive relationships, therefore work needs to continue from professionals to develop a mother's confidence and ability to cope on her own.

Feminists have highlighted how oppression and narrow minded views of women's roles, led to the presumption that a woman's identity os of mother and ultimately protector of their children. Is it time for gendered roles to be viewed differently and for men to be seen as responsible for such care giving? A worker's treatment of a mother can heavily influence their behaviour either positively or negatively. A common theme running through this chapter is women's experiences of the child protection system, and the need to be offered more sensitivity and empathy from workers. Assumptions should not be made about the mother's parenting ability because of the situation they are in. Although a child's safety is paramount, but as a mothers parenting ability has been negatively affected by domestic abuse, further work should be done to ensure that the strengths and attributes she has, are used to provide appropriate care for her child.

I agree with Munro (2012) that an ecological approach is needed. From experience, short term social work teams do not have the capacity or timescales to be able to complete detailed assessments that explore a mother's past and their current situation. But it would seem viable that longer term social work teams, need to be holistic in their approach to establish what home life is like for the mother, to be able to better understand a child's life and provide better outcomes for them. The notion of invisible fathers appears to be readily accepted, yet perpetrators within these homes have a great impact on both the child and mother. We can learn lessons from serious case reviews (SCR).

Although there are limited services in place for women, there are also insufficient services for men needing help to change their behaviour. It is unrealistic to expect a vulnerable victim to end an abusive relationship. Women need emotional and practical support that cannot be provided within the current environment of service cuts. Until such time the stereotype of victims of domestic violence who are seen as responsible for their situation can be challenged, I am not optimistic of significant change in this situation. Government, policy makers and large organisations employing social workers must take a lead to empower social work through adequate resources and effective leadership to enable the profession to help vulnerable victims of domestic abuse.

Recommendations

1. A greater recognition of funding streams for domestic abuse on a national level is required, as is the manner and priority they are given when devolved to local authorities. More resources and government funding would enable programmes to be held more frequently with a better range of support offered.
2. Further training to professionals working with domestic abuse is needed, to avoid further victim blaming. Emphatic and knowledgeable workers are more likely to be able to offer invaluable assistance, than those who are of the view that a mother is to blame. This is an idealistic recommendation that could be argued for every child protection issue, however with further training for social work students and more emphasis placed on domestic abuse in courses, would allow for this issue to be overcome.
3. Further studies and research completed on parenting of mothers suffering domestic abuse, to include a comparative study of their time with their perpetrator and the changes in their parenting after the perpetrators have left the relationship.
4. Implementation of Eileen Munro's (2012) recommendation of an ecological approach and holistic assessments to include the experiences of a mother in the household if domestic abuse is suspected.

References

Bell, M, Goodman, L & Dutton, M (2009) Variations in help-seeking, battered women's relationship course, emotional well-being, and experience of abuse over time. *Psychology of Women Quarterly*, 33, 149-162

Buchbinder, E & Eisikovits, Z (2004) Reporting bad results: the ethical responsibility of presenting abused women's parenting practices in a negative light. *Child and family social* work, 9, 4, 359-367

Burman, E, & Chantler, K (2005) Domestic violence and minoritization: Legal and policy barriers facing minoritized women leaving violent relationships. *International Journal of Law and Psychiatry*, 28, 59-74

Burton, S, Regan L & Kelly, L (1989) *Supporting Women and Challenging Men: Lessons from domestic violence intervention programmes.* Bristol: Policy Press

Campbell, A (2014) *Battered, bereaved, and behind bars.* http://www.buzzfeed.com/alexcampbell/how-the-law-turns-battered-women-into- criminals#.scJ7PkMea Accessed 27/03/15

Cleaver, H, Unell, I & Aldgate, J (2011) *Children's needs – Parenting capacity; Child abuse: Parental mental illness, learning disability, substance misuse, and domestic violence.* (2nd ed) Norwich: TSO

Collett, J (2005) What kind of mother am I? Impression management and the social construction of motherhood. *Symbolic Interaction*, 28, 3, 327-347

Cowdery, R & Knudson-Martin, C (2005) The construction of motherhood: Tasks, relational connection, and gender equality. *Family Relations*, 54, 3, 335-345

Damant, D, Lapierre, S, Lebosse, C, Thibault, S, Lessard, G, Hamelin-Brabant, L, Lavergne, C & Fortin, A (2009) Women's abuse of their children in the context on domestic violence: reflection from women's accounts. *Child and Family Social Work*, 15 12-21

Department of Education (2014) *Statistics - national statistics; Characteristics of children in need: 2013 to 2014.* London: DoE

Department of Health (DOH), (2000) *Framework for the assessment of Children in Need and their families.* London: DoH

Department of Health (2015) *No Secrets: Guidance on developing and implementing multi- agency policies and procedures to protect vulnerable adults from abuse.* London: Home Office, https://www.gov.uk/government/publications/no-secrets-guidance-on-protecting- vulnerable-adults-in-care Accessed 27/03/15

Domestic Abuse Intervention Project, (2011) *Home of the Duluth Model; Social change to end violence against women.* Duluth, http://www.theduluthmodel.org/training/wheels.html Accessed 26/03/15

Du Toit, L (2009) *Verbal Emotional Abuse.* http://lauradutoit.hubpages.com/hub/Emotional-Abuse Accessed 28/03/15

Edleson, J (1999) The overlap between child maltreatment and woman battering. *Violence against Women*, 5, 134-154

Epstein, D (1999) Cited in Johnson, S & Sullivan, C (2008) How child protection workers support or further victimize battered mothers. *Affilia*, 23, 3, 242-258, http://aff.sagepub.com/content/23/3/242.full.pdf Accessed 16/03/15

Ferguson, H (2011) *Child protection practice.* Basingstoke, Palgrave Macmillan

Harne, L & Radford, J (2008) *Tackling domestic violence: Theories, policies and practice.* Maidenhead, Open University Press

HCPC, (2012) *HCPC: Standards of Proficiency'* London: Park House. http://www.hcpc- uk.org/assets/documents/10003B08Standardsofproficiency-SocialworkersinEngland.pdf Accessed 27/03/15

HCPC, (2012) *Standards of Conduct, Performance and ethics*' http://www.hcpc- uk.org/assets/documents/10003B6EStandardsofconduct,performanceandethics.pdf Accessed 27/03/15

HM Government, (2013) *Working Together to Safeguard Children; A guide to inter-agency working to safeguard and promote the welfare of children*. Norwich: TSO

HM Government, (1989) *Children Act 1989*'

HM Government, (1998) *Human Rights Act 1998*

HM Government, (2002) *Adoption & Children Act 2002*.

HM Government, (2004) *Children Act 2004*.

HM Government, (2004) *Domestic Violence, Crime and Victims Act 2004*

Holden, G, Stein, J, Ritchie, K, Harris, S & Jouriles, E (1998) Parenting Behaviors and Beliefs of Battered Women. in Holden, G, Geffner, R and Jouriles, E (eds) *Children Exposed to Marital Violence: Theory, Research and Applied Issues*. p. 289-334. Washington DC: American Psychological Association

Home Office (2013) *Domestic Violence and Abuse*' https://www.gov.uk/domestic-violence-and-abuse Accessed 25/03/15

Home Office (2014) *Violence against women and girls*. https://www.gov.uk/government/policies/ending-violence-against-women-and-girls-in-the- uk Accessed 28/03/15

Horwath, J (2010) *The Child's world; The comprehensive guide to assessing children in need*. (2nd ed) London: Jessica Kingsley

House of Commons, (2010) *Sure Start Children's Centres; Fifth report of session 2009-2010*

Jenney, A, (2011) *Negotiating risk and safety in child protection work with domestic violence cases*. Toronto, Tspace, https://tspace.library.utoronto.ca/bitstream/1807/29764/3/Jenney_Angelique_C_201106_ PhD_Thesis.pdf Accessed 20/03/15

Johnson, S & Sullivan, C (2008) *How child protection workers support or further victimize battered mothers*. London: Sage

Kaufman Kantor, G & Little, L (2003) Defining the boundaries of child neglect; When does domestic violence equate with parental failure to protect?' *Journal of interpersonal violence*, 18, 4, 338-355,

Keeling, J & Fisher, C (2012) Women's early relational experiences that lead to domestic violence. *Qualitative Health Research*, 22, 1559-1567

Keeling, J & Wormer, K (2011) Social worker interventions in situations of domestic violence: What we can learn from survivors' personal narratives?' *British Journal of social work*, 42, 1354-1370

Krane, J & Davies, L (2000) Mothering and child protection practice: rethinking risk assessment. *Child & Family Social Work*, 5, 35-45

Landes, J (1998) *Feminism: The public and the private*. Oxford: Oxford University Press

Landsman, M & Hartley, C (2007) Attributing responsibility for child maltreatment when domestic violence is present. *Child Abuse & Neglect*, 31, 445-461

Lapierre, S & Cote, I (2011) I made her realise that I could be there for her, that I could support her: Child Protection practices with women in domestic violence cases. *Childcare in Practice*, 17, 4, 311-325

Lock, R (2013) *Final Overview Report of Serious Case Review re Daniel Pelka - September 2013*.

Coventry LSCB http://www.coventrylscb.org.uk/files/SCR/FINAL%20Overview%20 Report%20%20DP%2013 0913%20Publication%20version.pdf Accessed 25/03/15

Milner, J & Myers, S (2007) *Working with violence; Policies and practice in risk assessment and management.* Basingstoke, Palgrave Macmillan

Munro, E (2011) *The Munro Review of Child Protection: Final report, A child-centred system'* London, TSO,

Mullender, A (1996) *Rethinking domestic violence; The social work and probation response.* London, Routledge

Mullender, A (2002) Persistent oppressions: The example of domestic violence. in Adams, R, Dominelli, L & Payne, M (ed) *Critical practice in social work.* Basingstoke, Palgrave

Murphy, D, Duggan, M & Joseph, S (2012) Relationship-based social work and its compatibility with the person-centred approach; Principled versus instrumental perspectives. *British Journal of Social work*, 1-17, 07/03/12 http://bjsw.oxfordjournals.org/content/early/2012/03/07/bjsw.bcs003 Accessed 15/03/15

NHS, (2014) *Stress, anxiety and depression.* http://www.nhs.uk/Conditions/stress-anxiety-depression/Pages/understanding-stress.aspx Accessed 28/03/15

Ofsted, (2010) *Learning lessons from serious case reviews 2009-2010.* http://www.workingtogetheronline.co.uk/documents/Learning%20lessons%20from%20serious%20case%20reviews%2020092010.pdf 29/03/15

Parrott, L (2010) *Values and ethics in social work practice.* (2nd ed) Exeter : Learning Matters

Sernau, S, (2014) *Social inequality in a global age.* (4th ed) London: Sage

The Who Cares? Trust, (2015) Why is there so much movement in care?' http://www.thewhocarestrust.org.uk/pages/moving-on-dealing-with-multiple- placements.html Accessed 08/04/15

Valios, N (2011) *Are child victims of domestic violence being forgotten?'* Community care, http://www.communitycare.co.uk/2011/04/14/are-child-victims-of-domestic-violence- being-forgotten/ 29/03/15

Women's Aid, (2003) *Executive Summary: Failure to protect? Domestic violence and the experiences of abused women and children in the family courts'* (11.11.03) http://www.womensaid.org.uk/domestic-violence- articles.asp?section=00010001002200020001&itemid=1194 Accessed 24/03/15

Women's Aid (2015) *Domestic violence law reform campaign.* http://www.womensaid.org.uk/page.asp?section=00010001001000330002 Accessed 07/04/15

Yllo, K & Bograd, M (1988) *Feminist perspectives on wife abuse.* London: Sage

10
Online grooming: A consideration of everyday practice in child protection

Billy Hughes

Introduction

It is important to develop an understanding of 'online grooming' and the key characteristics involved in this crime. If social workers are to support and protect vulnerable children more effectively, preventing and identifying the signs of online grooming are fundamental. This chapter will examine a definition of online grooming and consider its prevalence in the UK and critically explore contemporary evidence to develop new insights and recommendations for change.

Background

The Internet is part of modern life and provides offenders with a platform to access children without leaving their homes. The use of the Internet and communication technology is now firmly embedded within the everyday lives of UK children. The Internet offers children entertainment, education and often facilitates their social life. Children access the Internet at school, at home and in the community. (Livingstone,2013:15; Facer,2012:397; McCarthy,2010:181: Katz,2013:1536). Attached to the many positive aspects of the Internet are online threats that seek children for exploitation. (CEOP,2013; NSPCC,2014: Whittle et al,2012:62). Ponte et al (2013:2) argues that views of the Internet tend to be polarised in society. People either see the Internet as a means of knowledge and learning or observe its negative consequences such as grooming and child pornography. Grooming is a process used to prepare a child for sexual abuse (CEOP,2013). Slavtcheva-Petkova et al (2014:59) concludes that 'the severity of online grooming is so significant that it deserves substantial resources and attention'.

Katz (2013;1536) suggests that children can be targeted online for trafficking, child pornography, sexual abuse and inappropriate sexual communication. Shannon (2008) reviewed 315 police reports. The research demonstrated a variety of ways in which online activities can facilitate abuse. In 179 cases the offender only had contact with the child through online contact that involved sexual conversations and exposure via webcam, in 22 cases an offender used the Internet to develop a sexual relationship with a known child and in 69 cases the offender and child met – resulting in sexual abuse. (Slavtcheva-Petkova et al, 2014:59) Katz and Shannon's research illustrates a variety of risks the Internet can pose to children that is neither monitored or controlled by adults responsible for the care of these children.

In addition, data gathered by Ofcom (2014) published in a document *'Children and Parents: Media Use and Attitudes Report'* reveal a significant increase in Internet use by children of all ages. In 1,660 interviews completed with parents and children aged 5 to 15, along with 731 interviews with parents aged 3 – 4. Since 2013 the ownership of a computer tablet has increased from 51% to 71% Furthermore, 4 in 10 children aged 5 to 10 own a smart phone, rising to 8 in 10 children aged 12 – 15, an increase from 2013. Children aged 8 – 11 are spending more time online than in 2013 and tend to prefer socialising online than watching television (Ofcom 2014). Desktop PC and laptop use by children continues to decline which means parents are less able to supervise their children and have less control over the material their children are exposed to.

Likewise, The CHILDWISE Monitor Report (Leggett and Ehren, 2015) highlighted that

> 81% used smart phone applications (You Tube, Snapchat, Facebook, Instagram and Minecraft), only 1% of children aged 7 – 16 had never accessed the Internet in 2014, 94% of children aged 7 – 16 accessed the Internet at home, including 73% who accessed in the Internet in their room. These statistics illustrate how younger children are starting to access the Internet more frequently and are on the increase. Children are increasingly accessing the Internet outside of the home without parental supervision. The opportunity for offenders to groom children has increased The NSPCC (2014) review of *'Serious Case Reviews'* found online abuse as a key factor. These reviews highlight how professionals need to raise awareness about online safety; online grooming can lead to sexual abuse; exploitation and child suicide; children are groomed for indecent images and an offender's sexual gratification.

A central problem in preventing online abuse is that grooming behaviours are usually identified after the abuse has taken place. (Williams, 2014;29) Furthermore, the underreporting of online sexual abuse and the child's awareness is an issue (Kloess et al, 2014:127). Parents are cautious about their children talking to 'strangers' in the community but are less concerned with their children's experience of online risk. (Whittle et al, 2012:65)

Evidence and research to support enquiry

'To what extent should online grooming be a consideration, of everyday practice, within child protection social work?' Craven et al (2006:291) definition of grooming is frequently referred to in research as a baseline. Craven et al (2006:291) proposed that before an offender begins to groom a child there has to be some level of motivation to abuse. Based on their review, Craven et al provided a clear definition of child sexual grooming,

> A process by which a person prepares a child, significant adults and the environment for the abuse of this child. (2006: 291)

Whittle et al (2012:63) describe grooming as a technique used by offenders to turn their fantasy into reality. Whilst Davidson and Martellozzo (2008) advocates grooming involves a process of socialisation during which an offender will interact with a child, to gain trust. Berson (2008) defines grooming as a clever process of manipulation, usually initiated through a nonsexual approach designed to gain the trust of a child. The child's inhibitions are lowered through desensitisation, power and control. Additionally, Kloess et al (2014) suggest the term 'grooming' has generally been used to describe offender's actions during the preparatory stages of sexual abuse.

The National Crime Agency annual plan (2014/15) states that the threat of online child sexual abuse and exploitation is high. Protecting children from online abuse is a priority where resources need protecting. The Child Exploitation and Online Protection Centre (CEOP) in their report (2013) indicated that they receive around 1,000 reports from children each year concerning online victimisation perpetrated by adults. In addition, a total of 2,391 reports received (submitted by the public), of which 64% related to grooming, making grooming the most reported activity to CEOP. A child met an offender in the community in 6.8% of cases and 48.5% began their relationship with an offender via social networking sites. It is concerning that children aged 8 – 11 years old do not know 12% (11 per child) of their social networking 'friends' and children aged 12 – 15 years old do not know 25% (72 per child). The majority of the children interviewed reported to communicate with people that online they do not know. Female victims were apparent in 80% of cases. (CEOP, 2013) These statistics are based on children having the confidence and awareness to report abuse. CEOP suggest many victims do not report incidents as they are unaware of an offender's devious motives. Similar ChildLine (2013) produced a report where 327 children had been exposed to grooming and exploitation in 2012/13. Many of the children disclosed meeting the offender via the Internet and building a 'trusting relationship' online. The majority of the children thought they were in a relationship with the offender and often referred to "being in love".

Grooming involves a process of interaction between the child and an offender over a period of time with the aim of gaining the child's trust. The grooming process can last months or sometimes as little as a day as the offender's aim is to gain leverage over the child. Kloess et al (2014) advocates that grooming is a technique that offenders master and contain a set of strategies and behaviors that they utilise at different stages of their interaction with the child. Katz (2013) proposes a linear online grooming process based on the findings of their research: (1) the offender will approach the child through the Internet (2) communication will take place to build a rapport (3) the offender will attempt to gain a phone number or schedule an offline meeting (4) the offender and child meet during which the child is sexually assaulted (p.1538). Furthermore, Whittle et al suggests grooming is 'multifaceted and complex' and grooming is difficult to identify (2012:63).

Craven et al (2006) generated a model of grooming and identified three types of grooming: (1) grooming the self (2) grooming of the surroundings and significant others and (3) grooming the child. This shows a link between the process an offender uses to prepare a child for sexual abuse and the process they use to prepare themselves for committing abuse. Common features of grooming refer to desensitising the child to the point there is an increased chance the child will engage in sexual activity. The offender will use techniques to maintain secrecy from the child, family and friends. The child will be manipulated, coerced or threatened into behaving into unexpected ways. Throughout the grooming process the offender may use bribery, gifts, money, flattery, sexualised games and threats to shape the child's cognitive functioning and behaviour. (Craven et al,2006; Smeaton,2012; Kloess et al,2014) This increases the offender's power and control over the child. The child becomes emotionally attached to the offender and unable to detach from such exploitation when they wish to do so. (Berson, 2008)

Based on the literature it can be assumed that an offender grooms a child in stages. The Internet provides a platform for children to be identified by offenders and to begin the grooming process. Grooming appears to be a skill whereby an offender uses techniques to build dependency and a fictitious relationship develops. The child becomes a victim, a slave to an offender's sexual desires (CEOP,2013) and a psychological 'smoke screen' inbuilt by the offender to prevent the child from seeing the reality.

The notion that offenders have different goals is becoming widely accepted. Quayle and Taylor (2003) suggest the Internet provides online sex offenders with an immediate solution to their fantasies. The Internet assists offenders with maintaining anonymity. Interestingly, a study conducted by Briggs et al (2011) suggest saw two types of Internet offenders. A 'contact-driven group' who are motivated to engage in meeting the child for sexual gratification and a 'fantasy-driven group' who are motivated to engage a child in cybersex without any intentions to meet offline. McCarthy (2010) states contact offenders have significantly more involvement with children online than non-contact (fantasy driven) offenders. Contact offenders are more likely to chat with children in a sexual manner, share child and adult pornography and attempt to meet children offline. However, regardless of the offender's intentions, Leonard (2010:255) concludes that Internet offending (fantasy driven) cannot be viewed as 'causing fewer traumas than contact offending'. Some offenders pose as a child whilst others pose as adults when approaching children online. Malesky (2007) report that only one third of the convicted offenders in his sample represented themselves as children, while even fewer offenders (5%) pretended to be younger in a study by Wolak et al (2008). Many children were aware they were talking to an adult. Conversely, Williams et al (2013) study recommends that offenders are still pretending to be children at the beginning of the grooming process. Therefore, this identifies two types of offenders – a true representation versus a deceptive representation of person as. (Kloess et al, 2014) The diversity of offenders makes the job of profiling potential offenders more difficult for protection agencies to identify.

Children groomed online are vulnerable. A basic definition of 'vulnerability' in relation to children has been defined by Munro (2011:7) as 'susceptibility to physical or emotional injury'. Cross et al (2009) suggest that vulnerable children are not a static group and can be vulnerable at anytime. According to Bradbrook et al (2008) children who are vulnerable or at risk offline are more than likely to be at risk online. Therefore, professionals including social workers are likely to come into contact with these children. Conversely, Palmer (2010) highlights that some victims of grooming would not be perceived as vulnerable offline. However, Berson (2008:10) proposes that an offender will focus on a child's 'loneliness or emotional neediness'. Offenders are skilled in locating social networking profiles of vulnerable children. Children from disadvantaged households with a history of abuse, poor self-esteem and confidence, less supervised by parents, in puberty suffer from psychological problems, experience poor relationships, victims of bullying and socially isolated or confused about their sexuality are all risk factors that may make a child vulnerable to online grooming (Slavtcheva et al,2014:59; Williams,2014:31; Livingstone,2013; McCarthy, 2010; Katz, 2013; Berson,2008:; Munro,2011: Davidson et al,2011; Barnardo's, 2013).

Throughout the counselling process children report feelings of shame, foolishness and being 'broken hearted'. In addition, Wells and Mitchell (2007) state that various health issues experienced by victims include a high prevalence of depression, anxiety or phobias, social isolation, parent-child conflict, sexualised and disruptive behavior. Supported by Howe (2005) suggest if a child experiences sexual abuse their physical, social, emotional and academic development is impaired. Whilst Judd and McGlashan (2003) and Dube et al,(2005) show 66% of children receive no education and have limited understanding of online risks.

> I would trust people after speaking with them for a while, perhaps 2 weeks, and then I'd know they were ok and would meet them.

> It would be alright if you met them out where there were lots of other people around. (Davidson and Martellozzo,2008:283).

Findings from the *Safer Internet Day: Campaign Evaluation* (2014) established 87% of children and 76% of teenagers felt they knew who to contact for advice if they experienced something online which made them feel uncomfortable. Furthermore, 60% of children said they were worried about Internet safety, with 7% saying they were very worried and 53% saying they were a little worried (Clegg,2014).

Kloess et al (2014) argues that to protect children online, parents' need strategies for monitoring their Internet use and are the first line of defence when protecting children online Berson (2008:7 . However, the advances in technology have left parents with gaps in technical knowledge in relation to the latest social networking sites, photo sharing services and smart phone applications. Furthermore, the NSPCC Share Aware campaign (2015) established that 'parents reported that it was difficult to find the reporting/blocking features' on the Internet (Cherry et al,2015). Bailey (2011) acknowledges that the Internet industry should additionally be supporting parents with introducing effective parental controls. It appears since his report in 2011, parents are still experiencing 'blocking features' on the Internet difficult to discover.

In summary 'vulnerability factors' place a child at a higher risk of being targeted by online groomers. Offenders have skilled strategies to locate children and build a fictitious relationship with the aim of sexual gratification. The impact of online abuse on children affects their emotional, psychological, social and physical development. Online grooming appears to be a real and significant risk to children. The Internet industry is continuously evolving and some parents are struggling to sufficiently protect their children online. However, the majority of children have reported they know how to access support if they experience something uncomfortable online. Based on the vulnerability factors established in this review, it is likely children subject to Child Protection or Child In Need plans are vulnerable to online grooming. It is therefore essential that this issue has greater social work awareness of the risk factors. The following is an analysis of the evidence will develop new insights.

Analysis of Evidence

The Internet is part of modern life for children and it is embedded within everyday behaviour. Children access the Internet at home, school and in the community. Technology has advanced and allows children to access the Internet instantly via smart phones and computer tablets. Katz (2013), Livingstone (2013), Facer (2012), McCarthy (2010), Whittle et al (2012) and Slavtcheva-Petkova et al (2014) all argue that there are many positive aspects attached to children using the Internet, however they equally support CEOP (2013) and NSPCC (2014) concerns of Internet threats such as online grooming.

Statistics presented by Ofcom (2014) and CHILDWISE (2015) illustrate the extent to which Internet use by children is increasing each year. The key messages highlights the use of desktop PCs and laptops are declining whilst tablet computers and smart phones are increasing. A child's Internet use on tablet computers and smart phones are more difficult for parents to monitor, these devices can be used in the privacy of their bedrooms and outside of the family home. Furthermore, younger children aged from 3 – 10 have access to the Internet and are possibly at risk from online threats in addition to older children and those with special needs. Applications such as Facebook and Instagram provide offenders with a catalogue of children to be targeted. However, CEOP (2013) only receive 1000 new reports from children each year concerning online victimisation perpetrated by adults. This is a small number of reports in comparison to the amount of children that access the Internet. I would argue that based on the grooming process children are unaware of an offender's intentions and realistically more than 1000 children have experienced a form of online grooming. (CEOP,2013; Williams,2014; Kloess et al,2014; Berson,2008).) Barnardo's *Sexual Exploitation Risk Assessment Framework* is a common tool used by local authorities which proposes mild, moderate and significant risk indicators.

Grooming is frequently referenced in research as a basis for further enquiry (Craven et al 2006). Such definition is easy to understand and can be utilised in social work practice. It provides the reader with a synopsis of grooming. Conversely, the definition appears to consider grooming in a wider context, such as grooming instigated in the community (offline). Furthermore, the definition was based on research conducted in 2006. 'Online grooming' has evolved and it would be beneficial for 'online grooming' and 'offline grooming' to have separate meanings in the literature. Whittle et al (2012) and Kloess et al (2014) each provide contemporary definitions of grooming but again, do not separate online and offline grooming. However, it has been established from reviewing definitions of grooming key words are gaining the child's trust, in 'preparing' a child for a form of sexual abuse, manipulation and desensitisation.

Arguably there has been legislative progress in terms of this issue. Online grooming was added to the Sexual Offences Act 2003. However, legislation does not account for non-contact harm (HMSO 2015) (Craven et al,2006). Furthermore, what if an offender communicates with a child once prior to meeting, is the act then valid? The process of grooming has previously been discussed and research suggests grooming will impact on a child's psychological, emotional and social functioning. It appears legislation does not acknowledge this but should be reviewed to consider criminalising offenders for any inappropriate sexual discussions with a child. However this may impinge on an individual's human rights. The 'gap' in legislation provides evidence to support why social workers need to utilise other legislation and guidance to protect children in their everyday practice. Guidance from Government (2009:30) states section 17 of the Children Act 1989, ensures that the needs of all children and young people who are being, or are at risk of being, sexually exploited are assessed and that appropriate multi-agency engagement and appropriate interventions are undertaken in line with the *Working Together* document (2013) and the *Framework for the Assessment of Children in Need and their Families*. The Sexual Offences Act 2003 does not appear to be satisfactory in the prevention and criminalising of online grooming. However, social workers in a child protection environment need to be aware of their legal responsibilities and it should be engrained in their practice that every child is at risk until assessments and evidence suggests otherwise.

Although there are definitions of online grooming available in literature, the grooming process appears to vary depending on the techniques and exploitative intentions of the offender. This makes assessment and gathering evidence a difficult task. Furthermore, an offender is able to groom a child within minutes or take years. Katz (2013:1538), Craven et al (2006) and O'Connell (2003) all generated a model of the grooming process. All 3 models offer a linear and sequential process. However, there are some differences. In addition, Craven et al and O'Connell's model was based on research completed in 2003 and 2006. Online threats to children and platforms used by offenders to initiate contact with children have developed. For example, social networking sites appear to have replaced chat rooms.

An offender will use different grooming techniques and present differently to children. Briggs et al (2011) research identified two types of offenders - contact and fantasy driven. Contact driven offenders approach a child with the intention of meeting the child for sexual gratification whilst a fantasy driven offender will engage in cybersex but will not meet the child offline. However, a child that has been groomed by a fantasy driven offender will still experience emotional and psychological harm. (Howe,2005) As supported by Leonard (2010), fantasy driven offending cannot be viewed as causing 'fewer traumas' than contact driven offending. It is important social workers acknowledge these offending characteristics as a child may not always display obvious risk indicators compared to that which fits neatly into a risk model.

Children are more at risk of online grooming today than ever before. Children who have been victims of online grooming display common risk indicators. (Bradbrook et al, 2008; Berson,

2008; Slavtcheva et al, 2014; Williams, 2014; Livingstone, 2013; McCarthy, 2010; Katz, 2013; Berson, 2008; and Munro, 2011) The government's report (DoE, 2014) on initial assessments completed by local authorities, show how children were placed at higher risk because of domestic violence, neglect, disability or illness, family acute stress, family dysfunction, socially unacceptable behaviour, poverty and absent parenting. Comparing these risk factors with those associated with online grooming, it is noticeable that there are similarities. Therefore, it could be argued that children subject to Child Protection or Child In Need plans are more at risk to online grooming then social workers are aware of.

Social workers need to provide appropriate interventions to children and families that have experienced, are experiencing or are at risk of experiencing online grooming. The literature reviewed established that online grooming does have an impact on a child's physical, psychological, social, emotional, motor and academic development. (Craven et al, 2006 Palmer, 2010; Wells and Mitchell, 2007; Howe, 200; Shea et al, 2004; Judd and McGlashan, 2003; Dube et al, 2005) A child's behaviour and future life choices are equally affected. It appears children whom experience sexual abuse may continue to access services as an adult for support. Online grooming activates an offender's opportunity to sexually abuse vulnerable children and the child's life is endlessly affected. However, as highlighted in a HM Government (2015) report titled *'Tackling Child Sexual Exploitation'*, early intervention is fundamental to protect children from abuse. Internet safety education to children should be provided by parents and/or professionals. Furthermore, Berson (2008:16) argues that successful prevention requires all parents and professionals who support children with Internet access to be educated about online safety. It is important to empower children with the knowledge to protect themselves online.

> Society neither prevents children from crossing the road nor permits them to run freely across the motorway. Rather, it takes the concerted efforts of parents, teachers, car designers, road authorities and town planners to strike an acceptable balance between children's freedom to navigate their neighbourhood and risks. (Livingstone, 2014:285)

Therefore, social workers in a child protection environment need to take responsibility for discussing online threats with parents and children. Social workers express less confidence when dealing with Internet based abuse and grooming. Social workers require extra training and practice guidance to assist them with investigating and post-investigation child sexual abuse and exploitation - including online grooming (Martin et al, 2014). Social workers lack confidence when investigating child sexual abuse, especially exploitation and online grooming, which is further supported by Marsh (2015). A key message from this study is that although a social worker's practice needs to consider online grooming as part of their everyday practice, social workers may not have the confidence, knowledge or adequate assessment tools for effective intervention.

Conclusion

The Key message from this chapter is children access the Internet at a younger age whilst having less supervision from their parents. This is often done in a private space. The use of smart phones and computer tablets have increased and the advancement in technology allows children to use the Internet outside of the family home unmonitored. The rise of social networking sites has created a platform for offenders to target children and exploit their vulnerability. Perpetrators increase their sophistication in methods to avoid detection whilst grooming.

Online grooming is a process where offenders use strategies to form a relationship with a child via the Internet; to gain their trust and desensitise them to sexual activities and manipulate them into secrecy. An offender's overall objective is to seek sexual gratification. Evidence demonstrate that the prevalence of online grooming is a contemporary issue but a true representation of children experiencing online grooming is uncertain due to the sophisticated strategies employed by offenders. Online grooming is a complex and difficult crime to identify and protect against. Furthermore, legislation does not criminalise offenders for the commencement of the grooming process and therefore this is not supported by the criminal justice system with prosecution. Legislation does not provide for the psychological impact that the grooming process has on children.

Furthermore, children subject to Child In Need (CIN) and Child Protection (CP) plans have greater risk factors to online grooming. The parents of children subject to CIN or CP may be less equipped to tackle the issue at home. This places children known to children services at a potentially higher risk of exploitation. Social workers are part of a child's support network, in partnership with other professionals and parents. Government reviews have suggested that social workers are not equipped with sufficient assessment and decision making skills to manage the problem. On line grooming is a serious problem aggravated by the lack of necessary specialist skills and knowledge in current social work practice.

The following thoughts are recommendations for change in key areas of practice.

- Social workers need training to identify the indicators of online grooming?
- Social workers in a child protection environment need to openly discuss online risks with parents and children to prevent grooming?

- Social worker's should be familiar with contemporary social networking sites and smart phone apps that children access?
- Social worker's should be familiar with the 2009 and 2015 HM government child exploitation guidance?

References

Aveyard, H. (2014). *Doing a Literature Review in Health and Social Care: A Practical Guide.* Maidenhead: McGraw-Hill Education.

Bailey, R. (2014). *Letting Children be Children.* (online) https://www.gov.uk/government/uploads/system/uploads/attachment_data/file/175418/Bailey_Review.pdf (accessed: 7 February 2015)

Barnardos (2013). *Sexual Exploitation Risk Assessment Framework.* (online) http://www.barnardos.org.uk/barnardo_s_cymru_sexual_exploitation_risk_assessment_framework_report_-_english_version-2.pdf (accessed: 6 February 2015)

Barnardo. (2014). *Support the Unsupported.* (online) http://www.barnardos.org.uk/what_we_do/advertising_campaigns/support-the- unsupported.htm *(accessed: 7 February 2015)*

Berson, I.R. (2003). Grooming cybervictims: The psychosocial effects of online exploitation for youth. *Journal of School Violence, 2,* 5-18.

Bradbrook, G. Alvi, I. Fisher, J. Lloyd, H. Moore, R. Thompson, V. et al. (2008). *Meeting Their Potential: The Role of Education and Technology in Overcoming Disadvantage and Disaffection in Young People.* Coventry: Becta.

Briggs, P. Simon, W. Simonsen, S. (2011). An exploratory study of internet initiated sexual offences and the chat room sex offender: Has the internet enabled a new typology of sex offender? *Sexual Abuse: A Journal of Research and Treatment*, 23, 72-91.

British Association of Social Workers (BASW). (2012). *The Code of Ethics for Social Work: Statement of Principles.* (online) http://cdn.basw.co.uk/upload/basw_112315-7.pdf (accessed: 11 April 2015)

Cherry, E. Fossi, J. Jetha, N. Lilley, C. (2015). *Net Aware: A Parent's Guide to Social Networking Sites.* (online) http://dwn5wtkv5mp2x.cloudfront.net/downloads/Research_Highlights/UKCCIS_RH75_NSP CC_Net_Aware_-_A_Parents_Guide_to_Social_Networking_Sites.pdf (accessed 10 February 2015)

Child Exploitation and Online Protection Centre CEOP. (2013). *Threat Assessment of Child Sexual Exploitation and Abuse.* (online) http://ceop.police.uk/Documents/ceopdocs/CEOP_TACSEA2013_240613%20FINAL.pdf (accessed: 7 February 2015)

Childline. (2013). *Childline Online Issues Report 2012-13.* (online) http://www.saferinternet.org.uk/content/childnet/saferinternetcentre/downloads/Research_Hi ghlights/UKCCIS_RH54_ChildLine_Online_Issues_Report_2012-13.pdf (accessed: 7 February 2015)

Clegg, H. (2014). *Safer Internet Day 2014: Campaign Evaluation.* (online) http://

dwn5wtkv5mp2x.cloudfront.net/downloads/Research_Highlights/UKCCIS_RH74_Safer_Internet_Day_2014_Campaign_Evaluation.pdf (accessed: 7 February 2015)

Craven, S, Brown, S, & Gilchrist, E. (2006). Sexual grooming of children: Review of literature and theoretical considerations, *Journal Of Sexual Aggression*, 12, 3, pp. 287-299, Academic Search Complete, EBSCOhost (accessed: 6 February 2015)

Cross, J. Richardson, B. Douglas, T. Vonkaenel-Flatt,K. (2009). *Virtual violence: protecting children from cyber bullying.* London: Beatbullying.

Davidson, J. Grove-Hills, J. Bifulco, A. Gottschalk, P. Caretti, V. Pham, T. Webster, S. (2011). *Online Abuse: Literature Review and Policy Context.* (online) http://www.europeanonlinegroomingproject.com/media/2080/eogp-literature-review.pdf (accessed: 7 February 2015)

Department of Education. (2013). *Working Together to Safeguard Children: A guide to inter- agency working to safeguard and promote the welfare of children.*

Department of Education. (2014). *Characteristics of children in need in England 2013-14.* (online). https://www.gov.uk/government/uploads/system/uploads/attachment_data/file/367877/SFR43_2014_Main_Text.pdf [accessed: 6 February 2015]

Dube, S. Anda, R. Whitfield, C. Brown, D. Felitti, V. Dong, M. Giles, W. (2005). *Long-term consequences of childhood sexual abuse by gender of victim.* (online) http://www.jimhopper.com/pdfs/dube_%282005%29_childhood_sexual_abuse_by_gender_of_victim.pdf (accessed: 7 February 2015)

Facer, K. (2012). After the moral panic? Reframing the debate about child safety online, *Discourse: Studies In The Cultural Politics Of Education*, 33, 3, 397-413, Academic Search Complete, EBSCOhost (accessed: 6 February 2015)

Health and Care Professions Council (HCPC). (2008). *Standards of Conduct, Performance and Ethics.* Available from: http://www.hcpc-uk.org.uk/assets/documents/10003B6EStandardsofconduct,performanceandethics.pdf (accessed: 11 April 2015)

HM Government. (2009). *Safeguarding Children and Young People from Sexual Exploitation.* (online) https://www.gov.uk/government/uploads/system/uploads/attachment_data/file/278849/Safeg uarding_Children_and_Young_People_from_Sexual_Exploitation.pdf

HM Government. (2015). *Tackling Child Exploitation.* (online) https://www.gov.uk/government/uploads/system/uploads/attachment_data/file/408604/2903652_RotherhamResponse_acc2.pdf (accessed: 6 February 2015)

Howe, D. (2005). *Child Abuse and Neglect: Attachment, Development and Intervention.* Basingstoke, Macmillan.

Judd, P. McGlashan, T. (2003). *A developmental model of borderline personality disorder: Understanding variations in course and outcome.* Arlingston VA: American Psychiatric Press

Kloess, J, Beech, A, & Harkins, L. (2014). Online Child Sexual Exploitation: Prevalence, Process, and Offender Characteristics, *Trauma, Violence & Abuse*, 15, 2, 126-139, Academic Search Complete, EBSCOhost (accessed: 6 February 2015)

Katz, C. (2013). Internet-related child sexual abuse: What children tell us in their testimonies, *Children and Youth Services Review*, 35, 9, 1536-1542. Doi: 10.1016/j.childyouth.2013.06.006.

Leonard, M. (2010). "I did what I was directed to do but he didn't touch me". *The impact of being a victim of internet offending.* Journal of Sexual Aggression, 16, 249-256.

Livingstone, S. (2014). *Developing social media literacy: How children learn to interpret risky opportunities on social network sites, Communications,* 39. Doi: 10.1515/commun-2014-0113.

Leggett, S. Ehren, J. (2015). *Childwise Report: Trends in media use.* (online) http://dwn5wtkv5mp2x.cloudfront.net/downloads/Research_Highlights/UKCCIS_RH73_Child wise_Monitor_2015.pdf (accessed: 7 February 2015)

Legislation.gov.uk. (2015). *Sexual Offences Act 2003.* [online]. http://www.legislation.gov.uk/ukpga/2003/42/section/15 (accessed: 5 January 2015)

Livingstone, S. (2013). *Online risk, harm and vulnerability: Reflections on the evidence base for child Internet safety policy, Zer: Revista De Estudios De Comunicacion,* 18, 35, pp. 13-28, Academic Search Complete, EBSCO*host* (accessed: 6 February 2015)

Malesky, A. (2007). Predatory online behaviour: Modus operandi of convicted sex offenders in identifying potential victims and contacting minors over the Internet. *Journal of Child Sexual Abuse,* 16, 23-32.

Martin, L. Brady, G. Kwhali, J. Brown, S J. Crowe, S. Matouskova, G. (2014). *Social workers' knowledge and confidence when working with cases of child sexual abuse.* (online) http://www.nspcc.org.uk/globalassets/documents/research-reports/social-workers-knowledge-confidence-child-sexual-abuse.pdf (accessed: 6 February 2015)

McCarthy, J. (2010). Internet sexual activity: A comparison between contact and non-contact child pornography offenders. *Journal of Sexual Aggression,* 16(2), pp. 181-195.

Munro, E (2011) The protection of children online: a brief scoping review to identify vulnerable groups. Research. Childhood Wellbeing Research Centre [online] http://www.ccinform.co.uk/research/the-protection-of-children-online-a-brief-scoping-review-to-identify-vulnerable-groups/ (accessed: 6 February 2015)

NSPCC. (2014). *Abuse and neglect: online harm.* (online) http://www.nspcc.org.uk/globalassets/documents/research-reports/how-safe-children-2014- indicator-09.pdf (accessed: 7 February 2015)

NSPCC (2014) Learning from case reviews where online abuse was a key factor. Key Documents. NSPCC [online] http://www.ccinform.co.uk/key-documents/learning-from-case-reviews- where-online-abuse-was-a-key-factor/ (accessed: 6 February 2015)

NSPCC. (2015). *Share Aware.* (online) http://www.nspcc.org.uk/preventing-abuse/keeping- children- safe/shareaware/?utm_source=google&utm_medium=cpc&utm_campaign=Grant_shareawa re2014&utm_term=nspcc_share_aware&gclid=CJ3a88 i23MQCFWIUwwodOlIAQw&gclsrc=a w.ds (accessed: 7 February 2015)

O'Connell, R. (2003). *A typology of cyber exploitation and online grooming practices.* University of Central Lancashire: Preston, England.

Ofcom. (2014). *Children and Parents: Media Use and Attitudes Report.* (online) http://

stakeholders.ofcom.org.uk/market-data-research/other/research- publications/childrens/children-parents-oct-14/ (accessed: 7 February 2015)

Palmer,T. Stacey, L. (2004). *Just one click. Sexual abuse of children and young people through the internet and mobile telephone technology*. Essex: Barnardo's.

Ponte, C, Simões, J, & Jorge, A. (2013). *Do questions matter on children's answers about internet risk and safety?*, Cyberpsychology, 7, 1, pp. 60-70, Academic Search Complete, EBSCO*host* (accessed: 6 February 2015)

Quayle, E. Taylor, M. (2003). Model of problematic Internet use in people with a sexual interest in children. *Cyberpsychology and Behaviour,* 6, 1, 93-106.

Shea, A. Walsh, C. MacMillan, H. Steiner, M. (2004). Child maltreatment and HPA axis dysregulation: relationship to major depressive disorder and post traumatic stress disorder in females. *Psychoneuroendocrinology,* 30, 162-178.

Slavtcheva-Petkova, V, Nash, V, & Bulger, M. (2015). Evidence on the extent of harms experienced by children as a result of online risks: implications for policy and research, Information, *Communication & Society,* 18, 1, pp. 48-62, Academic Search Complete, EBSCO*host* (accessed: 6 February 2015)

Smeaton, E (2012) Guide to safeguarding children and young people from sexual exploitation - Section two: Indicators, exploitation processes and impact of child sexual exploitation. Guides.

Community Care Inform [online] http://www.ccinform.co.uk/guides/guide-to-safeguarding-children-and-young-people-from- sexual-exploitation-section-two-indicators-exploitation-processes-and-impact-of-child-sexual-exploitation/ [accessed: 6 February 2015]

Wells, M. Mitchell, K. (2008). *How do high risk youth use the internet? Characteristics and implications for prevention. Child Maltreatment,* 13,pp. 227 – 234.

Williams, A. (2015). Child sexual victimisation: ethnographic stories of stranger and acquaintance grooming, *Journal Of Sexual Aggression,* 21, 1, pp. 28-42, Academic Search Complete, EBSCO*host* (accessed: 6 February 2015)

Williams, R. Elliott, I. Beech, A. (2013). Identifying sexual grooming themes used by Internet sex offenders. *Deviant Behaviour,* 34, 135 – 152.

Whittle, H, Hamilton-Giachritsis, C, Beech, A, & Collings, G. (2013). A review of young people's vulnerabilities to online grooming, *Aggression & Violent Behavior,* 18, 1, pp. 135-146, Academic Search Complete, EBSCO*host* (accessed: 6 February 2015)

Wolak, J. Finkelhor, D. Mitchell, K. Ybarra, M. (2008). Online "predators" and their victims: Myths, realities, and implications for prevention and treatment. *American Psychologist,* 63, 111-128

11
Reunification of looked after children with their birth parents
Samuel Tolerton

Introduction

The success and likelihood of a Looked after Child being reunified with their birth family, is a complex and emotive issue, which is effected by a multitude of factors. Additionally, the Department for Education (2013b) acknowledges that reunification decisions involve considerable uncertainty. When considering reunification, the best interests of the child , risks of further harm, benefits of its potential success and the positive changes the family has made need to be taken into account. Furthermore, consideration needs to be given to the difficulties previously encountered by the child in relation to abuse and neglect, trauma of separation and their experiences of being looked after. Approaching this topic from a wider perspective, other issues identified which are important in the success rates of reunification include; the reasons for being in care, number of episodes in care, type of placement, placement stability, sustained change within family home, resolution of parental issues, change in family structure, financial resources and economic wellbeing, assessment and support in reunification from services and the impacts of child age, ethnicity, and emotional and behavioural difficulties (Biehal, 2006).

This chapter will, focus on the impact of time in care, contact between parent and child whilst being looked after, and the motivation from the child and parent's perspective to reintegrate.

Background

In 2013, family reunification was the most common reason (35%) why a child ceased being looked after (DfE, 2013a) and this has been a long-standing trend (NSPCC, 2012). Although, Department for Education (2013b) report that the percentage of looked after children returning home dropped significantly from 49% in 2004 to 39% in 2008. This may be reflective of the Baby P factor (Jones, 2014), but applied to reunification risk adversity as opposed to entry to care rates.

The pattern of reunification being the most frequent outcome for looked after children, is also evident in the USA, whereby in 2001, 57% of children who left foster care were reunified with their parents (Pine, Spath and Gosteli, 2005). Pine, et al. go as far as labelling reunification as the 'goal' of foster care practice. SCIE (2012) however suggest that the reunification of a looked after child is the 'least successful permanence option', with findings from Farmer, et al. (2008) identifying that around half of children who suffered abuse or neglect prior to entry to care, encountered further abuse post reunification and a further half re-entered care.

Research by Wade, et al. (2010) identified that the outcomes, in regards to stability and well-being for children who have encountered maltreatment, are better for those who remain looked after, than those who returned home. This was found to be especially true for cases of neglect and emotional abuse. NSPCC (2012) report that 73% of children within their study said they were not ready to return home and 48% were not consulted at all prior to reunification. Research by Sinclair, et al. (2005) and Farmer and Wijedasa (2013) demonstrates that reunification is sometimes repeatedly attempted, resulting in failure and not necessarily always in the child's best interests. NSPCC (2012) warn that reunified children can face problems where professionals 'normalise' the abuse or neglect they suffer, by accepting the adverse conditions and experiences of the child. Subsequently, the threshold for intervention and support where the child has been reunified is higher in comparison to their first removal. Despite these issues reunification has not been the focus of significant policy or practice development (NSPCC 2012).

The Children Act 1989 (S.17:1B) stipulates a duty to promote the upbringing of children by their families. This is juxtaposed by varying levels and implications for birth families within current policies, relating to the permanence of Looked after Children, which attempt to tackle issues of delay (Boddy, et al., 2014). For example, Adoption Reform within the Children and Families Act 2014 (DfE, 2013c) and the earlier, Action Plan on Adoption: Tackling Delay (DfE, 2011a) put emphasis on early separation and timely placement for adoption. In the current political context of high profile child deaths, emphasis and successes of adoption, and budget cuts to services and resources that enable practical support to families, there is a danger that practitioners will increase risk adverse decisions. Murphy and Fairtlough (p.349, 2014) emphasise that 'the principle of 'no delay' in decision making and permanency planning must be balanced against the importance of promoting each child's right to be cared for by their parents wherever possible'.

Being looked after

Biehal (p.15, 2006) states that studies have 'consistently found that the probability of reunification is greatest immediately following placement and that statistically, the likelihood of discharge to either parents or relatives appears to decrease as time in care increases'. This assertion is supported by Wade, et al. (2010), for example, who found that reunification was altogether less likely where children had been looked after for a longer period of time. Similarly, Department for Education (2013b) report that 64% of children who were looked after for less than a year returned home, in comparison to 15% of those who were looked after for longer than a year. Schofield, et al. (2007) report however, that some children do return to their parents, even after spending a considerable amount of time being looked after and separated (up to eleven years within their study).

Under the Adoption and Safe Families Act (1997) in the USA, there is a 12-month time frame established as a window, in which counties must provide 'reasonable efforts' of support for reunification. Carnochan, et al. (2013) highlight that this policy is the subject of much criticism from practitioners and academics alike (e.g. Berrick, 2009, Risley-Curtiss, et al. 2004), expressing that 12 months is not a sufficient length of time for many cases to successfully reunify. Risley-Curtiss, et al. (2004), for example, discuss the barriers to reunification for parents with mental health problems and identify that the timeframes set out by ASFA (1997), present a significant obstacle to parents with mental health issues. This is due to the conflicting periods between ASFA (1997) timeframes and the time required for the necessary treatment of their condition, in addition to the length of time it took securing it.

Research by Cheng (2010) undertaken in the US, found that for children who have suffered maltreatment, stays in care of less than six months or over two years, resulted in repeated abuse or re-entering care, more frequently than those who spent between six months and two years in care. Biehal explains that although studies have been consistent in demonstrating that the longer spent in care, the less likely reunification will occur, she believes this is only true at a descriptive level. Instead however, it has become conceptualised as an explanatory variable, as the research findings have passed into the wisdom of many policy-makers and professionals. Therefore, Biehal (p.16, 2006) argues, 'the misconception that remaining in care longer than six weeks or six months, may in itself reduce a child's chances of reunification has become widely accepted'. I agree with Biehal's analysis, particularly in the recognition of how the duration of care is dependent and associated with other factors that relate to the child, parents and service. The length of time being looked after is therefore consequential of the other factors which inter-relate, causing reunification not to be in the best interests of the child. From wider reading, the other factors which impact upon the length of time a child spends being looked after, broadly include, but not limited to:

- Child characteristics of age, ethnicity, presence of disabilities, and emotional and behavioural difficulties and motivation for reunification.
- Positive parental change which is sustained, compliance with service plans and motivation for reunification.
- Service factors of case proactivity (not drift), stability of placements whilst in care, variation in local authorities i.e. thresholds, reasons for entry to care, placement type.

Also I believe that many of the studies and statistics which report on length of time in care and reunification rates fail to take account of the different reasons as to why children enter care. Rates of reunification relating to cases of abuse and neglect are therefore misrepresented, as there is a statistical bias, which includes children who enter care for reasons where the child only requires being looked after for a short period of time. For example, in Dickens, et al.'s study (2007), 34% of reunifications occurred within four weeks. Furthermore, this study excluded planned episodes of 'respite care' and noted that they thought 'one off' short-stay cases, were likely to have been under represented. The studies relating to length of time being looked after and reunification are therefore not directly scrutinized. Finally professional consciousness impacts on the proactivity of practitioners in considering reunification, which of course as a consequence, affects the amount of time spent being looked after. If practitioners hold the consciousness of the incorrect assertion, of time and reunification, this continues causing drift unless other permanency options are pursued. Where the permanency option of adoption is not being pursued due to the child being an adolescent for example, is having difficulty with stability in long-term foster placements (McWey and Mullis, 2004). This will cause the practitioner to focus their efforts and attention on the issues this presents, as well as other associated on-going problems i.e. substance misuse, which could cause drift and an occupation with these factors, as opposed to considering, or pursuing the potential stability that reunification could provide, if that is the child or young person's wishes.

Impact of contact

Under Schedule 2:15(1) of the Children Act 1989, the local authority has a duty to endeavour to promote contact between parents and looked after children, where it is reasonably practicable and consistent with the child's welfare. Contact Arrangements for Children (DfE, 2012) proposed that contact should be undertaken in a planned manner, with achievable goals which meet the best interests and welfare of the child. SCIE identify that developing and assisting positive family relationships whilst the child remains in care is an essential goal for reunification and that this can be facilitated through supervising contact (2012). Fahlberg (2012) also reinforces that 'healthy family relationships cannot be built without consistent contact among family members and therefore, it plays an important role in improving family life for children who enter care.

Biehal (p.39, 2006) acknowledges that 'the relationship between patterns of contact, parent-child relationships, child well-being and reunion is clearly a complex one' but beneficial (Fahlberg 2012:195). SCIE (2012) accurately state that 'while good contact does not necessarily lead to a return home, and poor contact does not prevent it, 'contact work' during and after care (including with a non-resident parent or previous carers) is important to successful overall return and lays the foundations for the continuing family support and professional relationship with the family'. However, Murphy and Fairtlough (2014) assert that existing research does not explore how contact is or could be used to prepare children for reunification. Humphreys and Kiraly (2011) also highlight that little research reports on the effectiveness of different patterns, durations and practice models of contact, especially for infants in care where reunification is being considered. In Biehal's literature review (2006), she found that literature relating to the impact of contact on reunification has largely been reflective, as opposed to being based on empirical research findings. Biehal suggests however that the research on contact and reunification tends to demonstrate that children, who have frequent contact with parents and a positive experience are more likely to be in care for less time (p.39, 2006).

Biehal (2006) cites that studies conducted in the 70s and 80s were overly influential in spreading the belief that, a lack of parental visiting diminishes the likelihood that children can be reunified with their families. More recently however, Wade, et al. (2010), found that where contact with birth parents was infrequent, children were less likely to be reunified. Furthermore, 90% of children who had contact with their birth families prior to reunification in Bullock, Gooch and Little (1998) found that contact had been assumed as predictive of reunification, but was actually due to it deriving from: 'the child's retention of both a role and territory within family, the family's perception of itself as a family, the inclusiveness of the social work plan and the easing of problems that led to separation' (p.37 in Biehal, 2006). Similarly, Cleaver (2000) found contact to be an important factor in return if it had a purpose, had the aim of improving the parent-child relationship and was positive for the child. In circumstances where parents were motivated about reunification, actively participated in the returning process and were willing to change and access support, contact helped the reunification process. Furthermore, when both contact and the returning process was regularly reviewed and involved both children and parents in the planning and decision making process, was even more beneficial. Davis et al (1996) found a correlation between levels of contact and reunification. However, within this study levels of contact were stipulated by the court and measured at a bivariate level with reunification. If the recommended frequency of contact was met, there was a strong association with reunification, in as much as ten times more likely than if levels were not met. However, in 44% of maternal and 38% of paternal visiting plans, where contact arrangements were adhered to, parents and children were not reunited. Davis et al (1996) suggest that reunification may have always been a doubt in these cases and that contact was stipulated to test parents' resolve to reunite with their children and therefore, the aim of contact was a form of evidence gathering as opposed to a therapeutic tool.

Humphreys and Kiraly (2011) advocate for the need for contact sessions to be therapeutically supportive, due the nature of their intimacy and potential for strong memories and emotions of abuse, trauma, separation and loss to be provoked, along with the more positive aspects of relationships and memories of happiness. Furthermore, Kenrick (2009) reports concerning findings of infant distress. Despite this, Durrell and Hill (2007) note contact supervisors are frequently underqualified and have received little training and state 'practice seems to be very much left to the discretion of the individual worker or agency' (2007, p.209). It seems therefore that contact is not necessarily predictive of whether reunification occurs, however it is an important factor in improving the dynamics within families and thereby its chances of success.

Impact of motivation and ambivalence

Biehal (2006) notes that the reasons for parental ambivalence are likely to be complex, suggesting a combination of factors, such as the strength of the parent-child relationship and bond, the severity and impact of parental problems and the extent of their social network available to support them. Children's sources of reluctance or ambivalence in relation to reunification are likely to stem from poor relationships, a result of earlier abuse or neglect, the nature of contact with parents whilst being looked after and feelings of resentment, anger, anxiety or fear. Fahlberg (2012) suggests that loyalty conflicts may exist within the child between their parents and foster carers, if they have developed a strong attachment with them and these are likely to manifest in feelings of ambivalence. Furthermore, the desire for reunification can coincide with periods of unhappiness in care, a series of placement breakdowns or a single disruption within an adoptive or 'permanent' foster placement.

Farmer, et al. (2012) determined that the motivation of children and parents for reunification has an impact on the likelihood of it occurring, although not necessarily on whether it is successful. If both parents and children are highly motivated in their reunification, SCIE (2012) report that it can produce positive outcomes.,

Sinclair et al (2005) supported by Bullock, Gooch and Little (1998) found that when parents were rejecting or ambivalent towards reunification, children tended to remain in care and sometimes the attitude of the parents additionally led to child ambivalence. Wade, et al. (2010) found that where there was recorded evidence on file that the child did not want to return home and that the child accepted their need to be looked after, the child was less likely to return home. In 20% of the reunification cases studied by Murphy and Fairtlough (2014), they found no evidence of the parent or child being consulted prior to reunification about its possibility, however take note that it may have happened, but not been recorded. In 40% of the cases, they found that both the parents and child's views were recorded and suggest that these influenced decision making and the support offered. A further 62% of cases demonstrated that the decision for reunification was highly influenced by pressures exerted by parents, children or both.

Murphy and Fairtlough's research (2014) however has significant limitations in regards to its use and the generalisations which can be drawn. It was undertaken using a case-file audit which examined a select sample of 42 looked after children, who had been successfully reunified with their families by a local authority. This equates to a small sample size and is only representative of one local authority's practice. As has already been demonstrated, rates of reunification and decision making vary greatly between authorities (Dickens, et al. 2007). Files were audited using a standardised process, examined in the same order for consistency purposes and by the same researcher. By using the same researcher for all files, the issue of different data interpretations being made by multiple researchers was reduced. However, the interpretation of files depends on researcher objectivity and Clark-Carter (p100, 2004) identify this is likely to cause an extent of observer bias, whereby the judgment of the researcher is effected by their knowledge and expertise. Furthermore, by using the methodology of case-file auditing, there are further limitations, as this is what has been recorded by a practitioner and therefore presents only one perspective on the progress of the case and reasoning behind why decisions were made. In addition, aside from commentary, there is no data-error measurement used within the study and therefore does not take account of entries which were not submitted, or inputted incorrectly.

Yatchmenoff (2005) and Dawson and Berry (2002), acknowledge how client compliance with case plans are often viewed as proxies for engagement; in the ability to acknowledge concerns and develop motivation for change. In enabling motivation to change, SCIE (2012) have highlighted the need for developing services which are tailored for parents, early on in the processes of intervention. Yatchmenoff (2005) also points out that it is frequently assumed by child welfare practitioners, that parents are unmotivated or do not want help, however there is evidence to suggest this is not the case and instead these perceptions are born out of anxiety or anger over child welfare agency involvement. Furthermore, Berry, et al. (2007) stress that parents and workers both view there to be an importance behind developing a common understanding of each other's views on the child's removal, reasons for it and working through parental anger. This is reflective of the social work dilemma of care and control (Ferguson, p.36, 2011) and how practitioners and parents will so often have conflicting views on what is in the child's best interests (Houston, 2003). Therefore, practitioners need to maximise their attempts at negotiation and empathy throughout their involvement with families, even when utilising the professions power and authority to protect the welfare of the child, in order to instigate parental engagement (Forrester, et al. 2008).

Analysis

In Biehal's literature review (2006), she suggests that quantitative studies of reunification sometimes use bivariate analyses (e.g. Davis, et al. 1996) and draw claims about the correlations of these with reunification. These studies do not take account of the multiplicity of factors which affect reunification and furthermore how these are inter-related. For example, considering the relationship between contact and reunification without regard to other factors which affect both of these, such as reasons for being looked after, frequency of contact, quality of contact, environmental considerations and levels of contact facilitation, will lead to unwarranted conclusions which do not take account of the wider picture when outcomes are discussed. Within the literature review, there are several inconsistencies between studies and results, relating to whether certain factors are indicative of reunification, or not. Biehal (p.21, 2006) proportions these inconsistencies to a consequence of poor methodologies, which fail to take a multivariate approach in conducting research on reunification.

Furthermore, many reunification studies suffer from bias due to using cross-sectional assessments as opposed to longitudinal methodologies. This is because the cross-sectional samples represent the population of children looked after at a single point in time. Due to this, these samples fail to take account of children who enter care for a brief period of time before returning home. Therefore an over representation of children who have been in care for long periods and under representation of children who experience a singular, brief period of time in care exists. Despite their underrepresentation, studies have tended to demonstrate the association between children spending less time being looked after with 'better' reunification success. This either demonstrates that there is a stronger correlation between time being looked after and reunification than is reported, or more likely that those studies which use cross-sectional sampling are the same studies which use bivariate analyses. Furthermore, cross-sectional sampling research tends not to take account of sibling groups and how this may impact upon reunification, but also the results within research and how this may generate a bias due to counting the effects of belonging to a singular family multiple times.

Ultimately, there is ambiguity in interpreting some of the statistics relating to rates of reunification, particularly when juxtaposed against the time spent in care. Furthermore, the figures relating to length of time spent looked after, should not necessarily be seen automatically as good or bad. They are it is assumed, outside the context of drift at least, what is necessary for the child and what is in their best interests, both in terms of the time needed being looked after until sufficient changes can be made and whether reunification happens or not.

Linked to this and as important to remember, 'reunification' or 're-entering care' are 'service outputs' and terminologies, consistent with target orientated practice and reflect quantitative statistics, instead of reflecting the wellbeing of the child (Tilbury, 2004). This demonstrates how the measures of agency performance, themselves have an impact upon how child welfare is constructed and understood. Therefore it is worth questioning and being critical in one's own practice of whether these terms and the findings they demonstrate actually represent the complex reality of a looked after child. Further, their birth parents circumstances and the associated dynamics of stability, development, wellbeing and the views of the child are equally important.

Schofield, et al. (p.639, 2007) speak of the pursuit of permanence, and how the multiple moves between placements can 'mean an emotional roller coaster of raised expectations and potential serial losses for the child until a settled and secure placement is reached. This process requires highly sensitive and skilled work by social workers, foster carers and residential workers if the child is to be able to sustain some coherent sense of themselves as a valued and loveable person'. Within reunification practice, this value is vital to hold in mind, as the hopes and desires of the child being reunified with their parent after a period of separation can, as research suggests, easily not work out, resulting in subsequent separations and a devastating sense of rejection and unworthiness for the child.

It appears that reunification is rarely considered as an option within parallel planning to secure permanence. Although reunification will not be possible in all cases, it seems that it is ruled out relatively early on during the period of time a child is looked after. The aspect of timeliness in relation to decisions over permanence and child development is important, although it appears in some cases the decisions taken not to reunify are taken too quickly. Reunification can by its nature take time, and therefore is important for a proactive reunification plan to have small, time-based actions to measure progress, ensure its achievability and remain strengths based. This will help to keep focus and prevent the case from drifting. Furthermore, reunification assessment and support in relation to reintegration, needs to be given the same focus that is currently given to adoption. Local authorities should invest more in reunification, as this will increase the likelihood of its success and achieve better outcomes for those children who return home. For example, in the local authority where Murphy and Fairtlough (2014) undertook their research, a looked after children's multi-agency panel responsible for approving all reunifications was created. This development ensured that a consistent and accountable approach to decision making in relation to considering the safety of reunifications ensued and a form of quality assurance to assessments was implemented. The planning, reviews and support for reunifications were also overseen and approved by the panel and I recommend that a similar approach is implemented nationwide. A method of regulation such as this will help to ensure that myths, such as the length of time being looked after is indicative of a reunification's success will be quashed. Furthermore, this idea chimes well with Improving Permanence for Looked after Children (DfE, 2013b) which states

> Local authorities need a clear organisational approach and framework for returning children home. Thorough assessment, purposeful preparation, clear expectations about parental change and the provision of intensive interventions and good quality support services all contribute to successful return home'.

Reunification literature, suggests that the chances of its success, are improved when a partnership has been developed between practitioners and parents. This level of relationship and trust however, may be difficult to achieve due to the previous experiences of the parent, when the child was removed from their care. In cases of abuse and neglect, authority and power is frequently used and necessary, in order to safeguard the child. However, I suggest that this affects the willingness and anxiety of the parent in developing relationships with future practitioners. These past experiences with child protection services are likely to adversely affect the belief and hope, and thereby motivation of the parent in being reunified with their child. Therefore, the practitioner will need to go to additional lengths in developing a relationship with the parent in cases of reunification for a partnership to develop. This will involve the provision of practical support, demonstration of empathy, degrees of empowerment and time in allowing this to be developed.

In addition to this, I concur with the research findings, undertaken by Boddy, et al. (2014), who suggested that reunification practice may improve if children and adult services were more integrated with one another. This would enable the gap between thresholds of services to reduce, thereby providing a more consistent approach.

Conclusion

This chapter has provided a snapshot of factors which interplay, that affect the possibilities and successes of looked after children being reunified with their birth parents. It is evident, that the provision of services and interpretations of the practitioner have a significant impact upon each of the three factors covered within this chapter, and how they indicate reunification success. Reunification is rarely achieved and often discounted too early in the planning process, consequently depriving children and their families of an alternative and possibly better option, for long-term permanence.

References

Adoption and Children Act 2002, TSO: London

Adoption and Safe Families Act (ASFA) – US Public Law 105-89, Accessed via, Child Welfare Information Gateway: https://www.childwelfare.gov/topics/systemwide/laws-policies/federal/

Berrick, J. D. (2009) *Take me home: protecting America's vulnerable children and families*, Oxford University Press: New York. Accessed on 27.02.2015 via: http://www.oxfordscholarship.com/view/10.1093/acprof:oso/9780195322620.001.0001/acprof-9780195322620-chapter-3

Berry, M., McCauley, K. and Lansing, T. (2007) Permanency through group work: a pilot intensive reunification program, *Child and Adolescent Social Work Journal*, 24:5, pp.477-493

Biehal, N. (2006) *Reuniting looked after children with their families: A review of the research*. National Children's Bureau: London.

Biehal, N. (2007) Reuniting children with their families: reconsidering the evidence on timing, contact and outcomes, *British Journal of Social Work*, 37:5, pp.807-823

Boddy, J., Statham, J., Danielsen, I., Geurts, E., Join-Lambert, H. and Euillet, S. (2014) Beyond contact? Policy approaches to work with families of looked after children in four European countries, *Children & Society*, 28:152-161

Bullock, R. Little, M. and Millham, S. (1998) *Children going home, the reunification of families*, Ashgate: Aldershot

Care Planning, Placement and Case Review (England) Regulations, 2010, TSO: London

Carnochan, S., Lee, C. and Austin, MJ. (2013) Achieving timely reunification, *Journal of Evidence Based Social Work*, 10, pp.179-195

Cheng, T.C. (2010) Factors associated with reunification: a longitudinal analysis of long-term foster care, *Children and Youth Services Review*, 32:10, pp.1311–1316

Clark-Carter, D. (2004) *Quantitative Psychological Research: A Student's Handbook*, Psychology Press: Hove

Cleaver, H. (2000) *Fostering family contact*, TSO: London

Davis, I., Landsverk, J., Newton, R. and Ganger, W. (1996) Parental visiting and foster care reunification, *Children and Youth Services Review*, 18:4, pp.363-382

Dawson, K., and Berry, M. (2002) Engaging families in child welfare services: An evidence-based approach to best practice, *Child Welfare*, 81, pp.293–317

Children Act 1989, TSO: London

Department for Education (2011a) *Action Plan on Adoption: Tackling Delay*, Department for Education: TSO. Accessed on 24.03.2015, via: www.gov.uk/government/uploads/system/uploads/attachment_data/file/180250/action_plan_for_adoption.pdf

Department for Education (2011b) *Statistical First Release: Children Looked-After in England Year ending 31 March 2011*, Office for National Statistics. Accessed on 05.04.2015, via: www.education.gov.uk/rsgateway/DB/SFR/s001026/index.shtml

Department for Education (2012) *Contact arrangements for children: a call for views*, Department for Education: London

Department for Education (2013a) *Statistical First Release: Children Looked-After in England Year ending 31 March 2013*, Office for National Statistics. Accessed on 23.03.2015, via: www.gov.uk/government/uploads/system/uploads/attachment_data/file/244872/SFR36_2013.pdf

Department for Education (2013b) *Improving Permanence for Looked After Children*, Department for Education: London.

Department for Education (2014c) *Children and Families Act 2014*, Department for Education: London.

Department of Health (1991) *Patterns and Outcomes in Child Placement*, HMSO: London

Dickens, J., Howell, D., Thoburn, J. and Schofield, G. (2007) Children starting to be looked after by local authorities in England: an analysis of inter-authority variation and case-centred decision making, *British Journal of Social Work*, 37:4, pp.597-617

Durrell, M. and Hill, B. (2007) Observing, recording and reporting: an analysis of practice relating to supervised child contact, *Ethics and Social Welfare*, 1:2, pp.209-215

Fahlberg, V. (2012) *A child's journey through placement*, Jessica Kingsley Publishers: London.

Family Rights Group (2014) *Reuniting children in the care system with their families*, 17. Accessed on 27.03.2015, via: www.frg.org.uk/images/Advice.../17-reuniting-children-and-families.pdf

Farmer, E., Sturgess, W. and O'Neill, T. (2008) *The Reunification of Looked after Children with their Parents: Patterns, interventions and outcomes*, Report to the Department for Children, Schools and Families, School for Policy Studies: University of Bristol

Farmer, E., Sturgess, W., O'Neill, T. and Wijedasa, D. (2012) *Achieving successful returns from care: what makes reunification work?* British Association for Adoption and Fostering: London.

Farmer, E. and Wijedasa, D. (2013) The reunification of looked after children with their parents: What contributes to return stability? *British Journal of Social Work*, 43:8, pp.1611–1629.

Ferguson, H. (2011) *Child protection practice*, Palgrave Macmillan: Basingstoke

Forrester, D., McCambridge, J., Waissbein, C. and Rollnick, S. (2008) How do child and family social workers talk to parents about child welfare concerns? *Child Abuse Review*, 17: 23–35.

Hess, PM and Folaron, G. (1991) *Ambivalences: a challenge to permanency for children*, Child Welfare, 70:4, pp.403-424

Houston, S. (2003) Moral consciousness and decision making in child and family social work, *Adoption & Fostering*, 27:61-70

Humphreys, C. and Kiraly, M. (2011) High frequency family contact: a road to nowhere for infants, *Child and Family Social Work*, 16, pp.1-11

Jones, R. (2014) *The story of Baby P: Setting the record straight*, Policy Press: Bristol

Kenrick, J. (2009) Giving babies stability in care from the start, *Adoption and Fostering*, 33, pp.5-18

Larrieu, J. A., Heller, S. S., Smyke, A. T., and Zeanah, C. H. (2008) Predictors of permanent loss of custody for mothers of infants and toddlers in foster care, *Infant Mental Health Journal*, 29:1, pp.48–60

McWey, L. and Mullis, A. (2004) Improving the lives of children in foster care: the impact of supervised visitation, *Family Relations*, 53:3, pp.293-300

Murphy, E. and Fairtlough, A. (2014) The successful reunification of abused and neglected looked after children with their families: a case-file audit, *British Journal of Social Work*, 44:2, pp.348-366

NSPCC (2012) *Returning home from care: what's best for children*, NSPCC. Accessed on 22.01.2015, via: http://www.nspcc.org.uk/preventing-abuse/research-and-resources/returning-home-from-care/

Pine, B., Spath, R. and Gosteli, S. (2005) 'Defining and achieving family reunification', pp.378-391, IN: Mallon, G. and Hess, P. (2005) *Child welfare for the 21st Century*, Columbia University Press: New York

Placement of Children with Parents etc Regulations Act 1999, TSO: London

Quinton, D., Rushton, A., Dance, C. and Mayes, D. (1997) Contact between children placed away from home and their birth parents: research issues and evidence, *Clinical Child Psychology and Psychiatry*, 2:3, pp.393-413

Risley-Curtiss, C., Stromwall, L. K., Hunt, D. T., and Teska, J. (2004) Identifying and reducing barriers to reunification for seriously mentally ill parents involved in child welfare cases, *Families in Society*, 85:1, pp.107-118

Schofield, G. (2005) The voice of the child in family placement decision-making: a developmental model, *Adoption and Fostering*, 29:1 pp.29-44

Schofield, G., Thoburn, J., Howell, D. and Dickens, J. (2007) The search for stability and permanence: modelling the pathways of long-stay looked after children, *British Journal of Social Work*, 37:4, pp.619–642

SCIE - Social Care Institute for Excellence (2012) *Returning children home from public care*, Social Care Institute for Excellence (Thoburn, J., Robinson, J. and Anderson, B.), Research Briefing 42.

Sinclair, I., Baker, C., Wilson, K. and Gibbs, I. (2005) *Foster children: Where they go and how they get on*, Jessica Kingsley Publishers: London

Sinclair, I., Baker, C., Lee, J. and Gibbs, I. (2007) *The Pursuit of Permanence: A Study of the English Child Care System*, London, Jessica Kingsley.

Tilbury. C. (2004) The influence of performance management on child welfare, policy and practice, *British Journal of Social Work*, 34:2, pp.225-241

Wade, J., Biehal, N., Farrelly, N. and Sinclair, I. (2010) *Maltreated children in the Looked-After system: a comparison of outcomes for those who go home and those who do not*, Social Policy

Research Unit: University of York

Yatchmenoff, D. K. (2005) Measuring client engagement from the client's perspective in non-voluntary child protective services, *Research on Social Work Practice*, 15, pp.84–96

12
Meaningful contact between the child and social worker: A critical review

Clair Lockyer

Introduction

Serious Case Reviews and reports on child protection services in the UK over the last decade have identified the child's voice and presence not being heard or seen in assessment (Laming, 2003; Laming 2009; Munro, 2010; Munro, 2011a; Munro 2011b;), therefore, decisions that are made for the child are not always deemed in the child's best interest (United Nations Convention on the Rights of the Child, 1989; Children Act, 1989, 2004; Ofsted, 2011). Currently children's social work practice is experiencing one of its biggest reforms to date (Social Work Reform Board, 2010). Social Workers are under increasing pressure and the need to evidence that the child has been physically seen has become a significant priority. The child's voice being heard is a necessary part of the role, but to achieve this, good meaningful contact needs to be applied. Current reform is tasked to support this happening, however Munro (2012) identified that although practice was heading in the right direction, the pace needs to be faster (p.3).

This chapter will look at the concept of meaningful contact between the child and the child's Social Worker and evaluates what it means to 'see the child' as this term is fraught with ambiguity.

The history behind the reform

Meaningful contact is nothing new but over seventy years of social work history would imply it is this very relationship that has let the child down. The death of twelve year old Dennis O'Neill in the 1940's led to the Monckton Report, with the Curtis Report of children in care following, both of which discussed the need for child-Social Worker relationships (Winter, 2011). Thirty years on from this a report into the death of seven year old Maria Colwell, identified similar problems in the child- Social Worker relationship with a lack of visits, failure to engage the child or see the child alone (Winter, 2011). A decade after this the report into the death of four year old Jasmine Beckford highlighted a lack of personal relationship between the child and the Social Worker (Winter, 2011). This continues with the death of Victoria Climbié in 2000 and Lord Laming's (2003) report highlighting there were too few visits that were short in duration but also the impact the organisational failings had on the child-Social Worker relationship. Since the Laming report, procedures and policy began to increase (Broadhurst et al., 2010a; Broadhurst et al., 2010b). However the profession appeared to then get caught up in paperwork and computer systems that hold information of children being protected rather than a focus on the child. Changes to the Ofsted inspections have been trying to tackle this problem (Ofsted, 2011).

However the death of Peter Connelly in 2007 led to a huge public outcry and a further report from Laming (2009) and further reforms (Social Work Reform Board, 2010; Munro, 2010; Munro, 2011a; Munro, 2011b). However nothing appeared to change. Further serious case reviews (Radford, 2010; Coventry LSCB, 2013) were published and highlighted by the media. A concerning picture of the state of children's social care work was beginning to emerge.

In June 2010 Professor Eileen Munro was tasked by the UK Secretary of State for Education, to conduct an independent review of child protection in England (Munro, 2010; Munro, 2011a; Munro, 2011b), with the aim to support the reform of the UK's child protection system. This reform appears to still be very much in progress moving into 2015. Munro's (2011b) final report offered 15 recommendations as to how children in the UK should be supported and protected, with the central themes running through the recommendations that the focus had to be on children. Recommendation 13 was for Local Authorities to *'review and redesign the ways in which child and family social work is delivered'* (p.13).

Children have to be seen, but seeing the child is more than just 'seeing', it's the meaning of the contact that will provide safety and support for a child. Ticking a box to say a child has been visited cannot be considered meaningful social work (Ferguson, 2010; Hall et al.,

2010). This led to Ofsted focusing on the quality of service children receive. Reform after reform has not in itself brought about changes expected in practice.

Meaningful contact in social work between the child and the child's social worker

History presents a concerning picture of social work. I shall now focus on one small albeit significant area in - what is meaningful social work in relation to contact and how does a Social Worker make their work meaningful to the child? Literature suggests this occurs through two avenues, direct work (Luckock & Lefevre, 2009; O'Sullivan, 2013) and relationship-based practice (Ruch et al, 2010).

The concept of direct work with children is an intervention essential in a post-modernist world. The child's voice has a right to be heard, as stated in law and policy i.e. Children Act (1989, 2004), United Nations Convention on the Rights of the Child (1989) which was ratified by the UK in 1991 and its principles are preserved in current childcare policy and *Working Together to Safeguard Children* (Department for Education, 2013). Since 2009 the social work reform (Social Work Reform Board, 2010) and currently the skills and knowledge consultation identifying *'relationships and effective direct work'* (Department for Education, 2014b:14) as a significant part to social work practice. Direct work has become the driving force to ensuring contact between the child and the child's Social Worker is meaningful. The use of direct work has been strengthened through the use of the ecological and child-centred approach in assessments whilst working with children (Department of Health, 2000). Direct work with the children has been researched to improve the child's relationship with Social Workers (Bell, 2002), something research states is important to children (Ofsted, 2011; Cossar et al, 2014). However, often in assessments the child's needs become blurred by the parents (McLeod, 2010).

Direct work with children who are in contact with statutory social care is fundamental to understand a child's situation in a meaningful way (Ferguson, 2011; Gibson, 2014). Social Workers have often been accused of avoiding intervention due to it being perceived as therapy (Ruch, 2009). However research by Ofsted (2008:7) examining fifty serious case reviews found direct work was absent. Further research by Ofsted (2010) concluded the child's voice was not heard (p.6) and the serious case review into the death of Daniel Pelka suggested direct work with him may have given him the opportunity to tell his truth (Coventry LSCB, 2013:53).

The term direct work with children is open to interpretation. Shemmings and Rhodes (2012) suggest direct work

'can include, exploring children's memories of events; helping children to 'process' traumatic experiences; helping children move into another family; undertaking 'life-story' work; helping with social aspects of the child's life'.

The skill of the Social Worker is essential to this task.

Since the social work reform, relationship based practice has been the buzz word applied in social work education, with Ruch et al (2010) writing a whole book on the concept *Relationship Based Social Work – Getting to the Heart of Practice*. There are limited research studies that have looked at the relationship between the child and the child's Social Worker and requires further investigation (Ferguson, 2011). Nevertheless the research that has been conducted over the last two decades within the UK and some Scandinavian countries reports, what children want from their relationship with their Social Worker is to be an emotional and empathic interaction (Sandbæk, 1999; Bell, 2002; Winter, 2010; Fern and Kristinsdottir, 2011) but instead is bureaucratic and impersonal.

Recent research by Cossar et al (2014) highlighted the importance of trusting relationships built between the child and the child's Social Worker in order for the child to be able to voice their thoughts and feelings. This study found the child protection process made children feel the Social Worker visit was more interrogational than relational. Also children disliked it when their Social Worker was inaccessible but still making decisions affecting their future.

Therefore despite the research telling us what children want in their relationship with Social Workers the profession still fails to provide a meaningful relationship with the child.

Seeing the child and direct work in child protection practice

Whilst there is research into effective ways Social Workers can communicate with children (Lefevre 2010; Winter 2011) research is still lacking in how children on child protection plans are best communicated with in terms of direct work with children. Working Together to Safeguard Children (Department of Education, 2013) guidance, highlights that where children are suspected to be at risk of harm and subject to a child protection plan, the Social Worker should *'undertake direct work with the child and family in accordance with the child protection plan,'* (p.42). However whilst the guidance states this should happen it does not expand any further on what this means.

Morson (2014) carried a small scale research of data from London

Local Authorities via requesting 'freedom of information' regarding child protection visits and from this discovered a lack of understanding of the child protection guidance by the authorities. The requests for this information illustrated the majority of children subject to child protection plans were seen by a Social Worker every ten working days; however each local authority will have its own guidance and policies in place to support this. The argument that in having policies and guidance for directing how often a child is seen, is not sufficient to make the contact meaningful.

Alongside the policies and guidance are complex information technology systems to record the information of 'the child seen', this information is recorded but is it meaningful? The statutory 'Working Together to Safeguard Children' (Department of Education, 2013) guidance has a requirement the Social Worker *undertakes direct work*. My challenge here is, does just seeing the child count for direct work or meaningful contact? The only impact we appear to measure is whether the child was seen not the impact on the child as a consequence of the visit.

Harry Ferguson has written extensively about what seeing the child and direct work means in practice. His research has highlighted how *'the home visit is virtually ignored'* (Ferguson, 2009:471). Nevertheless this is the very place we would expect meaningful contact to take place and yet what seeing the child and direct work means in practice is open to interpretation. Practitioners skills in engaging the child can also vary and affect meaningful contact, as can the age of a child because younger children are often seen with their parents present (Ferguson, 2014). Something Cossar et al (2014) also highlights.

Ruch's (2014) researched Social Workers experiences of working with children involved with child protection services and identified how meaningful contact between the child and the child's Social Worker can be challenging, identifying practitioners need for 'contextual awareness' to do this well, but because many visits take place in the home, Social Workers can be left feeling disempowered and therefore the contact with the child impaired. If a Social Worker is 'serious about being child-centred they have to be prepared to be affected' (Ruch 2014:2158, 2007 and 2012).

Phillips (2014) discusses how meaningful contact with the child includes observation of the child's body and its movement. Peter Connolly (Haringey LCSB, 2010) was seen by his Social Worker and other professionals similar to Khyra Ishaq (Radford, 2010) but unfortunately still died, indicating how meaningful contact needs to include close observation of the 'internal child' (Phillips, 2014:2263). Social Workers need to ask the right question 'Have I sufficiently seen the child' and in what I've seen is it meaningful?

Phillips relates this concept to movement and dance choreography and how this increases awareness and information of what the body is telling. Just like the case of Jasmine Beckford, where the Social Worker did not see natural movement of Jasmine. Seeing the body move and understanding the movement should support the understanding of how safe the child is, but Twigg (2006, cited in Phillips, 2014) argues official and prearranged situations to see the child can create less of an opportunity to view this movement accurately. Ruch's (2014) research supports this by illustrating the benefits of co-working visits with other professionals to enable further insights in picking up on what the child's body is telling you by 'getting under the layers' (p.2156). Ferguson's (2011) identifies this as crucial to practice to enable an appreciation of 'layers' and 'atmospheres' to alert us about a young persons lived experience (Ferguson, 2009; Ferguson, 2010).

Horwath (2011) identifies a number of barriers Social Workers face when 'seeing' the child during an assessment using the *Framework for the Assessment of Children in Need and their Families* (Department of Health, 2000). The findings identified, a range of issues such as a lack of purposeful contact by failing to 'see' the child in a meaningful way and not creating meaningful relationships; a lack of guidance and support; risk of harm identified but not need; and the completion of target driven assessments.

Horwath and Tarr (2014) look at 'child-centred' practice by Social Workers working in child protection. This highlighted that assessments were too general with an absence of understanding the identity of the child; superficial engagement by Social Workers when gathering the child's wishes and feeling; and a lack of awareness of individual needs of children. They further challenged how it is possible for Social Workers to make meaningful relationships with children when they are up against time pressures, for example, an Initial Child Protection Conference has to take place fifteen working days from the starting of the investigation. As previously stated Ruch's (2014) illustrates how co-working supports meaningful relationships with children and identified in current policy (Department for Education, 2013). The concept of joined up working needs to not only be within organisational systems but also within joined up practice.

Direct practice is highlighted as an area that needs further work. It would appear however that strength-based practice is finding ground in statutory child protection work. This approach is built on meaningful relationships by considering helpful solutions with the child to improve their well-being and situation (Kondrat, 2010; Payne, 2014). For example 'The Signs of Safety' model is being used in the UK by some Local Authorities (NSPCC, 2013) as a model promoting contact between the child, the Social Worker and the family as meaningful (Turnell and Edwards, 1999). This is an evidence based approach researched in New Zealand and tested within the countries child protection services as a model that works (Weld, 2008). However this would suggest the approach needs to be adopted by a Local Authority for the meaningful contact to occur, but there are many Local Authorities not using such a model and still opting for traditional approaches to child protection work so where is the evidence to suggest that the contact these Social Workers have with the child is meaningful?

Oliver and Charles (2015) research within a Canadian statutory child protection service considered how child protection Social Workers applied a strengths-based model to their practice, however findings appeared to demonstrate only a small fraction of those interviewed, achieved a strengths-based practice. These findings are similar to Murphy et al (2013) who argue that the concept of person-centred approach in statutory social work stating the strength-based approach is defined by non- directive practice and statutory intervention is often regarded as directive. This being the case how can the Social Worker make their work with children meaningful in a statutory setting? It would appear it is a fine balance between relational and directive at the same time, but this is not to say this cannot occur for the child and the Social Worker, but an approach where the child needs support but viewed as safe by the Social Worker requires specific skills (Howes, 2010). This is what the 'Consultation on Knowledge and Skills for Child and Family Social Work' (Department for Education, 2014b:14) identifies as fundamental to practice.

Fern's (2014) looks from an Icelandic child protection perspective and offers further insights into how meaningful contact with the child can take place by looking at a more child directed way of practice. This is where the child is not seen in the middle of the professionals but instead the problem is positioned here and the children alongside the family and professionals (Fern and Kristindottir, 2011). This is not how the UK's child protection system operates which takes a more child-centred approach with the child in the middle (Department of Health, 2000, Department for Education, 2013). The findings are interesting though and begin to develop an argument that meaningful contact with the child is more than just obtaining the child's wishes and feelings (Children Act, 1989, 2004; Department for Education 2013) but allowing the child to take a role in decision making. It also supports the concept of obtaining the child's wishes and feelings as not being a tokenistic form of participation and raises the issue of power and how this can affect relationships within a statutory role. Archard and Skivenes (2009) identify this exact point that the Social Worker will often be the person who decides if the child's view and wishes are to be taken seriously and therefore holding power. Social Workers can put themselves in the position of thinking 'I'm the adult and therefore I know best' and not thinking 'what does the child want?' This can create an oppressive system. To build the relationship with a child, where the contact is meaningful it is more than just challenging the 'doing' of the meaningful contact. Brandon et al (2009) identifies contact with the child can be full of parental opposition, absence co-operation and complex adults needs, so before the Social Worker even begins to make relationships with the child they have to navigate themselves through the complexity of the family situation. Achieving meaningful contact with the child as a statutory Social Worker appears more complex than just implementing changes in policy and systems (Dugmore, 2014). Even after direct work and relationship based practice has been highlighted as key skills and key requirements to the practice (Munro, 2011b; Department for Education 2013; Department for Education 2014b), the work that is involved in child protection is complicated, intimidating and often not welcomed.

Finally Social Workers need to be adequately trained to undertake not only meaningful contact but also the barriers families can create. Social Workers need training more in the forensic understanding of family dynamics, dysfunctioning, and skills in deception to be able to manage these challenging situations. Lefevre (2015) identifies short fallings in social work training. The education of student Social Worker's in regards to the direct work with the child is 'superficial' in its delivery and the meaning that comes into practice is lacking experience, confidence and skill in such work.

The operation of the system

Research into the system has identified many failings from resources, time limits and bureaucracy (Laming 2003; Laming, 2009; Broadhurst et al, 2010a; Broadhurst et al, 2010b). In the analysis of the literature around the importance of meaningful contact between the child and child's Social Worker, it is clear that one reason meaningful contact could continue to be hindered is due to technology. Broadhurst et al's (2010a) research mirrored Peckover et al (2008) and White et al (2008) that Social Workers felt the IT systems meant 'too little time for the real work of face-to-face communication with families' (p364). Ofsted could come and inspect a local authority through this IT system and therefore problems in real practice went unnoticed (Ofsted 2011), however this approach has been recognised as flawed and Ofsted have changed the inspection regime to include observing practice (Ofsted, 2014a; Ofsted, 2014b).

Ferguson's (2011) field work highlighted how failings due to bureaucracy creates an absence of relationship based empathic practice that is needed between the child and the child's Social Worker to produce positive outcomes for the child. This was also reinforced by the Munro reviews (Munro, 2011b) Munro, 2012:27).

So what does the research tell us about how the system is operating now and whether it is still operating against a child-centered approach? Ruch (2014:2156) found there was more of an emphasis on systems and procedures than how to form good relationships with a child. In some instances cases are closed too soon effecting the relationship the Social Worker has built with the child. Social Workers also experienced no time to do the work or to think about it, but when challenged viewed as a defence mechanism of Social Workers protecting themselves from the difficulties of child protection work

Although the research with children on child protection plans is limited, some correlation can be made with the research that has been conducted with children in care; due to the fact these children will have travelled the child protection journey at some point in their life. Winter's (2009) found that not all of the issues relating to the lack of meaningful contact between the child and the child's Social Worker are specially connected to organizational and resource issues but the Social Workers own attitudes and values regarding children will impact on whether the contact is meaningful. However you could argue that a Social Worker's attitudes and values can blur the boundaries inherent in the dynamics of a relationship rather than assume they are always helpful. Because it is our values that drive our moral action that can conflict with the task of social work.

Post Munro Review

My last argument will consider where is practice post Munro (2011b) in relation to meaningful contact between the child and the Social Worker. Before 2010 and the start of the Munro's reports and reviews (2010; 2011a; 2011b; 2012) it was described as the child protection system within the constraints of time barriers. Munro (2011b) found Social Workers spent too much time complying with procedures than spending time with the child to engage. It identified that the social work system as a whole needed shifting to a more child-centred approach, with a key message that offering early help to the child and the families in need of intervention were required. Local authorities have been working to improve multiagency and identifying families for Early Help Services (Home Office, 2014). However whilst the social work professional is striving towards achieving a child-centred approach this could be limited because of how the child protection system has been historically established. By 2012 Munro's progress review (Munro, 2012) of child protection started to identify a shift in practice with good child-centred practice being identified as vital rather than compliance driven by procedures. Working Together to Safeguard Children (Department for Education, 2013) was the point when the system had the chance to change to a more child-centred focus. However White (2014) argues that making meaningful contact with children and families is proving frustrating because of the managerial focus on organisational structures rather than the person.

Referral rates into statutory services have continued to climb, putting more and more pressure on the system (Munro, 2012) and in a time of economic austerity the solution of more resources needed to lower caseloads and creating more space for meaningful contact to take place seems unrealistic. Working with people is complex and social work will never resolve into equilibrium, it will only adjust, progress and change (Hood, 2014:31). For this reason possibly meaningful contact between the child and the Social Worker, will remain challenging as Social Workers need to adjust, progress and change practice to achieve what they all entered the profession for as well as all the other things they are tasked to achieve. This argument supported by Munro (2012) that organisations need to share responsibility for the practice children receive (p.13) and each member of the core group for a child protection plan is as responsible for achieving meaningful contact and not the Social Worker alone.

Munro (2012) discussed a 'reactive' child protection service would only deal with parts of the problem (p.17). I think this is interesting as perhaps this is why meaningful contact in a statutory setting is hard to achieve. The reaction is keeping the child safe and therefore interferes with the relationship which is also concerns well being. Social Workers can fall into the habit of reacting first and relationship building later or not at all. Two years post Working Together to Safeguard Children (Department for Education, 2013) direct and meaningful work with children involved in the child protection system is viewed from the research as challenging. Put another way there appears to be a struggle *'to shake off the compliance culture'* (Munro 2012:6) however Social Workers need to be bold and set out towards achieving this (Munro, 2012).

Analysis

My curiosity in exploring meaningful contact between the child and the child's Social Worker was developed whilst spending one hundred days in a statutory child protection team. Many children were visited fortnightly by a Social Worker and with the rise in referral rates the amount of children that required visits increased in significant numbers. This left me questioning how seeing a child on a statutory child protection visit under all the organisational pressures (Munro, 2011) enabled meaningful contact to take place. However through critically reflecting and reviewing the literature I have been left with the recognition that this is a complicated area not easily solved. Every part of the system needs as much attention as the other (Trevithick, 2014). The following quote highlights for me the inherent problem in why we cannot achieve meaningful contact with children:

> 'there should be toys and drawing materials to help the child or young person be more relaxed…there should be an opportunity 'to talk about what I want to talk about', in other words not just answering questions' (Isle of Wight LSCB, 2015:45).

There was also advice from the young people that Children's Services was to

> 'investigate more thoroughly… try harder… and not believe parents so much… listen before coming to conclusions' (Isle of Wight LSCB, 2015:46).

So whilst we know the bureaucracy, high caseloads, training issues and quality of supervision all play a crucial role in making it more difficult to achieve meaningful contact between the child and the Social Worker the question that also needs to be asked is why relationships are so difficult to make?

We know high caseloads and bureaucracy impacts on the time needed to build effective and meaningful relationships with children (Munro, 2010, p. 115), Social Worker's need enough time to build the relationship (small caseloads and less administration will support this). Manager's and Social Workers need to be focused on 'relationship-based practice' and willing to challenge the system to make this happen. As well as the emotional and knowledgeable skill to build the relationship or ask the very question have I done this, if not why not, what is stopping me? Social workers and their managers need to be confident and brave in challenging the status quo to realize Munro's ambition for spending more time with children than procedures and systems.

To keep the child at the forefront of practice requires skill and time. Knowing that a child is physically safe does not mean they are emotionally safe. The research on neglect (Action for Children, 2012) supports this argument. Children need to be seen by their Social Worker, to enable support of change, allow problem solving to take place, whilst encouraging empowerment and liberation of a child's well-being so a child can reach their full potential and avoid further dysfunction in their life (BASW, 2011:6). Nevertheless for the practice to occur Social Workers in statutory services need to daily ask themselves is the contact they have had with the child meaningful to them or just the organization and what purpose does it play?

It would appear that the history of child protection social work and the tragedies that have unfolded over the years have left the child protection system at breaking point. As previously mentioned one of the catalyst's for the social work reform in 2009 was the death of Peter Connelly in 2007. This has shown how the history of child protection social work can affect the current work on an enormous scale. It is fair to say in 2015, four years after Munro's review that the effect the death of Peter Connelly is still affecting the system. Usually after such an incident (child death or similar serious event) one would expect referrals and concerns for children to increase, because of increases of anxiety and risk however, the referrals never returned to where they were pre 2007 and this is having a lasting impact. The system is therefore overwhelmed (Jones, 2014). This means achieving meaningful contact in child protection is a battle as Social Workers struggle to manage the volume of work against a backdrop of austerity cuts with Local Authorities continuing to face further cuts over the years to come.

Conclusions and recommendations

We know that retention of staff is challenging. For the child to be seen, be viewed as safe and protected, and receive meaningful contact, social workers need to be a highly skilled and a well-informed work force who are professionally confident exercising good judgment. The reform, the Munro review, the implementation of Working Together to Safeguard Children 2013, the appointment of the Chief Social Worker and the social work education system, all appear to be positive steps for the profession and protecting children. However the profession needs to challenge what true evidence do we have that Social Workers are able to make meaningful contact with children and know that they are keeping them safe at every level? The new government inspectorate framework (Ofsted 2014a; Ofsted 2014b) should facilitate this approach and challenge the obstacles of good practice. Building and sustaining a good relationship with a child and his or her family is predicated on having physical contact that is meaningful to them and not something that is expedient to the service.

The evidence gathered and critiqued has left me with the following thoughts for the future for government and the profession:

1. Guidance is guidance not requirements and better understanding of this is needed by all those in the profession.
2. Social Workers need to continue to professionally challenge the compliance culture, with the view that to physically see a child does not necessarily mean they are safe.
3. Training, supervision and good management are all essential elements of a comprehensive system of support for social workers undertaking a difficult job
4. Direct work with children is more than just receiving children's wishes and feelings. Social Workers need to use direct work with children to identify what they recognise will help improve their life. The child is the expert on their life not the Social Worker.
5. Research is needed to explore how direct work with children through a relational approach can achieve better outcomes.

Bibliography

Action for Children. (2012) *Child neglect in 2011 - An annual review by Action for Children in partnership with the University of Stirling.* Watford

Archard, D, & Skivenes, M. (2009) 'Hearing the child', *Child & Family Social Work*, 14(4) pp. 391-399, Available from: http://SocINDEX with Full Text, EBSCO*host*, [Accessed: 2 April 2015]

Broadhurst, K., Watell, D., White, S., Hall, C., Peckover, S., Thompson, K., Pithouse, A. and Dolores, D. (2010a) Performing initial assessment: identifying the latent conditions for error at the front-door of local authority children's services, *British Journal of social Work*, 40(2) p. 352-70. Available from: http://doi: 10.1093/bjsw/bcn162 [Accessed: 2 April 2015]

Broadhurst, K., Hall, C., Watell, D. White, S. & Pithouse, A. (2010b) Risk instrumentalism and the humane project in social work: identifying the informal logics of risk management in children's statutory services, *British Journal of social Work*, 40(4) p. 1046-64. Available from: http://doi: 10.1093/bjsw/bcq011[Accessed: 2 April 2015]

Brandon, M., Bailey, S., Belderson, P., Gardner, R., Sidebotham, P., Dodsworth, J., Warren, C. and Black, J. (2009) *Understanding serious case reviews and their impact: a biennial analysis of serious case reviews 2005-07*. London: Department for Children, Schools and Families

BASW. (2011) *Code of Ethics*. Birmingham: BASW

Bell, M. (2002) Promoting children's rights through the use of relationship. *Child & Family Social Work*, 7. Pp.1–11. Available from: http:// doi: 10.1046/j.1365-2206.2002.00225.x [Accessed: 26 March 2015]. Children Act. (1989, 2004). Available from: http://www.legislation.gov.uk/ukpga/1989/41/contents. [Accessed: 6 March 2015]

Coventry LSCB. (2013) *Final Overview Report of Serious Case Review re Daniel Pelka* Available from: http://coventrylscb.org.uk/files/SCR/FINAL Overview Report [Accessed: 6 March 2015]

Cossar, J., Brandon, M. and Jordan, P. (2014) 'You've got to trust her and she's got to trust you': children's views on participation in the child protection system. *Child & Family Social Work*. Available from: http://onlinelibrary.wiley.com/doi/10.1111/cfs.12115/ [Accessed: 13 March 2015]

Department for Education. (2013) *Working Together To Safeguard Children*. Available from: https://www.gov.uk/government/publications/working-together-to-safeguard-children [Accessed: 4 April 2015]. Department for Education. (2014a) *Characteristics of children in need: 2013 to 2014*. Available from: https://www.gov.uk/government/statistics/characteristics-of-children-in-need-2013-to-2014 [Accessed: 4 April 2015]

Department for Education. (2014b) *Consultation on Knowledge and Skills for Child and Family Social Work – government response*. Available from: https://www.gov.uk/government/consultations/knowledge-and-skills- forchild-and-family-social-work [Accessed: 26 March 2015]

Department of Health, Home Office and Department for Education and Employment. (2000) *Framework for the Assessment of Children in Need and their Families*. London: The Stationery Office

Dugmore, P. (2014) Working together, or keeping apart? A critical discourse analysis of the revised working together guidance (2013). *Journal of Social Work Practice: Psychotherapeutic Approaches in Health, Welfare and the Community*, 28(3) pp.329-341. Available from: http://dx.doi.org/10.1080/02650533.2014.925863 [Accessed: 7 April 2015]

Ferguson, H. (2009) 'Performing child protection: home visiting, movement and the struggle to reach the abused child', *Child & Family Social Work*, 14(4) pp.

471-480, Available from: http/:///Academic Search Complete, EBSCOhost, [Accessed: 2 April 2015]

Ferguson, H. (2010) 'Walks, home visits and atmospheres: Risk and the everyday practices and mobilities of social work and child protection', *British Journal of Social Work*, 40(4), pp. 1100–17. Available from: http://doi:10.1093/bjsw/bcq015v [Accessed: 2 April 2015]

Ferguson, H. (2011) *Child Protection Practice*. Basingstoke: Palgrave Macmillan

Ferguson, H. (2014) What social workers do in performing child protection work: evidence from research into face-to-face practice. *Child & Family Social Work*. Available from: http://doi: 10.1111/cfs.12142 [Accessed: 28 February 2015]

Fern, E. (2014) 'Child-Directed Social Work Practice: Findings from an Action Research Study Conducted in Iceland', *British Journal of Social Work*, 44(5) pp. 1110-1128, Available from: http://SocINDEX with Full Text, EBSCO*host*, [Accessed: 2 April 2015]

Fern, E. and Kristinsdóttir, G. (2011) Young people act as consultants in child-directed research: an action research study in Iceland. *Child & Family Social Work*, 16, pp.287–297. Available from: http://doi: 10.1111/j.1365-2206.2010.00740.x [Accessed: 7 April 2015]

Gibson, M. (2014) Narrative Practice and the Signs of Safety Approach: Engaging Adolescents in Building Rigorous Safety Plans, *Child Care in Practice*, 20(1), p.64-80, Available from: http://DOI:10.1080/13575279.2013.799455 [Accessed: 13 March 2015]

Hall, C, Parton, N, Peckover, S & White, S. (2010) 'Child-Centric Information and Communication Technology (ICT) and the Fragmentation of Child Welfare Practice in England', *Journal of Social Policy*, 39(3), pp. 393-413, Available from: Academic Search Complete, EBSCO*host*, [Accessed: 13 March 2015]

Haringey Local Safeguarding Children Board. (2010) *Serious Case Review, Child 'A', November 2008*, London, Department of Education. Available from: https://www.gov.uk/government/publications/haringey-local-safeguarding-children-board-first-serious-case-review-child-a [Accessed: 13 March 2015]

Health and Care Professions Council. (2012) *Standards of conduct, performance and ethics*. Available from: London: http://www.hcpcuk.org/assets/documents/10003B6EStandardsofconduct,performanc eandethics.pdf. [Accessed: 2 April 2015]

Health and Care Professions Council. (2012) *Standards of proficiency*. Available from: London: http://www.hcpcuk.org/assets/documents/10003B08Standar dsofproficiencySocialworkersinEngland.pdf. [Accessed: 2 April 2015].Hood, R. (2014) Complexity and Integrated Working in Children's Services. *British Journal of Social Work*, 44, pp. 27-43. Available from: http://bjsw.oxfordjournals.org/content/44/1/27.full.pdf+html?sid=13ab1c01- 513f4e29-baeb-53f5eabed632 [Accessed: 9 April 2015]

Home Office. (2014) *Multi Agency Working and Information Sharing – Final Report*. Available from: https://www.gov.uk/government/publications/multi-agency-working-and-information-sharing-project [Accessed: 9 March 2015]

Horwath, J. (2011) See the Practitioner, See the Child: The Framework for the Assessment of Children in Need and their Families Ten Years On. *British Journal of Social Work*, 41(6) pp.1070-1087. Available from: doi:10.1093/bjsw/bcq137 [Accessed: 26 March 2015]

Horwath, J and Tarr, S. (2014) Child Visibility in Cases of Chronic Neglect: Implications for Social Work Practice. *British Journal of Social Work Work first published online July 9, 2014* Available from: *doi:10.1093/bjsw/bcu073* [Accessed: 7 April 2015]

Howes, N. (2010) Here to Listen! Communicating with Children and Methods for Communicating with Children and Young People as Part of the Assessment Process. In: Horwath, J. *The Child's World*. 2nd ed. United Kingdom: Jessica Kingsley Publishers Ltd. pp124-139

Isle of Wight Safeguarding Children Board. (2015) *Serious case review relating to the Q family*. Available from: http://www.iowscb.org.uk/serious_case_reviews [Accessed: 7 April 2015]

Jones, R. (2014) *The story of Baby P. Setting the record straight*. Bristol: Policy Press

Kolb, D.A. (1984) Experimental *Learning: Experience as the Source of Learning and Development*. Englewood Cliffs: Prentice-Hall

Kondrat, D. (2010) The strengths based perspective. In: Teater, B. *An Introduction to Applying Social Work Theories and Methods*. Maidenhead: Open University Press. pp.162-177

Mcleod, A. (2010) Thirty years of listening. *Adoption and Fostering*, 34 pp.67-73. Available from: http://doi: 10.1177/030857591003400312 [Accessed: 6 March 2015]

Laming, Lord, H. (2003) *The Victoria Climbié Inquiry: report of an inquiry by Lord Laming*. Available from: https://www.gov.uk/government/publications/the-victoria-Climbié-inquiry-report-of-an-inquiry-by-lord-laming [Accessed: 6 April 2015]

Laming, Lord, H. (2003) *The protection of children in England: a progress report*. Department for Children, Schools and Families. Available from: https://www.gov.uk/government/publications/the-protection-of-children- in-england-a-progress-report [Accessed: 6 April 2015]

Lefevre, M. (2010) *Communicating with children and young people: making a difference*. Bristol: Policy Press

Lefevre, M. (2014) Learning and development journeys towards effective communication with children. *Child & Family Social Work*. Available from: http://onlinelibrary.wiley.com/doi/10.1111/cfs.12202/ [Accessed: 13 March

2015]

Lefevre, M. (2015) Becoming Effective Communicators with Children: Developing Practitioner Capability through Social Work Education. *British Journal of Social Work* 45(1) pp.204-224. Available from: http://doi: 10.1093/bjsw/bct109 [Accessed: 13 March 2015]

Luckock, B. & Lefevre, M. (2009). *Direct Work: Social Work with Children and Young People in Care.* UK: British Association for Adoption and Fostering (BAAF)

Morson, W. (2014) *Freedom of information request based results regarding child protection visits.* Available from: http://www.tcsw.org.uk/standard-2col-rhm-blog.aspx?id=8589948395&blogid=24762&terms=morson%20research. [Accessed: 7 April 2015]

Munro, E. (2010) *The Munro Review of Child Protection. Part One: A Systems Analysis.* Department for Education (DfE). Available from: https://www.gov.uk/government/publications/munro-review-of-child- protection-part-1-a-systems-analysis [Accessed: 6 April 2015]

Munro, E. (2011a) *The Munro Review of Child Protection, Interim Report. The Child's Journey.* Department for Education (DfE). Available from: https://www.gov.uk/government/publications/munro-review-of-child- protection-interim-report-the-childs-journey [Accessed: 6 April 2015]

Munro, E. (2011b) *The Munro Review of Child Protection: Final Report – A Child Centred System.* Department for Education (DfE). Available from: https://www.gov.uk/government/publications/munro-review- of-child-protection-final-report-a-child-centred-system [Accessed: 6 April 2015]

Munro, E. (2012) *Progress report: moving towards a child centred system.* Department for Education (DfE). Available from: https://www.gov.uk/government/publications/progress-report-moving-towards-a-child-centred- system [Accessed: 6 April 2015]

Murphy, D., Duggan, M., & Joseph, S. (2013) Relationship-Based Social Work and Its Compatibility with the Person-Centred Approach: Principled versus Instrumental Perspectives. *British Journal of Social Work* 43(4), pp.703-719. Available from: http://bjsw.oxfordjournals.org/content/43/4/703.full [Accessed: 10 March 2015]. NSPCC. (2013) *Signs of Safety in England: An NSPCC commissioned report on the Signs of Safety model in child protection.* Available from: www.nspcc.org.uk [Accessed: 13 March 2015]

Ofsted. (2008) *Learning lessons, taking action: Ofsted's evaluations of serious case reviews 1 April 2007 to 31 March 2008.* Available from: http://webarchive.nationalarchives.gov.uk/20141124154759/http://www.ofsted.gov.uk/resources/learning- lessons-taking-action-ofsteds-evaluations-of-serious-case-reviews-1-april-2007-31-march-200 [Accessed: 26 March 2015]

Ofsted. (2010) *Learning lessons from serious case reviews 2009–2010.* Available from:

https://www.gov.uk/government/publications/ofsted-learning-lessons-from-serious-case-reviews-2009-2010 [Accessed: 26 March 2015]

Ofsted. (2011) *Messages for Munro: A report of children's views collected for Professor Eileen Munro by the Children's Rights Director for England*. Manchester: Ofsted

Ofsted. (2014a) *Inspecting local authority children's services: the framework*. Available from: https://www.gov.uk/government/publications/inspecting-local-authority-childrens-services-framework. [Accessed: 7 April 2015]

Ofsted. (2014b) *Raising Standards Improving Lives: Ofsted's strategic plan*. Available from: https://www.gov.uk/government/publications/raising-standards-improving-lives-ofsted-strategic-plan-2014-to- 2016 [Accessed: 7 April 2015]

Oliver, C. & Charles, G. (2015) Enacting Firm, Fair and Friendly Practice: A Model for Strengths-Based Child Protection Relationships? *British Journal of Social Work first published online March 4, 2015*. Available from: http://doi:10.1093/bjsw/bcv015 [Accessed: 27 March 2015]

O'Sullivan, A. (2013) Direct Work with Children. In Worsley, A., Mann, T., Olsen, A. & Whitehead-Mason, E. *Key concepts in Social Work Practice*, pp.62-65. London: Sage publications Ltd

Payne, M. (2014) *Modern Social Work Theory*. Basingstoke: Palgrave Macmillan

Peckover, S., White, S. and Hall, C. (2008) 'Making and managing Electronic Children: e-assessment in child welfare', *Information Communication and Society*, 11(3), pp. 375–94. Available from: http://Academic Search Complete,EBSCOhost, [Accessed: 7 April 2015]

Phillips, C.R. (2014) Seeing the Child beyond the Literal: Considering Dance Choreography and the Body in Child Welfare and Protection. *British Journal of Social Work* 44(8) pp.2254–2271. Available from: http://doi: 10.1093/bjsw/bct070 [Accessed: 7 April 2015]

Radford, J. (2010) *Serious Case Review in Respect of the Death of a Child: Case Number 14, Birmingham, Birmingham Safeguarding Children Board*. Available from: http://library.nspcc.org.uk/HeritageScripts/Hapi.dll/retrieve2?SetID=4B390302-5C53-415F-B579- 737EB35DA962&DataSetName=LIVEDATA [Accessed: 27 March 2015]

Reason, J. (2000) 'Human error: models and management', *BMJ: British Medical Journal (International Edition)*, 320(7237) p. 768, Available from: http://Academic Search Complete, EBSCOhost, [Accessed: 7 April 2015]

Ruch, G. (2007) 'Thoughtful' practice: child care social work and the role of case discussion. *Child and Family Social Work*, 12, pp 370-379. Available from: http://onlinelibrary.wiley.com/doi/10.1111/j.1365- 2206.2006.00466.x/pdf [Accessed: on 6 April 2015]

Ruch, G. (2012) Where Have All the Feelings Gone? Developing Reflective and Relationship-Based Management in Child-Care Social Work. *British Journal of Social Work* 42(7) *pp.1315-1332*. Available from: *http://doi:10.1093/bjsw/*

bcr134 [Accessed: 6 April 2015]

Ruch, G. (2014) "Helping Children Is a Human Process': Researching the Challenges Social Workers Face in Communicating with Children', *British Journal of Social Work*, 44(8) pp.2145-2162. Available from: http://doi: 10.1093/bjsw/bct045 [Accessed: 27 March 2015]

Ruch, G., Turney, D. & Ward, A. (2010) *Relationship Based Social Work: Getting to the Heart of Practice*. London: Jessica Kingsley

Ruch, G. (2009) *Post Qualifying Child Care Social Work*. London: Sage

Sandbaek, M. (1999) Children with problems: focusing on everyday life. *Children & Society*, 13(2) pp. 106- 118, Available from: http://Academic Search Complete, EBSCO*host*, [Accessed: 7 April 2015]

Shemmings, Y. and Rhodes, H. (2012) *Guide to confident direct work with children*. Guides

Community Care Inform Available from: http://www.ccinform.co.uk/guides/guide-to-confident-direct-work- with-children-6/ [Accessed: 27 March 2015]

Social Work Reform Board. (2010) *Building a Safe and Confident Future: One year on*. London, Department of Education

Trevithick, P. (2014) 'Humanising Managerialism: Reclaiming Emotional Reasoning, Intuition, the Relationship, and Knowledge and Skills in Social Work', *Journal of Social Work Practice*, 28(3) pp. 287-311, Available from: http://Academic Search Complete, EBSCO*host*, [Accessed: 2 April 2015]

Turnell, A. & Edwards, S. (1999) *Signs of safety: a safety and solution orientated approach to child protection casework*. 1st ed. New York: Norton & Company

Twigg, J. (2006) cited in: Phillips, C.R. (2014) Seeing the Child' beyond the Literal: Considering Dance Choreography and the Body in Child Welfare and Protection. *British Journal of Social Work* 44(8) pp.2254– 2271. Available from: http://doi: 10.1093/bjsw/bct070 [Accessed:: 7 April 2015]

United Nations Convention on the Rights of the Child. (1989) Available from: http://www.unicef.orf. [Accessed: 6 March 2015]

Weld, N. (2008) The Three Houses Tool: Building Safety and Positive Change. In: Calder, M.C. *Contemporary risk assessment in safeguarding children*. . Dorset: Russell House Publishing. p. 224-231

White, S. (2014) 'Introduction: Munro three years on', *Journal of Social Work Practice*, 28(3) pp. 267-269, Available from: http://Academic Search Complete, EBSCO*host*, [Accessed: 2 April 2015]

White, S., Hall, C. and Peckover, S. (2009) 'The descriptive tyranny of the common assessment framework: Technologies of categorisation and professional practice in child welfare', *British Journal of Social Work* 39(7) pp.1197-1217. Available from: http://doi: 10.1093/bjsw/bcn053 [Accessed: 2 April 2015]

Winter, K. (2009) Relationships matter: the problems and prospects for social workers' relationships with young children in care. *Child & Family*

Social Work, 14 pp.450–460. Available from: http://doi: 10.1111/j.1365-2206.2009.00628.x [Accessed: 2 April 2015]

Winter, K. (2010) The perspectives of young children in care about their circumstances and implications for social work practice. *Child & Family Social Work*, 15 pp.186–195. Available from: http:// doi: 10.1111/j.1365-2206.2009.00658.x [Accessed: 2 April 2015]

Winter, K. (2011) *Building Relationships and Communicating with Young Children: A Practical Guide for Social Workers*. 1st ed. United Kingdom: Taylor & Francis

13
Life story work in promoting strong attachments and identity in children

Gary Castle

Introduction

This chapter will look at the importance of life story work (LSW) in promoting identity and a sense of belonging in children's history for those in local authority care or adopted children. It will examine themes on attachment and provide key recommendations for change.

> 'Identity is whom the child believes him or herself to be. Without a clear explanation of where you came from, how can you have a true sense of self? (Levy and Orlans 1998 cited in Rose and Philpot, 2010:25).

What is life story work?

Children who live with their birth families have the opportunity to know about their past, and have a means of being able to understand it through discussions with their parents and others and to clarify past events in terms of the present. Children separated from their birth families are often denied this opportunity; they may have changed families; social workers; homes and neighborhoods. Their past may be lost, much of it even forgotten.

When children lose track of their past, they may well find it difficult to develop emotionally and socially into attachment. If adults cannot or do not discuss this past with them, it is reasonable for children to suppose that it may be bad or lost.

LSW is an attempt to give back some of this past to children separated from their family of origin. Gathering together facts about that life and the significant people in it helps them begin to accept their past and go forward into the future with this knowledge '(Ryan & Walker, 2007:3).

LSW has been used in many settings with adults and children, including reminiscence work with older people and as a therapeutic tool with adults with mental health and substance misuse problems. With children it has many different purposes. Cook-Cotton & Beck (2007:1) describe it as a model for 'facilitating the construction of personal narrative for foster children', which they discuss in the context of psychological and social development. It can also be used to explain a child's history, in adoption preparation, to address offending behaviour or to promote a sense of identity. It often results in the production of a book but, with technological advances, could take a digital format. This might include photos, drawings, a family tree, an ecomap and birth certificate usually accompanied with a narrative such as a later life letter explaining the child's history.

It came into use in the 1960's and became more widespread with the rise of permanency planning and direct work with children in the early 1980's. Direct work with children was underpinned by legislation through the Adoption and Children Act 2002 (ACA), which highlighted the importance of giving children comprehensive information about themselves. The importance of promoting a child's self-view was again given more weight in 2011, with the revised National Minimum Adoption Standards which state as its outcome that *'Children have a positive self-view, emotional resilience and knowledge and understanding of their background'* (National Minimum Adoption Standards, England 2011).

Life Story Work (LSW) literature and critical analysis

> Identity: 'The fact of being who or what a person or thing is' (The Oxford Dictionary of English).

'Who am I? Where did I come from? Where do I belong? All questions that are asked as we develop through childhood into adulthood'. Batsleer (2009) states that

> 'the transition to adulthood is a period of exploring and trying on the forms of adult identity that seem to be on offer to us, as well as a process of questioning and challenging them' (Batsleer, 2009:17).

But what if we do not possess the tools to do this and what if there were no answers to these questions? How would that affect our development and formation of self? According to Pasupathi (2007)

> 'the problem of personal identity is fundamentally a developmental problem. During later childhood and early adolescence, as people begin to construct a sense of their abstract and enduring characteristics, issues of personal consistency become important' (Pasupathi et al. 2007:85).

Theorists such as Chandler (2003) and Erikson & Erikson (1997) believe that issues arise and take on renewed importance in later life:

> 'thus, identity is a developmental problem in two ways: first, in that it first emerges at a particular age, and second, in that it remains a problem precisely because individuals continue to develop across the lifespan' (Pasupathi et al. 2007:86).

A healthy sense of identity is vital to everyone. A poor sense of identity can interrupt and impact a child's development and ultimately affect adulthood. Identity according to Ryan and Walker (2007) is a complex concept:

> 'it probably starts in individuals with the first separation of the 'inside' and 'outside' selves at about six months. This creation of the idea of 'self' is crucial to healthy development and where it is hindered by events and other people who are important (like mothers and fathers) not responding appropriately, severe *problems can arise*' (Ryan and Walker, 2007:5).

Child development

Theorists such as Erickson and Piaget (Research in Practice, 2015) suggest that early child development is fundamental in the formation of identity and if children do not meet certain milestones the implications later in life can be vast. Both Erickson and Piaget believed that personality develops in a series of stages. Erickson, an ego psychologist, believed there to be eight of these stages and as we reach each stage we meet a new challenge that can either help develop or hinder the formation of our identity. Stage 1 is described as Trust vs Mistrust:

> 'First feelings form about the world and whether or not it is a safe place, based on the level of familiarity, consistency and continuity of carers and care-giving. Positive experiences lead to a belief that security and hope or the strong belief that the world is a good place develop. Unreliable or inadequate care leads to fear and inner mistrust of the world, may be apprehensive, insecure and mistrustful' (Research in Practice, 2015:2).

Piaget, an influential researcher of child development in the 20th century also believed that

> 'children progress through a series of stages in their thinking, each of which corresponds to broad changes in the structure or logic of their intelligence' (Smith et al. 2003:391).

Piaget created a cognitive-developmental stage model theory that described how children's ways of thinking developed as they interacted with the world around them. Both believed that progressing through these stages is fundamental in development, if it was not possible to progress through these stages for reasons such as neglect or abuse then there would be significant impacts and challenges for that child as they move through life.

Not all theorists believe in the importance of these stages. Erickson and Piaget call them critical stages, while others such as Konrad Lorenz (Smith et al.2003:37) refer to them as sensitive periods. Attachment theory also plays a significant part in the development of children and the forming of identity. John

Bowlby's theory was based upon the concept that seeking attachment to others is a basic drive. (Payne, 2005:).

Children who are Looked After and Adopted will likely have experienced an insecure attachment and separation and loss. Rees (2009) suggests that

> 'those who have suffered neglect and abuse in their formative years will have been traumatised further and are often confused about their past. Such children tend to hold themselves responsible for any ill treatment they have suffered, have low self-esteem and a deep sense of shame' (Rees, 2009:21)

It is suggested that the addressing of identity through LSW can help resolve these issues. Pasupathi (et al. 2007:86)).

The past, present and future

LSW is a therapeutic method of intervention that can help Looked After and Adopted children develop and form identity.

Using a variety of tools such as Life Story Books to collect pictures of birth parents, grandparents, holidays, documentation (such as birth certificates) and favourite toys/artefacts, it is possible for the facilitator to explore the past and help the child develop some meaning around it.

Rose and Philpot (2010:27) suggest that to understand who you are, why you have lived where you have and with whom, it is not sufficient to simply say that your parents couldn't look after you, there needs to be meaning attributed to this.

According to Willis and Holland (2009), LSW in the form of books and memory boxes give identity meaning by providing: *'connections to worlds which they are not themselves able to access physically,* (Willis and Holland, 2009:50).

In a study by Gallagher and Green in 2012, LSW was deemed to have helped by acquiring a more accurate picture of their lives before they entered the home (Gallagher and Green, 2012:442).

LSW attaches importance to the past but according to Rose and Philpot (2010) *'how we define the past and what we think constitutes the past may differ.* (Rose and Philpot, 2010:16). Shotton's 2013 research also suggests that there is *'little consistency, in how life story work is carried out with Looked After Children'* (Shotton, 2013:353).

This experience was echoed in a local authority in South Wales. Willis and Holland's (2009:45) qualitative study of the experiences of 12 young people in foster care also had different workers delivering LSW including, social workers, support workers and life story practitioners, all using different methods and with varying degrees of input. This lack of consistency and the apparent variation of information given could potentially cause more harm than good in that by 'sanitizing' children's pasts and leaving them with an incomplete picture can further traumatise them. Many children will blame themselves for past actions of others, (Ryan and Walker 2007:5).

Willis and Holland's (2009:46) study describes the young people's views about LSW being mainly concerned with learning about themselves, their families and their pasts and dealing with emotions. Many of the young people had reported that they had found out new information about their past and about the current situation of their birth families. This information is about the

> 'people in the child's life, what happened to the child and the reasons why those things happened. It is not, and cannot be, a simple narrative or description' (Rose and Philpot, 2010:16).

Transitions through placements

LSW supports both the child and the carer as they travel through placements,. Within adoption the term 'bridging' is often used when linking the past, present and future and according to Ryan and Walker (2007) the adoption field has

> 'slowly come to the conclusion that successfully 'bridging' children is a crucial factor in them remaining in their permanent substitute family' (Ryan and Walker 2007:44).

Fahlberg, suggests that *'a child about to move into a new family is in a state of aroused anxiety* (Fahlberg, 1994) which can ultimately disrupt the placement. When talking about strategies to support children in maintaining long term placements, Fahlberg describes 'emotional permission' referring to a child attaching him or herself to the new family. This is expanded on by Donley (2007) who suggests that the early stages of placement should be characterised by

> 'disengaging the child from significant parental figures in the past, usually the birth mother, and assisting the child to engage with the 'new' mother' (Donley cited in Ryan and Walker, 2007:44).

I feel that this somewhat contradicts earlier messages because of the importance of establishing the past and the positive effects of this on forming identity.

Bowlby writes that

> 'Our sense of self is closely dependant on the few intimate attachment relationships we have or have had in our lives, especially our relationship with the person who raised us' (Bowlby, 2007:8).

That being said, the transition into a new placement for a child is full of difficulties and challenges and in order to ensure that they have the best possible chance of maintaining that placement a focus needs to be on developing new relationships. However, I feel that a balance between the two to ensure the formation of identity does need to be struck and LSW can facilitate this.

Unfortunately not all placements are successful ones. In 2014 researchers analysed national data on 37,335 adoptions over a 12 year period to show that 3.2 per cent of children, around 3 in 100, move out of their adopted home prematurely. According to SCIE (2015), foster placement breakdowns, or unplanned moves, are much less likely in younger children. In comparison, 'teenage' placements have a 50 per cent chance of breaking down (Social Care Institute for Excellence, 2015).

Shotton's (2013) research highlighted the usefulness of LSW in helping the young person prepare for change. A young person interviewed as part of the research stated that he had received LSW in this case the memory store approach in his previous placement '*as a way of helping him know what to expect in the next one*' (Shotton, G. 2013:361).

Shotton writes about a '*shared understanding of the importance of children having tangible memories to take with them to confirm their identity, comfort them, help say goodbye to their last carer and introduce them to their next one*' (Shotton, G. 2010:65) a theme also supported by Backhaus (1984:552).

Although there is a sound argument for the introduction of LSW as a method of supporting children through placements, there is an alternative view that suggests that LSW can be the catalyst to destabilisation. This argument was first brought to my attention whilst observing a session with an adoptive parent and her social worker who were trying to save the adoptive placement. During that meeting the social worker stated that '*if ever there was going to be a bump in the road, it would be when the process of LSW begins*' (Social Worker, 2014: IOW Local Authority). This perspective is backed up by Rose (2012), who states

> 'The danger of traumatising is at its highest at these times, and so the ability of the life story therapist, and the knowledge he has of the child, must be equal to the risk' (Rose, 2012:17), further supported by Backhaus (1984)

Emotional wellbeing

Children who possess a healthy sense of self-esteem feel that their carer's will love, care and protect them. Children who are Looked After or Adopted often have low self-esteem as a result of feeling unloved, unaccepted, It is theorised in Cook-Cotton and Becks article (2007) that

> '*self-esteem provides a guiding mechanism steering individuals through critical life choices and playing a large role in governing their behaviour.*

A reoccurring theme throughout LSW literature is that of how it can elicit the positive emotional wellbeing of fostered and adopted children. LSW as an intervention can help children to become more resilient by having evidence in the form of a life story book of their successes and achievements which they can turn to during more challenging times. Gallagher's and Greens (2012) study concurs with this and suggests that although many of the young people's stories had been dominated by adversity, some of them pointed out that their Life Story Book's also contained information about happier times in their lives. Some young people have found the process of LSW intrusiveness and to be overwhelming which has the potential to have the opposite effect on their self-esteem. One young person in Willis and Holland's (2009) study went to great lengths to destroy her life story book by tearing it up before throwing it away.

Building relationships

LSW is thought to be effective in developing relationships between children and the facilitators of LSW,. Shotton's 2010 study viewed LSW as being an opportunity to spend 'quality time' with their children and develop friendship, trust and insight into their children's lives.

A deeper insight into the formation of a relationship between an adoptive parent and child may help to explain how LSW helps to build relationships and ultimately support the formation of identity. Burnell and Vaughan (2008) wrote that

> 'although written for the child, a carefully prepared life story book will also help the adopters to see the child's story from a different perspective: the child's. Sharing this information and discussing it with the parents can also be a therapeutic experience for them, such as it gives them insight into their child and a greater sense of empathy (Burnell and Vaughan, 2008:228).

A negative aspect of the formation of these relationships is the possibility of another broken attachment. Through working in a Children in Care Team and having conversations with children who have been through numerous placements, a common theme with these children is that of 'trust'. One young person who I came into contact with had moved placements four times in one year and had 19 social workers since being taken into care. This young person and others that I had spoken to had initially invested in the process of forming relationships but ultimately withdrew when it became clear that the worker would not be 'hanging around'. I have also formed a relationship as a social work student with a child who is Looked After. A relationship that became strong and results in the child making positive progress. Ultimately I had to withdraw from this relationship when my placement came to an end. This has left me with feeling of guilt and remorse and the questioning of the ethics of the relationship. Did this leave another broken attachment for this child?

When LSW is carried out there is also the possibility that the child may become dependent on the carer or facilitator and that the success of the work is dependent on the relationship. In some cases LSW only takes place when it is facilitated by someone other than the child. In these cases that child becomes dependant on the facilitator to invest in the process and commit to it which can be a challenge especially with the ever increasing demands of social workers.

It is suggested that the level of input of workers is inconsistent and varied which can impact the success of LSW. In Gallagher and Green's study (2012), a common criticism of the LSW received was the way in which it had been organised, arguing that the participants had not been sufficiently engaged in it, that it needed to be gone into more depth and that it had been executed in a perfunctory manor (Gallagher and Green, 2012).

Constraints in regards to the time that a worker has available for LSW is highlighted in Backhaus's study. (Backhaus, K. 1984:553). It may be suggested that the time required to deliver LSW effectively has decreased significantly. Time must be invested into a professional's workload to make LSW effective and successful. Backhaus suggests that

> 'for such a relationship to exist, time must be invested. Most workers recognise the futility of expecting a child to participate in the Life Book process if trust had not been established' (Backhaus, K. 1984:553).

Later life letters

Later Life Letters form part of the wider LSW process and are seen by many as fundamental in the formation of adopted children's identity.

Later Life Letter's became a statutory requirement in England as part of the Adoption Agency Regulations in 2005 and are deemed fundamental in ensuring that the child, now a young person/adult can 'understand their history and make sense of their past, ensure their self-esteem and strengthen their resilience' (Moffat, 2012:1)

Because Later Life Letter's address events that have at some stage traumatised the child there is an argument that re-introducing these events to the, young person/adult, may re-traumatise them. If this is the case and in contrast to the support that is provided to the child through the early LSW process, is there the right level of support, in place for the young person during and after they have read the letter/Later Life Letter's give the young person specific details about the reason why they could not stay with their birth parents.

This question strikes a chord with me as I have recently read a Later Life Letter before it was given to the 16 year old deemed to be old enough to deal with what was enclosed. The letter explored the subject of identity, such as where she was born, who her mother and siblings were, her mother's culture and family. However, it also included specific details of the rape that lead to her conception, how her mother's family wanted nothing to do with her and how her mother decided to keep her other children and give her up for adoption. After reading this letter I asked myself the question, how much of this knowledge will really benefit the young person? She is settled in her life with her adopted family but has questions about her mother and father. How will this young person react to this information?

This raises the issue of power, and should the Social Worker have the option to hold back information for the best interest of the child? What is in the best interest of the child? How old is old enough to deal with this kind of information?

Traditional social work values influenced by Carl Rogers's Person-Centred Approach highlights the importance of 'Congruence' that being the willingness and ability to be genuine and open. Thompson (2008) states that

> 'If a positive working relationship based on trust and respect is to be developed, then a degree of such 'congruence' or genuineness must be achieved (Thompson, N. 2000:114).

This being the case, to hold back any information from the young person would be seen as highly unethical. Moffat (2012) addresses this issue in her guide to writing Later Life Letters and states that 'if details about paternity are left unclear, the young person is likely to either build up some fantasy picture, or to make a guess about who her father was, which (in some cases) may be much worse than the reality' (Moffat, 2012:19).

There rises another interesting debate about how negative information needs to be handled. Brodzinsky (2005) suggests that

> 'unless adoptive parents can find ways to help their children feel positive about their origins, these youngsters are likely to have more problems with self-esteem and identity' (Brodzinsky, 2005 cited in Moffat, 2012:35).

On the other hand, by only focusing on the positives and ignoring the facts of neglect and abuse, the young person may begin to fabricate their own history. Loxterkamp (2009) sees dangers in giving sanitised information.

> 'The account of the child's early years contains sanitised explanations that attempt to excuse the birth parents ('she was poorly') or that attempt to minimise the injurious behaviour ('they loved you but didn't know how to look after a child') and fall well short of meeting the standards of truth' (Loxterkamp, 2009 cited in Moffat, 2012:36).

This 'sanitised' information has just as much potential to cause harm to the young person as providing the truth. It can prevent the young person from understanding the real reasons for their adoption and affect the young person's ability to form secure attachments.

To introduce the hard hitting themes within later life letters, it is essential that the process of LSW has been undertaken and introduced at an early age. Without this, the information within the letter may be too much to comprehend. As much as we want to protect children, but have no right to withhold information which present a dilemma to the worker.

There needs to be a process of preparation in order for the child to be able to deal with the potential highly emotive information within the letter, no matter how ready social workers or adoptive parents feel they are.

Conclusion

LSW gives children the opportunity to gather accurate information about their birth families and enables children to develop an understanding of their pasts, piecing together their histories so that they can make sense of it and allowing them to move forward. It enables children to come to terms with their experiences, build new relationships and attachments and develop as healthy, secure individuals with a positive sense of self. Without LSW, children who have had traumatic pasts can become stuck and lost within their negative experiences, defined by Fahlberg (1994) as 'emotionally frozen'.

LSW is seen by adoption services as fundamental in achieving the best possible outcomes for adopted children, so much so that it has become a statutory requirement ensuring consistent and regular training around understanding and delivery. This however is lacking with Looked After Children where LSW is currently just a recommendation of good practice. To ensure that the same standards of delivery and training are upheld for Looked After Children, it is my opinion that LSW needs to be a statutory requirement across both areas.

Having two of the three perspectives within the adoption arena and coming into contact with Looked After Children on a daily basis, I have seen both the value of LSW in promoting identity but also the dangers if not delivered correctly.

I have had many conversations with adoptive parents, foster carers and social workers around the LSW process and more often than not, I receive a positive response to its potential, mixed with fear in regards to its delivery. In my opinion this has led to a failure in the appropriate delivery of the intervention. For LSW to move forward and to be more consistent, I feel that their needs to be more structure in place in regards to how we deliver the work, how it is regulated and how we engage with children through direct work.

The following passage from Fahlberg's book 'Helping children when they move on, provides an interesting perspective:

'The very fact that adults hesitate to share information about the past with a child implies to him that his past is so bad that he won't be able to cope with it. Whatever the past was – the child lived through it and survived, and so can live with the truth' (Fahlberg, 1981:51).

LSW is essentially a helping tool to bring clarity to a child's life history to help bring closure to past issues and build a new and stronger personal identity. However, the process of LSW is varied and inconsistency reliant entirely on the skill of the practitioner. The dilemma for the social worker is who owns the material and in what form makes it helpful to the child to share? Through withholding of information might protect the child from hurtful or damaging consequences but to not further risks damaging an already fragile identity. The social work literature fails to address this dilemma.

'We know that Looked After Children can overcome early experiences of trauma and adversity. Our participants demonstrate that children's histories do not have to predict their future, and that journeys through childhood to adulthood can be changed. We are learning that being looked after should be a time at which there is real opportunity for change' (Harper et al. 2006:60).

The following three key recommendations I are made to managers of Looked After and Adoptions services.

1. LSW for Looked After Children to be brought in line with the Adoption and Children Act 2002 and be made a statutory requirement.
2. Mandatory training to all that deliver LSW.
3. The Progress of LSW to be monitored and reviewed at every Looked After child's review (6 monthly).

References

ACA (2002) Adoption and Children Act 2002 (Online) Available at: http://www.legislation.gov.uk/ukpga/2002/38/contents (Accessed 20/12/2014)

Backhaus, K. (1984) *Life Books: Tool for working with children in placement.* Social Work, 29, 551-554

Batsleer, J.R. (2009) *Informal Learning in Youth Work.* London: Sage Publications Ltd.

Bowlby, J. (2007) *The Making and Breaking of Affectional Bonds.* London: Routledge

British Association for Adoption and Fostering (2015) *Statistics England (Online)* Available at: http://www.baaf.org.uk/res/statengland (Accessed: 18/03/2015)

Burnell, A. and Vaughan , J. (2008) *Remembering never to forget and forgetting never to remember: Re-thinking life story work.* In Luckock, B and Lefevre, M. (2008) *Direct Work: Social Work with Children and Young People in Care.* London: British Association of Adoption & Fostering (BAAF)

Children Act 1989 (CA) (Online) Available at: http://www.legislation.gov.uk/ukpga/1989/41/contents (Accessed 21/12/2014)

Cook-Cotton, C and Beck, M. (2007) *A Model for Life-Story Work: Facilitating their Construction of Personal Narrative for Foster Children.* Child and Adolescent Mental Health, 12, 193-195

Department for Education (2011) Adoption: *National Minimum Standards* England: Department for Education

Department for Education (2014) *Children looked after in England (including adoption and care leavers) year ending 31 March 2014* (Online). Available at: https://www.gov.uk/government/uploads/system/uploads/attachment_data/file/359277/SFR36_2014_Text.pdf (Accessed 3/04/2015)

Fahlberg, V. (1981) *Helping children when they must move on*. London: British Association of Adoption & Fostering (BAAF)

Fahlberg, V. (1994) *A Child's Journey Through Placement*. London: BAAF

Gallagher, B. and Green, A. (2012) *In, out and after care: Young adults views on their lives, as children, in a therapeutic residential establishment*. Children and Young People Review 34, 437-450

Happer, H., McCreadie, J. and Aldgate, J. (2006) *Celebrating success: what helps Looked After Children succeed*. Social Work Inspection Agency.

Moffat, F (2012) *Writing a later life letter: Good Practice Guide*. London: British Association of Adoption & Fostering (BAAF)

Oswalt, M (2015) Sensitive Periods in Child Development (Online). Available at http://www.sevencounties.org/poc/view_doc.php?type=doc&id=7923&cn=28 (Accessed 19/02/2015)

Pasupathi, M., Mansour, E. and Brubaker, J.R. (2007) *Developing a Life Story: Constructing Relations between Self and Experience in Autobiographical Narratives*. Human Developments, 50, 85-110

Payne, M. (2005) *Modern Social Work Theory* (3rd ed) Basingstoke: Palgrave Macmillian

Rachel Willis and Sally Holland. (2009) *Life Story Work: Reflections on the Experience by Looked After Children*. Adoption and Fostering 33, 44-52

Rees, J. (2009) *Life Story Books for Adopted Children: A Family Friendly Approach*. London: Jessica Kingsley

Research in Practice (2015) *Child Development Chart - Frontline resources (Online)*. Available at: https://www.rip.org.uk/resources/publications/frontline-resources/frontline-child-development-chart. (Accessed 20/03/2015)

Rose, R and Philpot, P. (2005) *The Child's Own Story: Life Story Work with Traumatized Children*. London: Jessica Kingsley

Rose, R. (2012) *Life Story Therapy with Traumatized Children*. Australian Journal of Adoption, 6:1

Ryan, T and Walker, R. (2007) *Life Story Work: A practical guide to helping children understand their past*. London: BAAF Adoption and Fostering

Shotton, G. (2010) *Telling different stories: The experience of foster/adoptive carers in carrying out collaborative memory work with children*. Adoption and Fostering 34, 61-68

Shotton, G. (2013) *Remember when .... Exploring experiences of Looked After Children and their carers in engaging in collaborative reminiscence*. Adoption and Fostering 37(4) 352-367

Smith, P.K., Cowie, H. and Blades, M. (2003) *Understanding Children's Development* (4th Ed). London: Blackwell

Social Care Institute for Excellence (2015) *Fostering Placement Stability (Online)*. Available at: http://www.scie.org.uk/publications/guides/guide07/placement/placement. (Accessed 26/03/2015)

The Oxford Dictionary of English. (2010) *Oxford University Press (Online)*. Available from: http://www.oxforddictionaries.com/definition/english/identity. (Accessed 12/12/2015)

Thompson, N. (2000) *Understanding Social Work: Preparing for Practice* (3rd Ed). Basingstoke: Palgrave Macmillian

University of Bristol (2014) *Report reveals adoption breakdown rate and the experiences of adoptive families in crisis (Online)*. Available at: http://www.bristol.ac.uk/news/2014/april/adoption-report.html. (Accessed 26/03/2015)

Wrench, K and Naylor, L. (2013) *Life Story Work with Children Who are Fostered or Adopted: Creative Ideas and Activities*. London: Jessica Kingsley

14
Talking Mats as a tool to hear voices of disabled children

Peter Holland

Introduction

The child's voice is incredibly important in all child care social work. Ascertaining the voice of the child is fundamental to safeguarding and needs assessment. This has been highlighted by child death enquiries for the past 50 years (Winter 2011, p23). Lefevre (2010, p1) highlights that listening to children can be a matter of life and death, and at the very least will improve the quality of assessment, planning and service provision, by allowing an expert (the child) to have their say. Ofsted (2011) highlighted that unheard children are at risk of significant harm or death subsequently Brandon et al (2012) identified that two thirds of the serious case reviews between 1st April 2009 and 31st March 2011 refer to the voice of the child not being heard or taken account of.

The need to hear the child is uncontested. It is emphasised in all significant children's social work legislation and policy such as the Children Act 1989 (strengthened by the Children Act 2004), United Nations Convention on the Rights of the Child 1989, Every Child Matters 2004 and Children and Families Act 2014. The Framework for the Assessment of Children in Need (DOH 2000); still relevant today as highlighted in Working Together 2015 (DfE 2015), is founded, from a strong research base, in ecological theory and emphasises the importance of understanding the child's world (Horwath 2010, p18). Furthermore, Eileen Munro's (2011) recent review of child protection practice emphasises the need to move toward child centred practice and Working Together 2015 (DfE 2015).

Social work with disabled children, in the realms of child protection and children in care, is generally conducted under the legislative framework of Section 17 of the Children Act 1989. Section 17 determines a disabled child's eligibility for an assessment as a child in need. The needs of the carer must also be considered under the Disabled Children and Carers Act 2000. In relation to children in need (Children Act 1989 s.17) and in conjunction with the Human Rights Act 1998 emphasises a need to work in partnership with parents and for interference into private life to be lawful, necessary and proportionate...Despite this supportive legislative and in the context of social work with disabled children it is far from straightforward.

A epidemiological study by Sullivan and Knutson (2000) identified that disabled children are 3.4 times more likely to be abused than non-disabled children. The research is widely accepted and regularly cited in policy and research (see DfE 2009, NSPCC 2003, OFSTED 2012, Oosterhoorn and Kendrick 2001, Stalker and McArthur 2012, Stalker et al 2010, Wonnacott et al 2013). The literature also identifies that though UK based research of this type is absent, Sullivan and Knutson's research in combination with other international studies demonstrates that disabled children are at an increased risk of abuse and under-represented in child protection.

The disabled child is at increased risk of abuse and yet is neither at the centre of practice, nor heard, despite it being considered vital facets of child care social work. A number of practice issues are identified as causing such inaction such as practitioner available time, professional skill and biased attitude. Given the duty to hear and safeguard disabled children many issues are raised for disabled children. Whatever identified method needs to be used must be simple and easy to use. This chapter analyses whether 'Talking Mats' is one way of helping to ascertain the voice, views and feelings of disabled children.

What are Talking Mats?

Talking Mats is an interactive, low tech augmentative and alternative communication (AAC) method. AAC methods replace or support speech. Talking Mats was developed by Speech and Language Therapist, Joan Murphy at the University of Stirling (see www.talkingmats.com). Talking Mats' first appeared in Murphy (1998) having been developed in 1996 from a project to examine peer interaction between nine adult AAC users in residential settings; the method has been developed and tested in subsequent studies, which are detailed in the literature review.

Talking Mats use three sets of symbols: a topic/issue (e.g. activities), options/influences (relating to the topic, e.g. dancing) and a visual scale of emotions (typically like/happy, unsure and dislike/sad). The topic and scale are laid out on a textured mat (such as a ribbed doormat (see www.duratex.co.uk) by the practitioner. The service user is asked consistent open questions about each option/influence ('How do you feel about?' etc.), and is handed the corresponding symbol to place under the appropriate emotion on the mat. The symbols are laminated and velcro backed to add further dimensions of texture. Service users can reflect and change the mat once all options have been placed. A photo is then taken to document the mat. Sub mats can be used for deeper exploration of unexpected choices.

Talking Mats with adults

The literature reveals that Talking Mat studies have focussed on a wide range of adults. This theme can be further reduced to two prominent groups, young adults and to adults of a more elderly disposition. Despite a child care focus it has been necessary to review the majority of these studies to understand their application, strengths and limitations of Talking Mats. The research regarding young adults is pertinent to disabled children whose social workers have an interest in transitioning to Adult Social Care. Successful use of talking mats has been used with adults with a combination of complex cognitive and communication impairments (Bell 2008 et al, Murphy and Cameron 2006), adults with learning disabilities (Bunning and Steel 2006, Cameron and Murphy 2002, Murphy and Cameron 2008, Watson et al 2003), adults with complex disabilities and mental health needs accommodated in a secure facility (Macer and Fox 2010), adults with dementia (Murphy et al 2007, Murphy et al 2010), adults with Huntington's disease (Ferm et al 2009, Ferm et al 2012), adults with aphasia (Murphy 2006), adults with acquired communication disorder (Harty et al 2011), frail and elderly people at the end of their lives (Murphy et al 2005), adults with cerebral palsy (Murphy 1998) and adults with motor neurone disease (Murphy 1999).

Talking Mats with children

Research is extensive including children and young people with learning, intellectual disability (Bunning et al 2008, Donahue et al 2013, Germain 2004, Mackay and Murphy 2012, Mitchell et al 2009, Pawson et al 2005, Small et al 2013, Whitehurst 2006), children with Downs Syndrome (Hooton and Westaway 2008), children with Autism Spectrum Disorder (Murphy et al 2010) young children, without learning disability (Iriss.org.uk, Nilsson et al 2012), children with complex health needs (Rabiee et al 2005, Ajodhia-

Andrews and Berman, 2009, Wright 2008), children with complex emotional and behavioural needs (Dinwoodie and Macer 2010, Coakes 2006), children and young people who use speech generating devices (Valiquette et al 2010) and a 14 year old with multi-sensory impairment (Taylor, 2007).

Talking Mats by design

The research suggests that in 1996 when Joan Murphy first conceived the idea of Talking Mats (1998), she created something worth far more than the sum of its parts. The mat and symbols design had more subtle benefits. The system is inexpensive to construct as highlighted by Murphy et al (2010). The mechanism of the Talking Mat is on face value very simple yet effective. The use of consistent language by the interviewer supported by visualisation provides service users with a clear structure and as is widely emphasised within the literature. It is a scaffold upon which to construct thoughts and feelings (Bell and Cameron 2007, Ferm et al 2009, Macer and Fox 2010, Murphy and Cameron 2008, Murphy et al 2005, Murphy et al 2010, Survivor Scotland and Talking Mats 2010).

The use of symbols is found to be helpful, breaking information down into manageable chunks, helping service users to express words they can no longer find and once upon the mat reduce demands on short term memory by providing a reminder of what's been discussed. This affords fluency to the conversation (Cameron and Murphy 2002, Dinwoodie and Macer 2010, Murphy and Cameron 2008, Murphy et al 2005, Hooton and Westaway 2008). Talking Mats is designed to work alongside existing communication systems. Completed Talking Mats are recorded by photograph. The photo can subsequently be reviewed and kept by the service user (Bunning et al 2008, Hooton and Westaway 2008).

Talking Mat Outcomes

The use of Talking Mats has allowed for rich first-hand information to be obtained relatively easily from service users for whom it would not normally be readily available (Ajodhia-Andrews and Berman 2009, Bell and Cameron, 2002, Bunning and Steel 2006, Bunning et al 2008, Bell and Cameron 2007, Bell et al 2008, Cameron and Murphy 2002, Germain 2004, Murphy and Cameron 2006, Murphy and Cameron 2008, Murphy et al 2005, Murphy et al 2007, Murphy et al 2010, Rabiee et al 2005,Taylor 2007, Valiquette et al 2010, Watson et al 2003 , Wright 2008). Due to the indirect and non-threatening nature of Talking Mats, it has been found possible to explore sensitive topics, resolve conflicts and explore and improve relationships.

Several studies used an effective coding framework (EFFC) to measure the overall effectiveness of service user communication when using Talking Mats compared to unstructured and structured conversation, or the service user's normal method of communication (Coakes 2007, Ferm et al 2009, Ferm et al 2012, Mackay et al 2012, Murphy and Cameron 2008, Murphy et al 2007, Murphy et al 2010). In all but one study (Ferm et al 2012), Talking Mats was found to be significantly more effective than other methods of communication.

The dementia studies (Murphy et al 2007, Murphy et al 2010) are corroborative in its results. This indicates reliability in terms of research methodology and the effectiveness of Talking Mats. This research also highlighted a reduction in perseveration when using Talking Mats and a reduction in uncontrollable tendencies to repeat or act. The increasing communicative effectiveness has meant that completing Talking Mats has been a meaningful process for service users. It is widely reported in the EFFC studies and others (Cameron and Murphy 2002, Hooton and Westaway 2008, Murphy et al 2005, Pawson et al 2005) that service users gain a sense of enjoyment and achievement.

Application of Talking Mats

Within the research reviewed, Talking Mats has been used to inform needs assessment, transition, future and person-centred planning, decision making, goal and target setting. The tool has also facilitated group work, therapeutic sessions, the review of inclusion activity, ability to access eLearning and IT and of medical care, the exploration of challenging behaviour, children's rights, quality of life, identity, culture, relationships and social networks, Topics discussed have included accommodation, activities and leisure, employment, education, family, friends and relationships, self, body parts, communication, independent living skills, social presentation, mental health, personal care, house work, mobility, transport, weather and food. Talking Mats have been undertaken in a wide range of settings including care, health and education. Talking Mats appear to have been used most effectively and innovatively when multi-agency colleagues have worked together to fully utilise the potential of the method, such as in Macer and Fox (2010) where a Speech and Language Therapist completed Talking Mats with 17 patients in a secure facility to capture their feelings

Adaptability

Research has shown that Talking Mats offers a platform for innovative practice. At a basic level Talking Mats can be simplified by reducing the three point scale to two points, thus removing the confusion of having a mid-point (unsure). This can been seen in Bell et al (2008), where the words representing the emotions are also changed to fit with the language of the service user (grumpy is used instead of sad). Cameron and Murphy (2002) removed the midpoint scale for 7 of their 12 service users. They give a structured approach and ease with which symbols can be created and the fact that it is on the surface a blank canvas. This has been subject to creative approaches to extend its use and with some success. It puts the child at the centre of the mat and places symbols representing relationships, activities and future aspirations around them. The distance placed from the centre represents value and influence

This is an interesting concept, however the research is small in scale, lacks statistical analysis and notes how service users struggled with the more abstract elements of the task, such as the focus on the future. Small et al (2013, p293) in reviewing this pilot as part of a wider study state that this idea is *'both rich in potential and beset by conceptual challenges'*; the challenges include having to recognise what a symbol represents and then attribute significance to it through the use of distance.

Reliability

The literature presented so far paints an encouraging picture. Talking Mats appears to be a novel, all encompassing, instant solution to communicating with services users with cognitive and/or communicative needs. However it does present issues in relation to research methodology in its reliability and validity.

The research reviewed is predominantly focussed upon single case studies (Ajodhia-Andrews and Berman 2009, Bell and Cameron 2003,

Bell and Cameron 2007, Bell et al 2008, Brewster 2010, Taylor 2007), practice examples (Iriss.org.uk, Hooton and Westaway 2008, Macer and Fox 2010) and small scale studies (Bunning and Steel 2006, Bunning et all 2008, Cameron and Murphy 2002, Coakes 2007, Dinwoodie and Macer 2010, Ferm et al 2009, Ferm et al 2012, Harty et al 2011, Mackay and Murphy 2012, Mitchell et al 2009, Murphy 2006, Murphy and Cameron 2006, Murphy et al 2005, Murphy et al 2007, Murphy et al 2010, Nilsson et al 2012, Rabiee et al 2005, Small et al 2013, Watson et al 2003, Wright 2008, Valiquette et al 2010). The largest studies are those of 48 adults with learning disability (Murphy and Cameron 2008) and of 188 children with learning disability in South Africa (Donahue et al 2013).

Pocock (2011) in her review of Murphy et al's (2010) dementia research questions the extent to which the findings can be generalised and applied to a larger cohort of dementia patients due to the scale of the study. The reliability of applying the data to larger cohorts is highlighted as an issue in a number of studies. There is however a counter-argument. Wright (2008) contends that service users with multiple and complex needs are not a homogenous group and therefore should not be subject to large scale studies or generalised findings. Bunning et al (2008), in a study of 20 young people with learning disabilities, aged 15-20, found higher non-completion rates for Talking Mats related to abstract topics such as future aspirations as opposed to more concrete topics such as activities liked and disliked. Cameron and Murphy (2002), Ferm et al (2009), Mackay and Murphy (2012), Murphy and Cameron (2008) and Survivor Scotland and Talking Mats (2010) found similar difficulties with abstract topics and choices. Few of the child related studies consider ability. Nilsson et al (2012) conclude that their STAI Talking Mat method is not reliable for children younger than 7.

Acquiescence is an issue that is referenced in several papers, including Mitchell (2010) being the increased likelihood, due to adult and societal oppression and control, that those with a learning disability will look to please by providing what they perceive to be the desired answer. However, Cameron and Murphy (2002) state that acquiescence wasn't an issue in their research, attributing this success to the design of the mat. The quality of evidence provided to argue this point is such however, that it appears to be mere opinion. Donahue et al (2013) did include an acquiescence testing question in their research rather the responses indicated only a low level of acquiescence. Researcher subjectivity and the complexity of, the validation of Talking Mats data is an issue that is raised in several papers (Hussein and Daud 2014, Murphy and Cameron 2008, Murphy et al 2007, Murphy et al 2010); subjectivity is particularly prevalent in Ajodhia-Andrews and

Berman (2009), who appear influenced by past experience and aspiration in analysing a child's seemingly random placement of symbols.

Finally, many of the studies reviewed have been completed by those who are associated with Talking Mats' creation or ongoing development (Bell and Cameron, 2003, Bell and Cameron, 2007, Cameron and Murphy 2002, Coakes 2007, Dinwoodie and Macer 2010, Macer and Fox 2010, Mackay and Murphy 2012, Murphy 2006, Murphy and Cameron 2006, Murphy and Cameron 2008, Murphy et al 2005, Murphy et al 2007, Murphy et al 2010, Survivor Scotland and Talking Mats 2010, Watson et al 2003,). Talking Mats is now a social enterprise and sells communication packages, software applications and training programs.

Ethical challenges

Wright (2008, p34) identifies that obtaining meaningful consent from those with multiple and complex needs is almost impossible. Germain (2004) and Murphy et al (2010) highlight that gaining informed consent from the service users in their research is problematic. Typically the consent of service users to undertake Talking Mats is assumed but raises ethical issues of informed consent. There are also issues in relation to permission to share first-hand information with others.

Barriers

Mitchell (2010) highlights the need for managers and policy makers to back the use of Talking Mats, although there appears some reluctance both from managers and practitioners (Macer and Murphy 2009, Survivor Scotland and Talking Mats 2010) to fully utilise Talking Mats. The most evident barrier is that of time. Time is a valuable resource. It has been regularly found that Talking Mat interviews take considerably longer than interviews via unstructured and structured conversation (Ferm et al 2009, Mitchell et al 2009, Murphy and Cameron 2008, Murphy et al 2007; Rabiee 2005).

There appears to be a perception related to the quality of evidence gathered by Talking Mats. One contributor to the Survivor Scotland and Talking Mats (2010, p11) research commented *'a client ... disclosed a sexual assault to me ... and my manger asked me not to use the pack* (of 6D cards) *as it would potentially contaminate the evidence'*. It is explained that a lengthy and difficult Police interview was arranged instead of the talking mat is 'user friendly' and less invasive approach.

Analysis

The Potential of Talking Mats

The literature presents a balanced view with respect of Talking Mats. On one hand Talking Mats have been used with a wide range of service users, including children and has been argued to be very effective at a particular level of communicative and cognitive functioning. This success is attributed to Talking Mats' design which affords consistency, structure, visual support and scaffolding for effective communication, particularly with respect of keeping service users on task and allowing ownership of the mat by the service user. This has led to rich and meaningful data being available. However these studies are small and a number are lacking rigorous statistical analysis and validation.

Talking Mats seemingly does not meet the needs of all service users with communicative and cognitive impairment and for those with mild impairments, structured conversation, which is far more time efficient, appears to be just as effective. For those with significant impairment Talking Mats is unable to promote the service users communication to levels deemed to be effective, however as it has greater benefits than other methods trialled in the research. Talking Mats does not appear to significantly remedy difficulties with abstract topics used in the process. The use of symbols is very much in the balance in terms of providing visual structure and support but also potentially limiting conversation. The service users who have participated in the Talking Mats research are far from being a homogenous group; generalisation of findings is therefore difficult, however nuanced snapshots of individual lives are possible.

'Talking Mats' and social work

The evidence so far is varied with regard to its benefits. Oliver's Social Model of Disability (Oliver et al 2012;p14) argues that it is the setup of society that is disabling, not a person's impairment. It is for the worker to change their thinking and skillset to enable direct work with disabled children (Lefevre

2010). Talking Mats has the potential to facilitate this. The method is also supported by Carl Roger's humanist approach (as cited in Payne 2005). The method is person centred and in searching for the service user's voice conveys congruence, positive regard and empathy. Talking Mats gives the service user control and seeks to visualise that which is unheard, anti-oppressive (Dominelli, 2009) and anti-discriminatory (Payne 2005).

The literature shows how Talking Mats has the potential to inform assessment, planning, review and transition in all key social work tasks. Furthermore the tool has been used to discuss a wide range of topics of interest to social work, for example, examined relationships, culture and identity. Nilsson et al (2012) have shown how anxiety might be explored. There is the potential that the likes of 'Strengths and Difficulties Questionnaires' (SDQs) (DoH 2000a) could be adapted to a Talking Mat format or that the NSPCC's *'Triangle's 'How it is'* series' (2002) could be used in conjunction with the tool. 'How it is' is a range of symbols, designed to expand the vocabulary of available symbols to include feelings, body parts and maltreatment or abuse.

Talking Mats have been utilised successfully in a multiagency context, where professionals have worked together to fully utilise the tool's potential with a specific service user group. Mitchell (2010) foresees Talking Mats improving cooperation and communication between health and social care practitioners, particularly Social Workers and Speech and Language Therapists, generating shared assessments with the latter providing advice and training. This approach could ensure that the method is tailored appropriately to individual children. Furthermore the research has shown the use of Talking Mats in care, health and education settings where there appears potential for all stakeholders in a disabled child's life to utilise Talking Mats to seek the child's view in a more consistent and effective manner.

Talking Mats is compatible with child protection investigations and a key component of child care social work. Guidance (CPS 2011) indicates that symbols based communication support is appropriate as long as leading questions are not asked and gesture is not restricted however they highlight that in a police investigation an intermediary would be required to coordinate this and that using symbols could be problematic in court. Finally, it is well documented by the likes of Rogowski (2010) that social workers in the current organisational context are under pressure from bureaucratic tasks and managerial compliance, limiting direct time with service users runs against the intensive nature of Talking Mats.

Evidence that Talking Mats can be used with disabled children suggests the method has a simple yet effective design. However the literature casts doubt on the reliability of Talking Mats and on how generalizable it can be. Wilson (2013).Murray (2014) states that 'it is impossible to provide a one size fits all approach'. A wide and varied toolkit of communication methods, including many non-verbal and creative techniques is advocated for by a number of authors such as Malaguzzi (cited in Lefevre 2010, p64-65) and Ferber et al (2011). Shemmings and Rhodes (2012), Shemmings et al (2011), Wilkins et al (2012) and Woodcock Ross (2011, p47) identify a range of potential alternate methods including using craft, poetry, games, questionnaires, drama/role-play, clay, emotions board games, dolls, observation, drawing and the 'three houses, faces and three Islands tools'.

Lefevre (2010) and Murray (2014) highlight that there are no absolute rules and that it is best to work out methods to suit the individual child or young person. Woodcock Ross (2011) adds that suitable materials relevant to the child's interests, age and cognitive ability should be used. Furthermore Watson et al (2006) and Morris (2003) conclude that the most important factor for success is the practitioner's attitude and they must believe that all children can communicate, be flexible, develop a wide range of resources and be prepared to make mistakes (Lefevre 2010, and Wilkins et al 2012) I would caution that effective communication with children requires skill such as listening, questioning, responding, use and reading of body language. A communication tool such as Talking Mats alone will only present part of a message from the child.

Talking Mats can be used to ascertain the voice, views and feelings of disabled people. On face value it is simple to use and through its innovative design is inexpensive, mobile, adaptable and effective. It has been used to collect rich first-hand information that has not been previously heard. Talking Mats is an intervention to explore the world of the disabled child, inform assessment, planning, review, transition and service provision and has the potential to help safeguard children through building effective relationships. The timing required to prepare bespoke symbols for different service users and to use the tool may make it less desirable in a fast paced social work environment, however they do offer extended and focussed service user engagement in an increasing complex and difficult world of need assessment.

It is difficult to assert that Talking Mats can be used regularly or reliably with disabled children. It appears that the child's needs will determine the suitability of Talking Mats on an individual case by case basis. They have been used in a wide range of settings and it appears that there is scope for many agencies to utilise this tool. If Talking Mats are to be used by Social

Workers more regularly there appears a need for closer working with those who know the child's communicative and cognitive abilities; notably education and speech and language services.

Conclusion

Talking Mats provides a creative alternative and could with the right skilland attitude provide exciting opportunities to present the disabled child's voice in a powerful and visual way. On balance Talking Mats should be a feature in the 'toolbox' of any disabled children's Social Worker, however as Murphy et al (2005) and Whitehurst (2006) conclude, great effort and care needs to be taken in the planning, preparation and interpretation of Talking Mats. Multiagency working is an effective way to be helpful. Talking mats can only ever be part of a holistic process of communication and not something in isolation.

Recommendations

I would recommend the following changes to local authority practice:

- Disabled Children's Team to have Talking Mat resources made available to everyone (Training, Mats, Symbols, Cameras)
- Disabled Children's Social Workers (or support staff) to undertake training in using Talking Mats with Disabled Children in line with their cognitive and communicative ability; to be ascertained from multi-agency colleagues, particularly education and SALT.
- Talking Mats to be considered as a potential platform when developing practice to be more in line with a child's communicative and cognitive ability.
- Social Workers to consider using Talking Mats with non-disabled children
- Further research is needed in to provide greater evidence of their benefits.

References

Ajodhia-Andrews, A and Berman, R, (2009), Exploring School Life from the Lens of a Child Who Does Not Use Speech to Communicate, *Qualitative Inquiry*, Volume 15 Number 5, June 2009 931-951

Bell, D, Turnbull, A and Kidd, W, (2008), Differential diagnosis of dementia in the field of learning disabilities: a case study, *British Journal of Learning Disabilities*, 37, 56–65

Bell, D and Cameron, L, (2003), The assessment of the sexual knowledge of a person with a severe learning disability and a severe communication disorder, *British Journal or Learning Disabilities*, 31, 123-129

Bell, D and Cameron, L, (2007), From Dare I say … ? to I dare say: a case example illustrating the extension of the use of Talking Mats to people with learning disabilities who are able to speak well but unwilling to do so, *British Journal of Learning Disabilities*, 36, 122–127

Brandon, M, Sidebotham, P, Bailey, S, Belderson, P, Hawley, C, Ellis, C and Megson, M, (2012) *New learning from serious case reviews: a two year report for 2009-2011*, Centre for Research on the Child and Family in the School of Social Work and Psychology, University of East Anglia and Health Sciences Research Institute, Warwick Medical School, University of Warwick

Brewster, S, (2004), Putting words into their mouths? Interviewing people with learning disabilities and little/no speech, *British Journal of Learning Disabilities*, 32, 166–169

Bunning, K, and Steel, G, (2006) Self-concept in young adults with a learning disability from the Jewish community, *British Journal of Learning Disabilities*, 35, 43–49

Bunning, K, Heath B and Minnion A, (2008) Communication and Empowerment: A Place for Rich and Multiple Media?, *Journal of Applied Research in Intellectual Disabilities* 2009, 22, 370–379

Calder, M, 2008, Risk and Child Protection, (2008), in Calder, M, (ed) *Contemporary Risk Assessment in Safeguarding Children*, Chapter 12, pp206-223. Russell House Publishing Ltd: Lyme Regis

Cameron, L and Murphy, J (,2002) Enabling young people with a learning disability to make choices at a time of transition, *British Journal of Learning Disabilities*, 30, 105–112

Children Act 1989, http://www.legislation.gov.uk/ukpga/1989/41 [accessed 01/04/2015]

Children Act 2004, http://www.legislation.gov.uk/ukpga/2004/31/ [accessed 01/04/2015]

Children and Families Act 2014, http://www.legislation.gov.uk/ukpga/2014/6/

[accessed 01/04/2015]

Coakes, L, (2006) *Evaluating the ability of children with social emotional behavioural and communication difficulties (SEBCD) to express their views using Talking Mats*, Final report to NHS Forth Valley

Contact a Family, (2011) *The impact of isolation on families with disabled children across the UK*,

DfE, Department for Education, (2004) *Every Child Matters – Change for Children*, http://webarchive.nationalarchives.gov.uk/20130401151715/https://www.education.gov.uk/publications/standard/publicationdetail/page1/dfes/1081/2004 [accessed 01/04/15]

DfE, , (2009) *Safeguarding Disabled Children, Practice Guidance.* Department for Education: HMSO.

DfE, , (2015) *Working Together to Safeguard Children 2015 – A Guide To Inter-Agency Working to Safeguard and Promote the Welfare of Children.* Department for Education: HMSO.

Disabled Children and Carers Act 2000, http://www.legislation.gov.uk/ukpga/2000/16/ [Accessed 01/04/2015]

DOH, , (2000) *Framework for the Assessment of Children in Need and their Families.* Department of Health: HMSO.

DoH, , (2000a) *Framework for the Assessment of Children in Need and their Families Pack*, Department of Health .http://webarchive.nationalarchives.gov.uk/+/www.dh.gov.uk/en/publicationsandstatistics/publications/publicationspolicyandguidance/dh_4008144 [accessed 01/03/15]

Dickens, J, (2013) *Social Work Law and Ethics*, London: Routledge

Dinwoodie, D and Macer, J, (2010) Talking Mats for Literacy Target Setting, *Literacy Today*, March 2010.

Donohue, D, Bornman, J and Granlund, M, (2013) Examining the rights of children with intellectual disability in South Africa: Children's perspectives, *Journal of Intellectual and Developmental Disability*

Dunhill, A, (2009) What is communication? The process of transferring information, in Dunhill, A, Elliott, B and Shaw, A, (eds) Effective Communication and Engagement with Children and Young People, their Families and Carers, Learning Matters, pp17-30.

Duratex, (2015) http://www.duratex.co.uk/indoor-door-mats/98-ribbed-polypropylene-door-mat.html [accessed 01/04/2015]

Febrer, Y, Cook, A, Feeley, F, Denham, C, Shemmings D and Shemmings, y, (2011) *Using tools in direct work with children. Guides.* Community Care Inform [online] http://www.ccinform.co.uk/guides/using-tools-in-direct-work-with-children/ [accessed: 9 March 2015]

Ferm, U, Wallfur, P, Gelfgren, E and Hartelius, L, (2012). Communication Between Huntington's Disease Patients, Their Support Persons and the Dental Hygienist Using

Talking Mats, http://www.intechopen.com [accessed 01/04/2015]

Ferm, U, Sahlin, A, Sundin, L and Harteliusk, L, (2009) Using Talking Mats to support communication in persons with Huntington's Disease, *International Journal of Language & Communication Disorders*, First Article, pp.1–14

Germain, R, (2004) An exploratory study using cameras and Talking Mats to access the views of young people with learning disabilities on their out-of-school activities, *British Journal of Learning Disabilities*, 32, 170–174

Harty, M, Griesel, M, van der Merwe, A, (2011) The ICF as a common language for rehabilitation goal-setting: comparing client and professional priorities, *Health and Quality of Life Outcomes* 2011, 9:87

Hooton, J, and Westaway, A, (2008), The Voice of the Child with Downs Syndrome, *Downs Syndrome Research and Practice*.

Horwath, J, 2010, Assessing Children in Need: Background and Context< Chapter 1, pp18-33, in Horwath J, 2010, *The Child's World*, Second Edition, Jessica Kingsley, London

Howe, D, (2006) Disabled Children, Maltreatment and Attachment, *British Journal of Social Work*, 36, 743–760

Hussein, H and Daud, M, (2014) Examining the Methods for Investigating Behavioural Clues of Special-schooled Children, *Field Methods*, 1-16

http://www.inclusive.co.uk/product-list-a-z [accessed 01/04/2015] IRISS.ORG. UK, *Case study: Empowering vulnerable children and their parents using Talking Mats*, http://www.iriss.org.uk/resources/empowering-vulnerable-children [accessed 01/04/2015]

Lefevre, M, (2010), *Communicating with Children and Young People: Making a difference*, London: Policy Press

Macer, J and Fox, P, (2010), Using a Communication Tool to Help Clients to Express Their Health Concerns, *Learning Disability Practice*, vol 13, no 10, November 2010

Macer, J and Murphy, J, (2009) *Training care home staff to use Talking Mats® with people who have dementia*, Joseph Rowntree Foundation, www.jrf.org.uk

Mackay, M and Murphy, J, (2012) Talking Mats® and The World Health Organisation International Classification of Functioning Disability and Health - *Children and Youth*, www.talkingmats.com [accessed 01/04/2015]

Mallen, A, (2011) 'It's Like Piecing Together Small Pieces of a Puzzle'. Difficulties in Reporting Abuse and Neglect of Disabled Children to the Social Services, *Journal of Scandinavian Studies in Criminology and Crime Prevention* Vol. 12, pp. 45–62, 2011

McCool, S, (2008) Communication impairments in children in residential care: an overlooked aspect of their education and well-being? *Scottish Journal of Residential Child Care*, Volume 7 No 2 August/September 2008

Mitchell, W, (2010) 'I know how I feel' Listening to Young People with Life limiting

Conditions who have Learning and Communication Impairments, *Qualitative Social Work* 9(2).
Mitchell, W., Franklin, A., Greco, V. and Bell, M. (2009) Working with children with learning disabilities and/or who communicate non-verbally: research experiences and their implications for social work education, increased participation and social inclusion, *Social Work Education*, 28, 3, 309-324.
Morris, J, (2003) Including All Children: Finding Out About the Experiences of Children with Communication and/or Cognitive Impairments, *Children and Society*, Vol. 17 (2003) pp. 337–348
Munro E, (2011) *Munro review of child protection: final report - a child-centred system*. Department of Education: London.
Murphy J. (1998) Talking Mats: speech and language research in practice. *Speech and Language Therapy in Practice* Autumn, 11–14.
Murphy J. (1999) Enabling people with motor neurone disease to discuss their quality of life. *Communication Matters* 13 (2), 2–6.
Murphy, J. (2006) Perceptions of communication between people with communication disability and general practice staff, *Health Expectations*, 9, pp.49–59
Murphy, J and Cameron, L, (2006) The Acute Hospital Experience of Adults with Complex Communication Needs, *Communication Matters*, vol 20, no 2, August 2006
Murphy, J and Cameron, L, (2008) The effectiveness of Talking Mats_ with people with intellectual disability, *British Journal of Learning Disabilities*, 36, 232–241
Murphy, J, Gray, C and Cox, S (2007), *Communication and dementia: How Talking Mats can help people with dementia to express themselves*. Joseph Rowntree Foundation [www.jrf.org.uk]
Murphy, J, Gray, C and Cox, S (2008) Talking Mats and Dementia, *Communication Matters*, Vol 22, No 1, April 2008
Murphy, J, Oliver, T and Cox, S, (2010) *Talking Mats and involvement in decision making for people with dementia and family carers*, Joseph Rowntree Foundation [www.jrf.org.uk]
Murphy, J, Tester, S, Hubbard, G, Downs, M and MacDonald, C, (2005) Enabling frail older people with a communication difficulty to express their views: the use of Talking Mats™ as an interview tool, *Health and Social Care in the Community* 13(2), 95–107
Murray, P (2014) Guide to the voice of the disabled child. Guides. *Community Care Inform* [online] http://www.ccinform.co.uk/guides/voice-of-the-disabled-child/ [accessed: 9 December 2014]
Nilsson, S, Buchholz, M, and Thunberg, G, (2012), Assessing Children's Anxiety Using the Modified Short State-Trait Anxiety Inventory and Talking Mats: A Pilot Study, *Nursing Research and Practice*, Volume 2012,

NSPCC/Triangle, (2002) *'how it is' an image vocabulary for children about: feelings, rights and safety, personal care and sexuality*, NSPCC, London

NSPCC, (2003) *'It doesn't happen to disabled children' Child protection and disabled children*, NSPCC, London

OFSTED, (2011), *The voice of the child: learning lessons from serious case reviews*

OFSTED, (2012), Protecting disabled children thematic inspection

Oosterhoorn, R, and Kendrick, A, 2001, No Sign of Harm: Issues for Disabled Children Communicating About Abuse, *Child Abuse Review* Vol. 10: 243–253 (2001)

Pawson, N, Raghavan R, Small, N, Craig, S and Spencer, M, (2005) Social inclusion, social networks and ethnicity: the development of the Social Inclusion Interview Schedule for young people with learning disabilities, *British Journal of Learning Disabilities*, 33, pp.15–22

Pocock, M, (2011) *Talking Mats – a communication tool for people with dementia*, Community Care, http://www.communitycare.co.uk/2011/06/24/talking-mats-a-communication-tool-for-people-with-dementia/ [accessed 01/04/2015]

Rabiee, P., Sloper, P. and Beresford, B. (2005) Doing research with children and young people who do not use speech for communication, *Children & Society*, 19, 5, 385-96

Rogowski S (2010), *Social Work: The Rise and Fall of a Profession?*, Bristol Policy Press

Rose, W, (2010) *The Assessment Framework, Chapter 2*, , in Horwath J, 2010, The Child's World, Second Edition, pp34-55. Jessica Kingsley: London

Shemmings, D, Shemmings, Y, Wilkins, D, Febrer, Y, Cook, A, Feeley F and Denham, C ,(2011) *Using tools in direct work with children. Guides. Community Care Inform* [online] http://www.ccinform.co.uk/guides/using-tools-in-direct-work-with-children/ [accessed: 9 March 2015]

Shemmings, Y and Rhodes, H (2012) Guide to confident direct work with children. Guides. *Community Care Inform* [online] http://www.ccinform.co.uk/guides/guide-to-confident-direct-work-with-children-6/ [accessed: 9 March 2015]

Small, N, Raghavan, R and Pawson, N, (2013), An ecological approach to seeking and utilising the views of young people with intellectual disabilities in transition planning *Journal of Intellectual Disabilities* 17(4) 283–300

Stalker, K, and McArthur, K, (2012) Child Abuse, Child Protection and Disabled Children: A review of recent research, *Child Abuse Review* Vol. 21: 24–40 (2012)

Stalker, K, Green, P, Lister, Erpiniere, J, McArthur, K , (2010) *Child Protection and the needs and rights of disabled children and young people: A Scoping Study*, Abridged Report, University of Strathclyde.

Sullivan P and Knutson J, (2000) Maltreatment and disabilities: a population-based epidemiological study. *Child Abuse and Neglect*. 2000 Oct; 24(10):1257-73

Survivor Scotland and Talking Mats, (2010) *Survivor Scotland and Talking Mats: Supporting people with learning disability to disclose issues of concern*, http://www.

talkingmats.com/wp-content/uploads/2013/08/Talking-Mats-and-Survivor-Scotland-final-Report.pdf [accessed 01/04/2015]

Talking Mats TM, (2015) *www.talkingmats.com* , accessed 15/03/2015

Taylor, K, (2007), The participation of children with multi-sensory impairment in person-centred planning, *British Journal of Special Education*, Volume 34, Number 4

Trevithick, P, (2009), *Social Work Skills: a practice handbook*, 2nd Edition, Open University Press: Buckinghamshire.

United Nations Convention on the Rights of the Child, 1989, http://www.ohchr.org/en/professionalinterest/pages/crc.aspx [accessed 01/04/2015]

Valiquette, C, Sutton, A, and Ska, B, (2010) A graphic symbol tool for the evaluation of communication, satisfaction and priorities of individuals with intellectual disability who use a speech generating device, *Child Language Teaching and Therapy* 26(3) 303–319

Watson, D, Abbott, D, Townsley, R, (2006) Listen to me, too! Lessons from involving children with complex healthcare needs in research about multi-agency services, *Child: care, health and development*, 33, 1, 90–95

Watson, J, Cameron, L and Murphy, J, (2003) Don't Just Make The Font Bigger, *Learning Disability Practice*, vol 6, no 7, September 2003

Whitehurst, T, (2006) Liberating silent voices – perspectives of children with profound & complex learning needs on inclusion, *British Journal of Learning Disabilities*, 35, 55–61

Wilkins, D; Goodman, L and Hooper, R, (2012) Direct social work with disabled children: The experiences of a specialist team. Guides. *Community Care Inform* [online] http://www.ccinform.co.uk/guides/direct-social-work-with-disabled-children-the-experiences-of-a-specialist-team/ [accessed: 9 March 2015]

Wilson, C (2013) A different language: Implementing the total communication approach, *Scottish Journal of Residential Child Care*, June 2013 – Vol.12, No.1

Winter, K, (2011) *Building Relationships and Communicating with Young Children: A practical guide for social workers*, Routledge: London

Wonnacott, J, Patmore, A, Kennedy, M, (2013) *Assessing the Needs of Disabled Children*, in Calder, M and Hackett, S, (eds) Assessment in child care: using and developing frameworks for practice, 2nd Edition pp185-200. Russell House: London.Wright, K, (2008) Researching the views of pupils with multiple and complex needs.

Is it worth doing and whose interests are served by it? *Support for Learning*, 23, 1

15
'Seeing the Child Alone'
Jacqui Gaunt

Introduction

This chapter will explore the policy of 'seeing the child alone' and its role in child protection; I draw on a range of research, social work theory and serious case reviews. The purpose is to identify best practice and recommendations.

I will first analyse how serious case reviews are used to gain insight into repeated failings to protect children and whether seeing children alone might facilitate greater child protection. Many have revealed the failings of inter-agency communication and co-operation in sharing information. Ferguson points out, 'before information can be shared, someone has to find that information. And to do that you have to go and see the child....' (Ferguson, 2011: 38). The second section explores the practice of seeing a child alone, and how to make this a meaningful experience in terms of gaining an understanding what it is life like for the child and how to maximise opportunities to build effective communication and relationships.

I will then examine the importance of building a successful relationship with the child and one which makes 'seeing the child alone' a worthwhile and productive practice. Munro reports (2011) what children and young people told her review: that what they value most are 'good relationships with professionals they can trust'.

Serious Case Reviews: Lessons to be learnt

What are the main obstacles to seeing the child alone? What are the realistic confines of what is practical and preferable? Seeing 'a child alone' needs to be analysed within the context of what Ferguson states: 'The complexity of social work practice and service users' lives' (2013:119). If there is any point at all in 'seeing the child alone' it is as a significant part of keeping children safe. 'Of all the rights that children now have the one that they rate the most is the right for protection from abuse.' (Munro: 2011:4) Further, Munro reports that children and young people express the view that most important for them are good relationships with professionals they can trust. Munro emphasises the importance of 'creating the right environment for a child to feel that it is "'safe to tell"'. The Children Act 1989 provides a legal duty to ask children their 'wishes and feelings'. This gives a legal imperative to the idea that it is essential to see children alone.

Repeated enquires and reviews assert that professionals did not speak to the children enough. Munro, (2011:6) stresses, '...the importance of listening to the child continues to be repeated in serious case reviews'. In a report by OFSTED (2011), five main messages are highlighted with respect to the voice of the child:

- 'The child was not seen often enough by the professionals involved, or was never asked their views or feelings.
- Agencies did not listen to adults (such as advocates or teachers) who tried to speak up on behalf of the child and who had important information to give.
- Parents (or carers) stopped professionals from seeing and listening to the child.
- Workers paid too much attention to the needs of the parents, and not enough on the needs of the child.
- Agencies did not understand well enough what was going on to protect the child.'

In Lord Laming's extensive report (2003) on the death of Victoria Climbié, many issues regarding 'seeing the child' were raised. It was often difficult for social services to keep track of Victoria who moved house fairly frequently and whose aunt would orchestrate visits and meetings in order to meet her own needs and hide the abuse of Victoria. 'Many parents will resent the worker's involvement and show resistance and hostility' (Howe, 2010:331). When the social worker gained access to Victoria, there is no report of her being directly contacted and spoken to. None of the professionals working with her were able to reflect her wishes and feelings.

The government Inquiry into Victoria Climbié' acknowledges that: '...the authorities charged with her care almost without exception failed to talk to Victoria directly...' Lord Laming reported on the work of one of the social workers on the case that: 'We can only guess at what more Ms Arthurworrey might have learned had she spoken to Victoria on her own. But the fact is she did not speak to Victoria at all during that visit and now 'deeply regrets not doing so'. (Laming 2003:159). Munro (2008) warns against the dangers of 'hindsight error': after we know the outcome of a situation, it is often easy to point out what should have been done. However, why Victoria was not regularly visited, spoken to or attempted to build a relationship with her, was not clear.

Observations from social workers in Laming's Inquiry noted Victoria's 'posture as submissive, very quiet and timid' when she was around her aunt (Laming 2003:73). This and other observations pointed to the controlling nature of Victoria's aunt but this did not alert them to the fact that seeing her alone, away from her aunt, was essential to understanding what life was like for her.

Victoria's first language was French, however, this should not have deterred professionals from speaking to her. Laming (2003) makes the recommendation that interpreters must be employed if English is not the child's first language. Time and skill is needed to build a relationship with a child that will support them and encourage sharing their experiences with you. These aspects of social work were not afforded to Victoria '...the children's 'expert' knowledge should have been a vital part of the compilation and comprehension of the whole picture'. Brandon et al (2005). Ferguson (2005) explores how social workers were repelled by Victoria, she was suffering from scabies, incontinent, unkempt and smelly. Difficult feelings are generated, by the distress one feels, when one is confronted by the realisation, that the child you are protecting disgusts you. Ferguson (2005) uses the phrase 'contamination fears' to explain this idea and promotes a psycho-social approach to explain how Victoria's abuse was missed - 'There is a whole unwritten history of disgust and fear of contamination in child welfare work.' (p.790).

It is a well-documented incident that Peter Connelly had chocolate on his face when the social worker visited and asked that it should be removed. However, this request was not followed through, and so she never discovered the injuries that were being hidden (Haringey Safeguarding Children Board, 2009). Building a relationship with the child and family, ensuring his face is wiped to view what it might be disguising might have made a difference to the protection of 'baby Peter.' Especially important for small children and babies is the routine of picking them up, holding them and talking to them. Indeed, this is essential, so why was it not done? Ferguson (2011) asserts that what could have made a difference to Peter was for the social worker '...to have touched and cleaned the child's face herself, and to have enquired more deeply into the presence of men in the home' (p.101)

The serious case review (SCR) for Blake Fowler identified repeated failings concerning the issue of seeing the child alone. Social workers' approach to seeing Blake was sporadic, he was not seen alone on repeated occasions after significant safeguarding concerns were raised (Southampton Safeguarding Children's Board, 2013). The SCR explains how professionals were distracted by the parents' problems with domestic violence and this detracted from the abuse that Blake was suffering. OFSTED (2011) explored how in several SCRs, problems that the parents were experiencing became the main focus of concern and masked the suffering or risks to the children. Beckett warns against professionals falling into the trap of avoiding 'the child who is the cause of the concern, and form[ing] a kind of alliance with the parents' (2013:49).

Blake was aged seven when he died, was coached by his parents to collude with them and make excuses for his injuries, however, as a young child it is not surprising that he sometimes just told things from his own point of view: 'I get bruises off my dad, but I don't care' (Southampton Safeguarding Children's Board, 2013:26). However, this and other direct disclosures from Blake, and from family members concerned for his welfare, resulted in no further action from professionals. Seeing the child alone and hearing their voice is not sufficient in itself to keeping them safe. As part of the analysis of the many issues arising from this review 'Was practice child-focussed, for example were the child(ren)'s wishes and feelings ascertained and given appropriate priority? Was consideration given to what it was like to be a child living in the family?' (Southampton Safeguarding Children's Board, 2013:68).

The practice of seeing the child alone

The above serious case reviews call into question what exactly is seeing a child? Just having sight of a child is not enough. Phillips (2014) explores the importance of having practice questions around what is being seen. These include: 'What do I need to look for? How will I do so? Who initiates and shapes my seeing? Both what I see and how I see? Can I see the child's everyday life? Can I see bodily effort? Pedestrian movement? What am I afraid to see? Is there enough bodily information to make a defensible decision?' (2014:2267). It is possible that a social worker asking these questions might have made a difference to the outcome.

Ferguson (2011) uses the phase 'intimate social work' to explain the process of getting into people's lives, their homes, their bedrooms, their kitchens and their fridges and to get to know and understand. It may not always be easy to enter these spaces with confidence, '...the issue is how intimate they are prepared to be in entering family members' most private spaces and getting as physically close to children as possible to ensure they are safe'. (Ferguson 2011:68). This physical contact would have supported identification of abuse in many cases, some of which I have analysed, and a relationship where frank and honest dialogue, touch, holding, playing, and doing together is commonplace could fundamentally change the course of some children's experiences (Ferguson, Ruch 2013; Howe 2010; Turney 2012). 'In dialogue, we are subjects seeking understanding and to be understood rather than objects seeking to act upon or be acted upon' (Hoggett 2008).

It is essential to consider the age of the child when deciding what seeing the child alone is like. Children under one-year old are statistically over-represented in child protection plans (NCPCC, 2014), but seeing them alone can be more complex. Parents may carefully guard a small baby and it may be difficult to persuade them to allow you to physically pick them up. Their lack of verbal communication and physical mobility means that physical contact becomes more vital, '...findings suggest that young children are more likely to experience unmet needs in relation to their health and in regard to family and social relationships.' (Cleaver et al, 2011).

As children get older, play-based interaction become more appropriate as children express themselves through play, and as children get more mobile they may need opportunities to be physically active during or before meaningful conversation can take place. 'Depending on their age, stage of development, cognitive abilities and environment, they may have neither the language to name their experience nor the intellectual or affective frameworks through which to interpret or process them.' (Lefevre, 2004:334).

Munro (2011) advises that direct work is a way to aid communication with children. 'There is a variety of tools that can be used to help children communicate their views' (Munro 2011:89). Fahlberg makes the following observation:

> over the course of the young person's growing-up years, repeated intervals of direct work maybe necessary to help him/her learn about him/herself, to integrate early-life experiences with current perspectives of self and others, and to help identify the life-long issues he/she will face as a result of early-life events.(1991:334)

This is further explored by Lefevre (2008) who asserts that a bag of props and resources can act as a focus for building relations and talking to children. These could include: pen/crayons and paper, finger puppets, play dough, small figures or animals, also worksheets and computers which can enhance interaction.

Different considerations accompany the teenage years. The rapid development and, at times, volatile behaviour can make this stage more difficult to negotiate for all involved. Adolescence is also viewed as a time when, due to the rapid neurodevelopment, the brain is malleable and the changes that are taking place, if positively influenced, can support improvement in attachment styles and emotional development. (Fraser & Robinson 2009; Fonagy 2004). Building rapport, using empathy and unconditional respect, being able to tune into humorous banter and slang that is embedded in youth culture, and establishing a shared goal, will all be important in time spent alone with them. (Woodcock Ross, 2011).

Developing effective relationships

This now leads me to explore why it is important to establishing good, professional relationships with children and other service users, as Munro puts it, in order to 'try to understand their experiences, worries, hopes and dreams, and help them change'. (Munro, 2011: 87).

There are different justifications for building successful relationships with children and families. Pragmatically it is important to develop relationships that promote opportunities for seeking change and protecting children. Beyond the pragmatic there are broader ethical principles that apply here. 'This moves the notion of relationship away from the merely instrumental and recognises its potential contribution to emotional and psychological understanding, self development and wellbeing' (Turney 2012:150). Practice that is relationship-based crucially recognises the ethical status of the service user, whether voluntary or involuntary, to be regarded as an individual - 'To be seen as an 'end in themselves' rather than simply as a means to the end of protecting their children from harm' (Turney 2012:150). This draws on the enlightenment philosopher of Immanuel Kant's established principle of the 'categorical imperative' - to treat people as an end in themselves, rather than only as a means to an end as a moral rule to act (Walker 1998)). Respect for persons in this and other senses is, indeed, a fundamental moral principle well established in social work (BASW Code of Ethics, 2012). A relationship-based approach based on ethical principles is identified by Turney (2012: 152) and one of her key claims is that an ethical relationship should be based on three elements: recognition, respect and reciprocity. These are important as they contribute towards readdressing the power differential between social worker, service user and between adult and child.

Recognition needs to be given to the nature of power in social work relationships. Structural assumptions are often at play, which perceive some people as more powerful than others. Fook (2002) questions 'what practices, cultures, systems and structures are upheld by these assumptions?' (p106). Indeed, what actual power relations are preserved or created by them? Relationships that are valued for their own sake and contain recognition, respect and reciprocity help to redistribute power more equally amongst the social worker and the child. However, power is also, what gives some force to authority and as Ferguson explains: 'good authority' is essential to the child protection role. (2011: 173).

Ruch (2013) explains how the psychodynamic approach is important to children's social work as it explain the complexity inherent in behaviour being driven from both conscious and unconscious motivations that are further confounded by the intrapersonal nature of this work. These processes can, sometimes, generate a range of defensive behaviours in service users and it is how these are managed by the social worker that creates the opportunities (Howe, 2008; Ruch, 2005 & Trevithick 2003). Reflective practice is important here because '...reflective practitioners are those who can situate themselves in the context of the situation and can factor this understanding into ways in which they practise' (Fook 2002: 40). The psychodynamic concepts of 'transference' and, particularly, 'countertransference' help one to understand relationships (Freud 1915). Mandell (2008) explains how 'countertransference' has a role to play in relationships and it is not always positive, as it can distort or blur our perceptions of events. Trevithick explores this idea further, looking at a positive aspect of countertransference and explains, 'countertransference reactions, in so far as they correctly mirror another person's thoughts and feelings, enable us to experience some of the emotions that another person might be feeling or thinking' (2003: 170).

This involves a 'use of self' (Mandell, 2008; Ruch, 2000) in a relational and therapeutic approach to social work that aimed, as Parton and O'Byrne (2014:6) explored, '...to find ways of using words to empower lives, to safeguard and support, to bring good futures into view'. Howe (2008:161) explains that, '...those who experience problems recognising, experiencing and regulating their emotions are likely to benefit from forming relationships with those who are emotionally available and responsive, intelligent and psychologically minded'. The use of self facilitates the social worker to offer this level of support.

Ferguson (2010) explores the importance of physical touch and holding to relationships that facilitate emotional development. Also, Ferguson (2010) explores the importance of touch to keeping children safe and his work on 'intimate child protection', advocates touch as part of examining the child for possible injury. Ferguson examines the idea of the disgust and fear that can prevent the social worker touching a child as part of their role. Others question the legitimacy of touch, stating that it may leave children feeling uncomfortable or vulnerable to grooming if boundaries around touches are not clearly drawn. (Lefevre, 2010) Also, it may increase the power differential, where a social worker will touch a child, but children are not free to initiate touches back. (Lynch and Garrett, 2010). Fear of allegation needs to be considered. Fear seems to feature widely in the debate about touch, where professionals may touch service users as part of daily interactions but not admit to it (Piper and Stronach, 2008). It could be asserted that the situation of touch needs to be placed within the wider context of the child's past experiences, age, stage of relationship with you and what they need in terms of reassurance and demonstration of empathy.

Children need to feel touchable and need to have a strong understanding of what is and what is not appropriate touch. There are blurred lines here as professional touch requires adults to be fully aware of how to touch different people in different situations and for different purposes and be able to apply this to practice. It is important to seek the child's view on being touched and for this to always be the guiding factor if, when or how, they are touched. However, it is also for the social worker to set the boundaries if a child is too familiar. Ferguson claims he is, 'pro-touch' and asserts that 'professional touch is a skill that rests on the creative integration of tactile contact performed simply and generously in everyday natural ways, but with determination in the realisation that its use is a vital part of what keeps children safe and feeling cared about and loved' (Ferguson, 2011:110). It can, therefore, be an essential part of seeing a child alone.

A positive approach to relationships is important. Parton and O'Bryne (2000:17) show the importance of '…identifying, or showing interest in, what is going right rather than what is going wrong; what is right about a person's life can mend what is wrong'. This proves an empowering and respectful way of understanding a child's situation and can slowly support change. An opportunity, as Parton and O'Byrne suggest to '…empower them to reclaim and redefine who they are and how they want to act.' (2000:11) A collaborative approach is also important to support change. As Parton and O'Byrne (2000:11) advises the need to '…participate in their social worlds, and cooperative construct social realities.' Through a collaborative approach the issues that have been shared and 'contained' with in the relationship can be offered for joint appraisal and assessment of a way forward. A decision that is reach jointly in this way can be a shared burden and an owned solution that is more likely to result in progress. As explored by Braye and Preston-Shoot (2005), involving young people in their lives, exploring and reflecting with them, makes good practical sense too, as it draws on the insider expertise that children have about their own lives.

Crucially important is affording enough time to build effective relationships. This issue is most pertinent in a political climate that puts great emphasis on the importance of austerity, and where government cuts dominate the political and ideological agenda (Banks 2011). It is indeed important to deliver child protection services that are affordable. Banks explores the recent policy and practice that is '…characterised as stressing the importance of measurable outputs, targets and cost effectiveness in the provision of public services' (2011:5). However, as it is realised that a 'good relationship' is crucial to keeping the child safe, then creating other focuses that prevent this is counter productive. This links to the issue of proceduralism where too much time is spend at the computer by the social worker in activities that keep them away from physically being with the children. It is important that the practice of seeing the child alone is given enough time and is prioritised over other pressures.

A child-led approach

The Children Act 1989 and The Munro Review 2011, assert that the welfare of the child must be paramount. I believe that best practice involves taking this approach a step further and promoting the importance of practice that is not only child centred, but crucially, 'child-led'. This will alter the emphasis in relationship between social worker and child, from being one that it wholly led and developed by the adult, to one that starts with the child and as much as is possible is led by them. This emphasis is typically missing in the serious case reviews.

The notion of child-led practice draws on developmental theorists such as Vygotsky (1978) and Bandura (1977) who emphasize the social nature of learning. Vygotsky (1978) explored the notion of 'scaffolding' that explains how children's learning is supported by interactions with others. It can in Vygotsky's theories be either children or adults that act as the 'scaffold' and provide the support and stimulation for the child to progress and develop crucial skills such as communication, emotional regulation and expression. For adults to provide the scaffold they would strive to understand where a child is at developmentally, and use this knowledge to support them through interaction that builds on the child's understanding, interest and ideas. This gives emphasis to the importance of the social worker having a good knowledge of child development and expected developmental norms. The supporting or scaffolding children's emotional and social development is an important part of social work practice. This facilitates an understanding of what it is like in the child's world. I believe understanding this, is to understand when the child is safe and how to keep them safe. Scaffolding a child's development supports the children to be able keep themselves safe, and promote their own wellbeing. The theory of scaffolding involves getting along side the child, listening and following their lead, whilst also providing structure, direction and support. This facilitates a trusting relationship where the child can share their world, thoughts and feelings with their social worker.

Recent child development policy (DCSF, 2008, 2009, 2012) explored these issues of balancing child-led and adult-led activities. Adult led activities that are thoughtfully provided can scaffold a child's social and emotional development and understanding. For example, various forms of 'direct work' can be used to support the child to understand and express their views and feelings. If the adult is too dominant, adult-led time could be filled with activity that for the child is 'hands on and brain off' (DCSF, 2009:5). In other words the child's engagement is passive, contrived and forced and the result is unlikely to be the child expressing its own thoughts and feelings. Child-led activities give the child more opportunity for free expression, they are more likely to reveal the child's interests, ideas, feelings and level of understanding. Child-led activity can provide opportunity for you to see what the child sees. This could be a simple as asking the child to show you round and tell you about their house. Or if they are playing, ask if you can join their game and then follow their led. Or saying, 'when I visit next, what would you like us to do?' and let the child choose. Having choice, gives the children a sense that they have some power and control and promotes trust in your relationship.

Summary and concluding thoughts

Child-led practice can be operationalized in three following ways.

- Activity that are based on understanding a child's developmental stage and that scaffolds their social and emotional development to help them progress such skills. Also, to scaffold their skills of language and communication to facilitate free expression, could include using non-verbal communication, pictures etc. The training and resources of newly qualified as well as experienced social workers are essential to achieving this.

- The need to promote opportunities that are varied and flexible so that the child can have a central role in their own planning. This should include 'choice' for the child, so that they can view the time that is spent 'seeing the child alone' as their time. Letting the child lead the play when ever possible, and let them be the teacher/leader showing you how things work at school/home etc.
- Lastly, with babies and very young children, touch becomes essential to practice. You cannot expect to keep a small child safe if you do not, over time, build a relationship where you handle, hold and have close contact with them. Intimate child protection becomes essential to keeping these children safe (Ferguson 2011).

These activities are basic elements of good interaction with children and should take precedence over administration in the high priority task of regulation to record data set against targets that do nothing to improve the quality of life of a child.

This chapter has explored the policy of 'seeing the child alone' and argues for a relationship-based, child-led approach that engages the child fully in the time that the social worker spends with them. Giving the child a voice and a sense of ownership and choice is crucial so that the time spent alone is effective and focused. However, until social workers spend more direct one-to-one time with children there will be a continued risk of sad cases like Victoria Climbié's occurring.

References

Balloch, S. (1998) Pahl, J. & McLean, J., Working in the Social Services: Job Satisfaction, Stress and Violence. *British Journal of Social Work*, 28: 329-350

BASW (2012) *The Code of Ethics for Social Work*. BASW: Birmingham

Bandura, A. (1977) *Social Learning Theory*. New Jersey: Prentice Hall

Banks, S. (2011) 'Ethics and the Age of Austerity: Social Work and the Evolving New *Public Management. Journal of Social Intervention: Theory and Practice* –

2011 – vol 20, issue 2 pp5-23

Beckett, C. (2013) *Child Protection: an introduction*. London: Sage

Bell, M., Shaw, I., Sinclair, I., Sloper, P., & Rafferty, J (2007) *An evaluation of the practice, process and consequences of the ICS in councils with social services responsibilities*. Report to the Dept for Education and Skills Welsh Assembly Govt., May 2007

Blom-Cooper, L. (1985) *A Child in Trust: The report of the panel of inquiry into the circumstances surrounding the death of Jasmine Beckford*, LB Brent, London

Brandon, M., Dodsworth, J. and Rumball, D, (2005) Serious Case Reviews: Learning to Use Expertise. *Child Abuse Review*, Vol 14: 160-176

Braye, S. & Preston-Shoot, M. (2010) *Practising Social Work Law*, 3rd. Edn. Basingstoke: Palgrave Macmillan

Chambers, D. (2012) *A Sociology of Family Life: change and diversity in intimate relations*. Cambridge: Polity Press

Children Act (1989). London: TSO

Cleaver, H., Unell, I. and Aldgate, J. (1999) *Children's Needs - Parenting Capacity: The impact of parental mental illness, problem alcohol and drug use, and domestic violence on children's development*. HMSO: HMSO

Collier, R. and Sheldon, S. (2008) *Fragmenting Fatherhood*. Oxford: Hart Publishing

Cunningham, H. (1995) *Children and Childhood in Western Society since 1500*. Harlow: Longman

Cunningham, J. & S. *Social Policy and Social Work*. Sage: London

DCFS (2009) *Learning, Playing and Interacting*, London: The National Strategies. HMSO: London

Demos, D. H. and Cox, M. J. (2000) Families with young children: a review of research in the 1990s. *Journal of Marriage and the Family* 62: 876-895

Report of the Committee of Inquiry in to Care and Supervision Provided in relation to Maria Colwell, DHSS. (1974) HMSO: HMSO

Duncan, S. and Smith, D. (2006) *Individualisation versus the geography of 'new' families*. Twenty First Century Society 1: 167-189

East Sussex County Council (1975) *Children At Risk: report of inquiry into the case of Maria Colwell*. East Sussex County Council

Fahlberg , V. I. (1991) *A Child's Journey through Placement*. Perspectives Press: London

Ferguson, H. (2005) Working with Violence, the Emotions and the Psycho-social Dynamics of Child Protection: Reflections on the Victoria Climbié Case. *Social Work Education*, Vol 24, No 7, October 2005, pp 781-795

Ferguson, H. (2011) *Child Protection Practice*. Palgrave: Macmillan Basingstoke

Ferguson, H. (2013) Ch 12, *Social workers as agents of change*. In: Gray, M. and Webb, S.A. (Eds.) (2013) The New Politics of Social Work. Palgrave

Macmillan: Basingstoke
Fonargy, P. (2004) *Attachment Theory and Psychoanalysis*. Karnac: London
Fook, J. (2002) *Social Work: critical theory and practice*. Sage: London
Framework for the Assessment of Children in Need and their Families. (2000). London: D of H
Freud, S. (1915) *The Standard Edition of the Complete Psychological Works of Sigmund Freud*. Hogarth Press: London
Hargie, O. (2011) *Skilled Interpersonal Communication*. 5th edn. London: Routledge
Greer, G. (1970) *The Female Eunuch*. MacGibbon & Kee: London
Haringey Safeguarding Children Board, (2009) London Borough of Haringey: London
Harrison, C. (2008) Implacably hostile or appropriately protective? Women managing child contact in the context of domestic violence. *Violence Against Women* 14: (4), 381-405
Holmes, L., McDermid, S., Jones, A., & Ward, H. (2009) '*How Social Workers Spend Their Time*. DfCSF: London
Hoggett, P. (2008) *Relational thinking and welfare practice*. In: Clarke, S. Hahn, H. & Hoggett, P., (eds) Object relations and social relations: the implications of the relational turn in psychoanalysis. pp 65-86
Horwath, J. (2010) *The Child's World*. 2nd ed. Jessica Kingsley: London
Howe, D. (2010) The safety of children and the parent-worker relationships in cases of child abuse and neglect. *Child Abuse Review*, 19: 5, 330-341
Howes, N. (2010), *Here to Listen!* In Howarth, J. (ed). The Child's World. Chapter 12. Jessica Kingsley: London
Isle of Wight Serious Case a Review Relating to the Q family, (2015). I o W: IoWSCB
Kant, I. (1781) *The Critique of Pure Reason*, translated by N Kemp-Smith. St Martins Press: New York
Kehily, M. J. (2010) Childhood in crisis? Tracing the contours of 'crisis' and its impact upon contemporary parenting. *Media, Culture & Society* 32, 171-85
Kolakowski, L. (1978) *Main Currents of Marxism*. Oxford: Oxford University Press
Laming, H. (2003) *The Victoria Climbie' Inquiry : Report of an enquiry by Lord Laming*. HMSO: London
Lefevre, M. (2004) 'Playing with sound: the therapeutic use of music in direct work with children. In: *Child and Family Social Work*, vol 9: 333-345
Lefevre, M., Richards, S. & Trevithick, P. (2008) '*Using play and the creative arts to communicate with children and young people*. www. scie.org.uk
Lefevre, M., Tanner, K. & Luckcock, B. (2008) 'Developing social work students' communication skills with children and young people' In: *Child and Family Social Work*, vol 13: 166-176,
Lefevre, M . (2010) *Communicating with children and young people: making a difference*. Bristol: The Polity Press: Bristol

Lynch, R. And Garrett, P.M. (2010) ' More than words: touch practices in child and family social work'. In: *Child and Family Social Work*, 2010, 15: 389-398,

London Borough of Brent (1985) *A Child In Trust: report of the panel of enquiry investigating the circumstances surrounding the death of Jasmine Beckford*. LBB: London

Mandell, D.(2008) 'Power, Care and Vulnerability: considering use of self in child welfare work. *Journal of social Work Practice*. Vol 22, no. 2: 235-248

Munro, E. (2008) *Effective Child Protection*, 2nd ed. Sage: London

Munro, E. (2011) *The Munro Review of Child Protection Interim Report: The Child's Journey*. Department for Education: London

Munro, E. (2011) *Young Person's Guide to the Munro Review of Child Protection*, Department for Education: London

OFSTED, (2011) *The Voice of the Child: Learning Lessons from Serious Case Reviews*, TSO: London

Parton, N. (2014) *The Politics of Child Protection*: Palgrave Macmillan: Basingstoke

Parton, N.and O'Byrne, P. (2000) *Constructive Social Work towards a new practice*. Palgrave Macmillan: Basingstoke

Pease, B. (2013) 'A History of Critical and Radical Social Work' in: The New Politics Of Social Work, Ed. By Gray, M. & Webb, S.A. Bh: Palgrave Macmillan: Basingstoke

Piaget, J. (1962) *Play, Dreams and Imitation in Childhood*. Routledge: London

Philips, C.R. (2014) 'Seeing the child beyond the literal: considering dance choreography and the body in child welfare and protection'. In: *British Journal of Social Work*, 2014, 44: 2254-2271. Palgrave Macmillan: Basingstoke

Ruch, G. (2007) 'Reflective Practice in Contemporary Child-care Social Work: The Role of Containment. *British Journal of Social Work*, 37 (4) 659-680

Ruch, . (2013) "Helping Children is a Human Process': Researching the Challenges Social Workers Face in Communicating with Children'. In: *British Journal of Social Work*, 2013, March, 1-18

Scott, P. D. (1975) The Tragedy of Maria Colwell, *British Journal of Social Work*, 15, (1) 88-90

Sheldon, B. & MacDonald, G. (2009) *A Text Book of Social Work*. Routledge: Abingdon

Southampton Safeguarding Children's Board, (2013) Blake Fowler Inquiry Report. SSCB

Storo, J. (2013) *Practical Social Pedagogy*. Policy Press: Bristol

Trevithick, P. (2003) 'Effective relationship-based practice: a theoretical exploration' In: *Journal of Social Work Practice*, vol 17, 2 (163-176)

Trevithick, P.(2011) 'Understanding Defence And Defensiveness in Social Work'. In: *Journal of Social Work Practice*. Vol. 25, (4) : 389-412

Trotter, C. (2006) *Working with Involuntary Clients*, 2nd edn. Sage: London

Turney, D. (2012) 'A relationship-based approach to engaging involuntary clients: the contributing of recognition theory. In: *Child & Family Social Work*, 17: 149-159

Upton, S., Varma, V., and Davey, R. (2003) *The Voice of the Child: handbook for professionals*. London: Routledge

United Nations Convention on the Rights of the Child (1989). unicef.org

Vygotsky, L. (1978) *Interaction Between Learning and Development, From Mind and Society* pp79-91 Harvard University Press: Cambridge MA

Walker, R. (1998) *Kant: Kant and the moral law*. Phoenix: London

Westwood, J. (2014) *Children In Need of Support*. Palgrave Macmillan: Basingstoke

Woodcock-Ross, J. (2011) *Specialist Communication Skills for Social Workers*, Palgrave Macmillan: Basingstoke

Zeller, V.A. (1985) *Pricing The Priceless Child: the changing social value of children*. Basic Books: New York

16
Exploring digital technology and its potential to improve outcomes

Anthony McMurdo

Introduction

Hill and Shaw (2011) state that the use of digital technology in social work is neglected in academic discourses, and undervalued in practice. I agree whilst hypothesising that current and emerging digital technology can be utilized more effectively to improve social work practice, and consequently improve outcomes for service users. To explore this hypothesis effectively it is first important to define the terms. Social work is broadly defined as an academic discipline and practice based profession concerned with the facilitation of change and development in society by promoting social justice, empowerment, and liberation (International Federation of Social Workers, 2014). Digital technology is defined in a simplified manner as electrical technology that uses binary data to function, which includes technology such as computers and mobile phones (Woodford, 2006).

The examination of digital technology and its potential for change in social work is said to be of vital importance to the continued development of the profession and practice (Hill & Shaw, 2011). To justify this claim Hill and Shaw (2011) state that by its very nature of being concerned with society, social work must recognise the ubiquity of digital technology and the impact it has upon society at macro and micro levels. However others are not as positive with pessimism stemming from a humanist perspective, an approach that fears digital technology will dehumanize social work (Steyaert & Gould, 2010). These conflicting perceptions will be a theme addressed throughout this chapter, which will explore a multitude of current and potential uses of digital technology in social work.

What is digital technology?

Digital technology uses electronic binary language to function, to store, communicate, and process data (Woodford, 2006). Essentially the label of digital technology can be applied to the vast majority of electronic technology found in modern society (Kare-Silver, 2011). This includes digital technology commonly used by social workers such as the internet, telephones, computers and mobile devices (Hill & Shaw, 2011). Currently it is suggested that these digital technologies are predominantly used by social workers to record data and as a communication tool (ibid).

Bunz (2014) promotes digital technology as having significant benefits for society in relation to its impact on economy and productivity. Bunz (2014) also notes that on a social level digital technology is often depicted as a threat that will negatively impact upon social interactions and human behaviour. As stated previously social work is concerned with both the macro and micro facets of society, as such social workers need to be mindful of these perceptions, in addition to the influence and transformative power of digital technology (Hill & Shaw, 2011).

The digital divide

According to Prensky (2001; 2011) a generational digital divide impacts the value individuals ascribe to digital technology, in addition to their capacity to utilise if effectively. Here Prensky (2001) claimed that digital technologies rapid growth in modern society created a divide between what he termed digital natives and digital immigrants. According to Prensky (2001) digital natives are those born in the 1980's into a digital society, for whom digital technology use is natural because they have utilised it throughout their life path. Digital immigrants however grew and developed in a less digital society, as such they do not naturally 'speak' the digital language (ibid). According to Prensky (2001) this results in older individuals being less competent with, and appreciative of, digital technology.

Steyaert and Gould (2010) link this to social work and social policy in their claim that historically, social work commentators have perceived the profession as being pessimistic about digital technology. Hill and Shaw (2011) also identify this pessimism whilst stating that it is an outdated barrier to improving practice. Dunn, Braddell and Sunderland (2014) researched the perceptions and use of digital technology in social work settings, gathering data from social workers and managers using desk research, site visits and questionnaires. The data highlighted a disparity in digital skills, with managers perceiving age divisions as correlating with social workers digital competences (ibid). Furthermore Dunn et al's (2014) research also indicated that managers perceived younger social workers as being more likely to seek and utilise the potential benefits of digital technology.

Dunn et al's (2014) evidence supports the notion of a generational digital divide in the social work profession. Although Salajan, Schönwetter and Cleghorn (2010) argue that this popular duality theory is an oversimplification of a skill divide influenced by more complex processes. Evidence supporting this comes from Guo, Dobson and Petrina (2008) who directly tested the digital divide theory by assessing the digital competency of 2583 students, aged between twenty and forty. Students aged 20-24 scored 22.05 on a digital competency questionnaire; with students age 30-40 scoring 22.36 (ibid). In essence these results could be seen to discredit the notion of a generational digital divide, suggesting that age is not always a primary factor for divides in digital skills and attitudes towards technology.

It is important to note that Prensky (2011) claims his digital divide theory must by its very nature have a limited period of validity, whereby it is inevitable that a time will come where all humans alive would have been born into a digital society. Despite this inevitability, research still indicates that social work students are not as digitally competent as those in other sectors (Margaryan, Littlejohn, & Vojt, 2011). In essence the notion of a generational digital divide appears to be a complex theory; perhaps it is transitory, non-existent or a brief phenomenon. However what is important to appreciate is that a digital skill divide exists in some form.

Social work training in a digital age

For Candra and Sharma (2007) education is a philosophical concept regarding the acquisition of knowledge and personal development. Buckley and Caple (2007) agree whilst defining training as a process tailored towards the development of a distinct set of skills for a specific task. The Health and Care Professions Council [HCPC](2016) outlined the importance of high quality social worker training in a review of programmes, which indicated that 96% of programmes required changes to comply with their standards. A need for change in social work education is also voiced by the Secretary of State for Education Nicky Morgan who unveiled plans to invest heavily in this area (Morgan & DfE, 2016). The government reportedly plans to improve social work training through increased funding and the formation of a new social work governing body (Morgan & DfE, 2016). It is my view that this suggested improvement and restructuring of social work training should also look to digital technology to facilitate learning.

Digital technology in social work education

Braye and Preston-Shoot's (2016) findings suggest that digital presentations are the most common digital technology found in social work education. Inoue-Smith and Wang (2016) agree whilst stating that Microsoft PowerPoint is the predominant software used by lecturers in the digital age. In a study of lecturer's perceptions and use of PowerPoint over more traditional methods, such as a whiteboard or chalkboard, Inoue-Smith and Wang (2016) provide evidence to suggest that PowerPoint can have significant pedagogical value. Whereby lecturers reportedly kept students engaged in learning through stimulating and interactive content. However this value appeared reliant, much like previous methods, on the lecturer's ability to use PowerPoint effectively as a teaching device (ibid).

However Brandl, Schneid and Armour (2015) report that 85% of their undergraduate sample preferred lecturers to use whiteboards instead of digital presentation. Here students reportedly felt digital presentations inhibited engagement and were filled with unnecessary information (ibid). Furthermore Braye and Preston-Shoot (2016) note that PowerPoints are potentially used instead of more creative digital technologies due to time constraints, inferring that PowerPoint lectures are not the most productive use of digital technology in universities. This perspective is also present in Henderson, Selwyn and Aston's (2015) study of 1658 Australian university students' perceptions of what digital technology supported learning. The results indicated that productivity and organizational uses were most appreciated by the students (ibid). Henderson *et al* (2015) concluded that this indicates the notions of creative and transformative influences of digital technology, present in popular discourses, are not overtly present in education.

Here it must be considered that discourses of social work education place significant value on autonomous learning (Worsley & Littler, 2013). This is defined as self-directed learning that sees the individual become their own educator, who seeks the knowledge required to advance their skills and understanding (Peters, 2001). When considering this perhaps for social work education it could be theorised that the negative aspects of digital presentations, outlined by Brandl *et al* (2015), are not as impactful. I suggest this because studies consistently indicate that the ability to revisit digital presentations to revise and guide future learning is a strength of the medium (Brandl *et al*, 2015; Henderson *et al*, 2015). In essence this suggests that digital presentations and their overabundance of information (ibid), provide social work students with signposts to further learning they can seek autonomously.

Advancing social work education with digital technology

Henderson *et al* (2015) state, that digital technology has not fulfilled its perceived potential as a transformative element that could revolutionize education. When considered with the notion that digital technology has just modernized traditional pedagogical approaches (Brandl *et al*, 2015), it becomes apparent that it is important to investigate if more can be done to harness digital technology in a transformative manner. In Social Work education the University of Kent (2016) appear to be undertaking work to answer this question, through the development of interactive digital child protection simulations. These simulations are part of a package being developed called 'Virtually Safe' which includes games currently called Rosie 1, Rosie 2 and Rosie: My Courtroom (ibid).

According to Reeves (2016) these simulations have been created to revolutionise social work education, by utilising digital technology to provide a learning experience that allows students to safely explore Child Protection situations. An example of this can be found in Rosie1 where students are able to undertake an initial home visit to investigate concerns of sexual abuse in the virtual environment (Centre for Child Protection, 2014). Moreover according to Reeves (2016), the aim of these simulations is to allow students to bring together placement and university learning through an interactive experience. This experience reportedly facilitates critical thinking, reflection, analysis and other important learning mechanisms in a fashion not facilitated by traditional methods used in social work education (ibid). Loveless (2002) agrees that the use of computers and digital games, such as those discussed here, can enhance learning. It is suggested that this, in addition to computers ability rapidly automate tasks and present the data required for learning, allows students to spend a more time directly engaged with meaningful learning experiences (Easingwood, 2007). The behaviourist learning theory of connectionism claims that a result of this will be the increased use and subsequent development of higher-order thinking skills (Pritchard, 2009).

Higher-order thinking skills are defined as the cognitive abilities used to understand and evaluate information, in addition to being able to analyse and synthesis information (Lincoln, 2008). These higher order thinking skills also include the ability to perform a competent application of learning and knowledge in practice. Moreover, Lincoln (2008) states that these skills can be developed through the use of digital technology. According to connectionism theories digital games or simulations would increase an individual's higher-order thinking and competence through repetitive practice linked to feedback (Pritchard, 2009). This is, according to Pritchard (2009), due to the digital game providing an experience that will strengthen the stimulus response associated with the skills being practiced. In essence this can be seen to provide strong theoretical evidence for the benefits of using digital simulations in social work education, to practice the many skills needed to be a competent professional.

In addition to theoretical evidence, real world studies into the impact of digital simulations on learning must be considered. Initial evidence to highlight the benefits of digital technology comes from Vogel *et al's* (2006) meta-analysis of 32 studies into the influence of digital games on learning. Here Vogel *et al* (2006) concluded that digital games clearly triggered higher learner motivation and engagement. Moreover, the learning provided by digital games and simulations reportedly resulted in increased cognitive development (ibid). This is supported further by Gegenfurtner, Quesada-Pallarès and Knogler's (2014) meta-analysis of 15 studies and 25 years of research into digital simulations, which correlates

Vogel et al's (2006) findings. Gegenfurtner et al's (2014) study concluded that digital simulations have high levels of efficacy which results in a significant level of skill transferability to real world practice. In essence these studies appear to provide strong evidence to validate the claims of Reeves (2016).

Focusing directly on the digital simulation Rosie1, Reeves, Drew, Shemmings and Ferguson (2015) completed a small scale study into its use by eight social workers, five health visitors, and eleven control participants from different sectors. During this study eye tracking devices were coupled with digital algorithms to record the emotional responses of participants. Here social workers were recorded as spotting signs of neglect a mean of 35 times, with the control sample having a mean of 18. Moreover social workers where almost twice as likely to display neutral emotional responses to situations, with the control sample being approximately five times more likely to respond with anger (ibid). This can be used to highlight a strength of the Rosie1 simulation, in that it is able to provide an immersive experience that can trigger emotions and therefore learning (Gegenfurtner et al, 2014).

However, Reeves et al's (2015) study inadvertently raises a limitation of digital simulations. That they are unable to adequately read, respond, or simulate body language. Haaster (2014) agrees by noting the importance of the embodied experience for learning, stating that digital games and role play may not provide learning from the nuanced body language and physical presence of the person being communicated with. This is supported by Fitch, Canada, Cary and Freese's (2016) study of role play using digital technology in social work education, which provided strong evidence to suggest that learners find more benefit in role plays that allow the exploration of body language whilst communicating. Here it must be highlighted that in a recent pilot of a Government social work accreditation scheme 20% of participants failed a traditional role play assessment with actors (McNicoll, 2016). When considered together this provides some validity to concerns regarding digital technology dehumanizing social work practice (Steyaert & Gould, 2010).

Assessments in social work

According to Parker (2008) assessment is a core function of social work, which permeates every aspect of the role through a need to constantly assess and plan for outcomes and interventions based on a vast array of causal or influential factors. For Smale, Tuson and Statham (2000) it is key to understand that social work assessments can have profound impacts, such as a child being removed from their family. According to public data there is a 20% rise in care cases being heard in court (Munby, 2016). These are hearings regarding the potential removal of a child from their family due to safety concerns, which statistics show have risen from 6786 in 2006-7 to an estimated 15485 in 2016-17 (ibid). Munby (2016) states that it is implausible to claim this rise is solely due to significant increases in children experiencing significant harm, and is indicative of the Baby P case having a profound impact on Local Authority behaviour. Moreover Munby (2016) states that Local Authority and social worker behaviour must have a causal relationship with this rise in children being assessed as needing to be separated from their family (ibid). This evidences a need to explore how social workers undertake assessments, whilst investigating the potential influence of digital technology.

Gathering data

I would argue that assessments can be improved through digital technologies. Smale et al (2000) perceive data collection as a primary task of social work that is clearly crucial to the assessment process. Furthermore, data collection is predominantly completed through a form of interview conducted by the social worker. During these assessment interviews social workers are required to use a broad range of skills to investigate and discern a wide range of facts to use in assessments (Martin, 2010).

Data collected must be accurate and capture the voice of those being assessed (Martin, 2010). Kadushin and Kadushin (2013) agree and state that note taking during interviews can ensure accuracy, whilst demonstrating to the interviewee that you value their views. Broadhurst et al's (2010) research highlights the importance of accurate recording, with a serious case review stressing the need to do this competently and in a timely manner (Wonnacott & Watts, 2014). Social workers report that it is this case recording and administrative aspect of their role that causes time constraints, which results in a reduced ability to complete work with families effectively (Unison & Community Care, 2014). As such it could be suggested that social workers would benefit from a digital technology that saves time and accurately records interviews.

According to the Health and Social Care Information Centre [HSCI](2013) digital dictation can offer accurate transcripts of meetings, with time and cost savings. The HSCI (2013) define digital dictation as the use of a microphone and voice recognition software to convert speech to text, which they see as being beneficial for social workers. Qualitative evidence supporting the use of digital dictation comes from Dr Camphor (2013), who perceives the tool as a valuable technology that has allowed him to focus on the patient instead of taking notes.

Vogel, Kaisers, Wassmuth and Mayatepek (2015) provide substantial evidence to suggest digital dictation can improve data capture for social work interviews. Here Vogel et al (2015) analysed 1,455 reports from 28 medical practitioners, 718 using digital dictation and 737 typed traditionally, with the analysis indicating digital dictation was 26% faster. Additionally digital dictation was reportedly more accurate, with professionals using digital dictation also displaying more positive moods (ibid). Research indicates that both doctors (Nuance Healthcare Solutions, 2015), and social workers (Unison & Community Care, 2014), spend a significant amount of time on data entry and recording. Moreover they reportedly feel this negatively impacts upon the time spent with service users which may be detrimental to overall outcomes (Unison & Community Care, 2014; Nuance Healthcare Solutions, 2015). When considered together this provides strong evidence supporting the view that digital dictation can improve social work practice.

However it is important to note that research highlights a significant difference in the levels of trust service users report for social workers when compared to medical professionals (Ipsos MORI & British Medical Association [BMA], 2011). Whereby 1020 individuals were polled and 88% of these reported they would trust doctors to tell the truth, compared to only 60% viewing social workers as truthful (ibid). Mellon (2016) states that the current perception of social work, and the bureaucratic processes involved with risk assessment, has created a mutual distrust between social workers and service users. When considered together this indicates that service users may be mindful of what they disclose to social workers, which may be exacerbated if conversations are captured through digital dictation (Fontes, 2008). However digital dictation captures an accurate that would result in a more balanced power dynamic, increased trust, and ultimately better outcomes (Scharer, 2015).

Analysing data

In addition to gathering data, a primary role of the social worker is to critically analyse information (Turney, Platt, Selwyn, & Farmer, 2011). This analysis is crucial because it directs provisions and interventions towards a family, with a robust analysis creating improved outcomes and poor analysis leading to inferior outcomes (ibid). In the context of statutory social work, assessment and analysis is usually focused on child protection whereby risk screening and reduction is a primary motivator or focus for practice (Mellon, 2016). In this context risk is defined as the probability of a factor to cause harm to an individual (Social Care Institute for Excellence [SCIE], 2007).

This definition of risk is also enshrined in the Section 47 of the Children Act 1989, which outlines the legal requirement for Local Authorities to investigate when there is reason to believe a child is at risk of harm. There is currently a need to address the significant increase of children being assessed as at risk of significant harm, and the concern that a high proportion of cases should perhaps not have been assessed as being as high risk as they have (Munby, 2016).

Munby (2016) and Mellon (2016) both perceive social worker analysis of risk as being significantly influenced by media, public, and political discourses surrounding the case of Baby P. Here it is hypothesised that social workers have become too risk adverse due to a culture of blame resulting from narratives around tragic outcomes, such as Baby P's death, as being the fault of poor quality social work risk analysis (ibid). Evidence supporting this view comes from Macleod, Hart, Jeffes and Wilkin (2010) whose research into the impact of Baby P's death highlighted a shift to more risk adverse practice and lower thresholds for care proceedings. According to Turney *et al's* (2011) research it may be possible to view effective multi-agency practice as a means to avoiding this, by facilitating more accurate and holistic assessments.

Ultimately Turney *et al's* (2011) research can be used to validate the suggestion that multi-agency practice would result in a more robust analysis, and therefore improved outcomes. This theme is also present in Munro's (2011) review of Child Protection, in which she highlights a need for professionals to work in partnership to identify and manage risk. For Hill and Shaw (2011) this can be facilitated through digital technologies capacity to share information between professionals with relative ease. According to Hill and Shaw (2011) the digital technologies commonly used by social workers and other professionals, to share data and communicate, are computers and mobile phones. Moreover some Local Authorities use digital forms and record keeping systems that are designed to promote joint access or simplified sharing of records, which can promote multi-agency analysis (ibid) and improve risk analysis (Home Office, 2014),

Looking to the future there are discourses promoting and attempting to use digital technology and complex algorithms to analyse digital data to automate risk analysis (Peachey, 2016). Whilst others perceive the use of digital technology in risk analysis as negative impacting on the validity of the analysis and dehumanizing social work processes (Steyaert & Gould, 2010).

Laming's (2003) inquiry into the death of Victoria Climbé can be seen to agree with the concerns raised by Styaert and Gould (2010). Here Laming (2003) claims that interpersonal communication, that occurs through face to face discussions between professionals, facilitates a mutual understanding of information. This is reportedly lost in digital communication as cues from body language are missing (ibid). This view is supported further by Turney *et al's* (2011) research, that recorded digital technology used by social workers to capture data forced them to standardise information to fit predetermined boxes. A consequence was that over time records failed to capture a holistic view of the child and lost elements of the family's narrative (ibid). Moreover social workers reportedly felt that the digitization of the profession reduced the amount of time working directly with families (Turney *et al*, 2011). Essentially this evidences a significant weakness of digital technology being used in social work assessments.

Digital direct work

According to the College of Social Work (2014) assessments are used to plan for interventions targeting change, whilst further exploring the child's wishes and feelings. Being able to do this in a robust and effective manner, to improve outcomes, is a key role of social work (Parker, 2008). Smale, Tuson and Statham (2000) point to direct work as fulfilling this role by engage with a child, the family, and their network, to confront issues impacting upon them. Moreover direct work, if facilitated well, is perceived as a powerful agent of change (ibid). Bronfenbrenner (1986) outlines how a child's developmental path can be impacted by their environment. Coleman and Hagell (2007) agree and highlight that children who experience forms of maltreatment can face negative outcomes, such as emotional and behavioural difficulties. These outcomes can be said to have macro and micro impacts on the child's life path (ibid). Ultimately social workers must be capable of delivering direct work that identifies risk factors and support the child to manage negative outcomes caused by their experiences.

The literature suggests that in social work practice direct work is associated with using worksheets, art, and play, to explore the child's views and support their understanding (Tait & Wuso, 2012; Luckock & Lefevre, 2008). This is seen as promoting relationship building, allowing the child's views to be heard, and for change to be nurtured (ibid). Digital technology does not seem to be considered in common discourses around direct work, nor have I observed it being used frequently during my social work training. The exception to this is within direct work with children with disabilities, where digital technology is commonly used to encourage interactions and improve communication (Adams & Leshone, 2016). It is my view that the use of digital technology can be greatly expanded, to improve outcomes and increase the social workers 'toolbox'. The HCPC (2016) can be seen to agree through their recommendation that social workers should be knowledgeable of developments in digital technology.

Video games as direct work

It is my contention that video games can be used in direct work by social workers to improve outcomes. For Newman (2013) video games are defined simply as a game played on a computer. Figures indicate that video game revenue in the UK reached £2.96bn in 2016, compared to £2.25bn for the video industry and £1.1bn for music (Entertainment Retailers Association, 2017). This evidences how widespread video game use has become, which is highlighted further by figures stating that in 2016 78% of children aged 5-15 played video games, as did 45% of 3-4 year olds (Ofcom, 2016). Essentially supporting the notion that social workers should consider video games as a potential tool, due to their high usage among children.

In considering this it could be suggested that video games could facilitate a personalised approach, an approach perceived as promoting change (Beresford, 2014). In her research Harvey (2015) states that video games are frequently subject to moral panics, whereby they are considered a threat to normative social functioning, whilst also promoting violence. Perhaps multiple moral panics, and professional uncertainty of video games, has resulted in a lack of exploration of the medium by social workers. If we consider that the US Supreme Court ruled that there is no conclusive evidence for video games causing violence (Epstein & Walker, 2012), a notion also present in multiple studies (Kutner & Olson, 2008; Ferguson & Kilburn, 2009), this suggests video games should not be dismissed as a direct work tool.

Stoll and Collett (2013) agree, stating that video games can be used to support an understanding and improvement of a child's wellbeing. Video games can be used by children to support emotional regulation and facilitate positive outcomes such as relaxation and stress reduction (ibid). These themes are also present in Dawson, Cragg, Taylor and Toombs' (2007) research recording children and adults expressing a view that video games aid relaxation, by facilitating escapism from the frustrations and strains in life. Research into recovery from daily stressors also highlights how escapism through video games can support an individual's ability to manage negative stressors (Collins & Cox, 2013; Reinecke, 2009). In essence, the evidence indicates social workers could engage in video game play as with children to offer beneficial support and reduce stress (Horn & Reyes, 2014). This is supported by Reilly and Dolan (2015).

Video game use is also play, with play being a philosophical concept involving activities that help children to make sense of the human condition, their experiences, and the world they inhabit (Eichberg, 2016). Fromberg and Bergen (2006) agree whilst defining play simply as an activity engaged in instinctively for enjoyment, with an important focus on child development. Essentially, it can be considered that video games could be utilised by social workers to improve outcomes by enhancing a child's insight into their life experiences (Goldstein, 2012, Van Deventer & White, 2002).

Horn and Reyes (2014) agree in their claim that the treatment of trauma and associated symptoms of maltreatment, can benefit from a focus on exploring the maltreatment itself. Initial evidence supporting my claim comes from research into game based therapy with children who had experienced sexual abuse (Misurell, Springer, Acosta, Liotta, & Kranzler, 2014). The study strongly indicated that game based therapy allowed children to develop insight into their abuse, whilst also reducing negative outcomes such as anxiety, depression, anger, stress, and behavioural issues (ibid). These outcomes correlated strongly with a research review highlighting substantial evidence of commercial and specially designed video games being used to promote recovery in children who had experienced abuse (Horne-Moyer, Moyer, Messer, & Messer, 2014).

Horne-Moyer *et al* (2014) further highlights the potential to improve an abused child's social functioning and behaviour through video games. However whilst discounted earlier moral panic around video games causing negative behaviours must be considered, because 'Folk Devils and Moral Panic' contain elements of validity as a catalyst for their creation (Cohen, 2011). Social cognitive theory of learning supports this claim as behaviour is learnt from observations of modelled behaviour, such as violence in video games (Hobart, 2012). Investigations by Kutner and Olson (2008) support this whereby 60% of their sample reportedly played violent video games and displayed aggressive behaviours, which was in contrast to 39% who didn't access violent games. Evidence also suggests additional factors, such as poor parenting, have a significant role in the video games create violence debate (Paton, 2008; Wood, 2008). Ultimately this highlights a need for professionals to be mindful of video game use.

Virtual reality

Virtual reality [VR] refers to multiple topics in computer science discourses, with a broad definition describing VR as a computer generated environment that can be experienced and manipulated by the user (Jerald, 2016). In the context of this section VR will refer specifically to head mounted display [HMD] technology. According to Jerald (2016) VR-HMD's once perceived as science fiction fantasy have been researched in some form since the early 1900s, and have recently experienced a resurgence in interest. This resurgence has been spurred by the technology required to make a VR-HMD, offering a compelling experience, becoming relatively affordable (Jerald, 2016; Frick, 2016).

2016 saw the release of the first affordable and convincing consumer VR-HMD solutions, Oculus Rift and PlayStation VR (Frick, 2016). Additionally Google released the template for an inexpensive cardboard HMD, which uses any smartphone to operate as the screen and computer component (Jerald, 2016). Appendix 1 provides an overview of the historical and current VR-HMD designs, to clarify what technology is being addressed in this section. Current predictions suggest that the VR industry will grow from a global revenue of £4.1 billion in 2016, to around £130 billion in 2020 (International Data Corporation, 2016). This suggests that VR would fit the definition from the HCPC (2016) of a technology social workers need to be conscious of.

Here it is useful to provide a description of using a VR-HMD for those who have not experienced it. To do so it is helpful to draw upon the definition of VR proposed by NASA's Advanced Supercomputing Division [NAS](n.d), who claim the term itself can incorrectly have connotations of not being real, of a fake reality. However it is stated that in fact in the context of VR the term relates to providing an experience that feels real even though it is not (ibid).

NAS (n,d) expand upon their explanation to state that a VR experience provides cues to the cognitive systems which are interpreted as a sense of reality, with the visuals not having to be life like to trigger a perception in the brain of the VR being somewhat real.

To draw upon personal experiences to provide a simplified explanation, a VR rollercoaster provides feelings of an abrupt drop similar to real life, and a sudden shark appearance in a VR scuba dive elicits fright. According to Bohil, Owen, Jeong, Alicea and Biocca (2009) these responses are created due to VR presence, which in its simplest form is defined as the user having the feeling of being in the VR environment. Here the VR-HMD can mediate reality to a varying degree based on a combination of factors, such as software and hardware, which can facilitate presence and immersion into a VR experience that triggers psychological and physiological responses (Bohil *et al*, 2009; Diemer, G, Peperkorn, Shiban, & Mühlberger, 2015).

For social workers, direct work can at times focus on supporting children to navigate the complex emotions and symptoms resulting from their life path (Corcoran, 2000). Here social workers often work with children who have experienced forms of maltreatment, such as abuse and neglect. As noted earlier, maltreatment can be a catalyst for symptoms such as anxiety, depression, post-traumatic stress disorder [PTSD], in addition to behavioural and emotional difficulties (Misurell *et al*, 2014). Interestingly, evidence suggests that in addition to eliciting psychological and physiological responses, VR can be used therapeutically to alter human responses to stimuli (Bohil *et al*, 2009; Diemer *et al*, 2015). As such it is feasible to claim that social workers could potentially use VR to support maltreated children.

According to Mason (2007) PTSD is often linked to child abuse trauma, with symptoms such as anxiety, intrusive thoughts, avoidant behaviour, in addition to behavioural and emotional difficulties, impacting on normative functioning. Social workers can support children to manage these symptoms through Cognitive Behaviour Therapy [CBT]. VR is capable of decreasing PTSD symptoms, through exposure to stimuli related the PTSD trauma catalyst (Botella, Serrano, Baños and Garcia-Palacios, 2015). This can be direct exposure to the traumatic event, or indirect through stimuli that triggers trauma memories. This research states VR therapy facilitates changes in emotional processing to reduce PTSD symptoms (ibid).

As such VR would possibly be seen by Mason (2007) as a CBT tool clinical social workers could use with children experiencing PTSD. However, Botella *et al* (2015) note that only one study has been completed regarding VR-HMD PTSD therapy for children. This study was completed by López-Soler, Castro, Alcántara, and Botella (2011), in which they adapted VR software used for adult PTSD sufferers for children. This small scale study used VR CBT with a thirteen year old male who had been removed from his family due to maltreatment and domestic violence. The VR environment used objects, colours, and sounds the child linked to negative experiences to perform graded exposure, to promote understanding and emotional regulation (ibid).

López-Soler et al's (2011) results indicated a significant decline in PTSD symptoms after prolonged VR therapy. Anxiety levels reportedly dropped from a score of 45 to 10, with depression, self-esteem, and social functioning scores also showing significant improvements. Interestingly the study also highlighted the child's perception of his parents throughout the VR treatments became more negative (ibid), perhaps indicating increased insight into his experiences. This study highlighted the potential of VR therapy for the symptoms of child maltreatment. However Botella et al (2015) note that VR therapy can also be traumatic due to its method of exploring trauma. Essentially this suggests VR is currently an inappropriate tool for social workers to use, without first having significant clinical experience in PTSD treatment.

Lastly, I would like to propose my own hypothetical VR technology which could be used by social workers to facilitate parental change and positive outcomes, by promoting empathy, reflection, and learning around poor parenting. An initial diagram of this proposed tool can be found in appendix 2. This tool would require a child to wear glasses that captured VR compatible footage, which would be achievable to produce when considering available technology (Stein, 2016). These would be worn in the home and the child could trigger recording at times of chastisement or poor parenting. The parent could then experience the child's perspective through a VR-HMD, whilst being guided by the social worker to explore the child's perceptions and different approaches to parenting.

My proposed VR solution can be likened to Parent-Child Interaction Therapy [PCIT]. PCIT aims to improve parent-child relationships through observations of interactions being conducted through a one-way mirror, with parents being given feedback on how to improve interactions (Bjørseth & Wichstrøm, 2016). Research indicates that PCIT can successfully modify parenting strategies and children's behaviour (ibid), in addition to being effective with families whose abusive parenting styles cause child maltreatment (Ware, Fortson, & McNeil, 2003). Here abusive parenting includes using physical and verbal strategies such as biting, slapping, threatening, swearing, shouting, and criticizing (ibid). Ware, Fortsona and McNeil (2003) present a compelling argument highlighting how PCIT teaches parents more appropriate responses to their child, which results in a rewarding interaction that creates change. In theory this evidence could be applied to my proposed intervention.

Where PCIT's approach can be seen to be based on experiential learning and improved stimulus responses, my VR solution would differ as it focuses on empathy being a catalyst for change. Asmussen (2011) perceives this as a positive approach through the sentiment that change would occur if parents could experience their child's perspective. Increasing parental empathy for their child's experience can reduce the risk of significant harm (Ward, Brown, & Hyde-Dryden, 2014). VR can promote empathy by providing an immersive perspective of another's experience (LaValle, 2017). In his TED Talk, Milk (2015) agrees stating VR is a powerful medium where change can be created by empathy. Essentially, evidencing a strength of my proposed VR intervention.

Milk (2015) also highlights the potential for VR induced empathy to facilitate reflection and experiential learning. Here it is important to draw upon Kolb's (2015) Experiential Learning Cycle, which claims individuals learn through their experiences and subsequent reflections on them. According to Nancarrow and Rifkin (2012) this theory is widely accepted, as such this supports the strengths of VR interventions. However it must be noted that participants will know a recording device is present, which discourses on human interactions may suggest impacts upon human behaviour. Evidence to support this comes from a study of Police wearing body cameras, during which it was reported that the use of Police force dropped by over 50% (Police Foundation, 2013). Here it was suggested that both the Police and public's behaviour was changed by the presence of a video capture device (ibid). This potentially highlights a significant weakness of my proposed VR solution.

Conclusion

Digital technology is a valued element of human life in western society (DfE, 2013; Bunz, 2014). Some are concerned that it is negatively impacting human behaviour, whilst eroding the social nature of humanity (Steyaert & Gould, 2010). The conflicting views of digital technology may be due to a generational divide that will dissipate over time (Prensky, 2011), however evidence also contests this (Salajan, Schönwetter, & Cleghorn, 2010). Contrasting debates and perspective such as these will continue, however it is unlikely that digital technology and its influences upon humanity will just cease to exist. As such it is crucial to explore the digital world.

Social work education has not embraced the advancement of digital (Henderson et al, 2015; Brandl et al, 2015), perhaps to its detriment. Social work education should prepare professionals to undertake assessments, a core function of the role (Parker; 2008). Key to assessment is data collection and recording, which evidence suggests is time consuming and impacts upon practice (Broadhurst et al, 2010; Unison & Community care, 2014). Evidence suggests social workers could use digital dictation to reduce time spent on collecting and recording information (HSCI, 2013; Camphor, 2013). Moreover digital dictation can improve trust between service users and social workers (Scharer, 2015), which is currently lacking (Ipsos MORI & BMA, 2011). Although it must be highlighted that digital dictation could inhibit disclosures by making service users mindful of being recorded (Mellon, 2016).

Once gathered data must be analysed, in which Munby (2016) calls for improvements. Turney et al (2011) state that multi-agency practice can improve analysis, with the Home Office (2014) reporting that shared digital recording systems have improved joint analysis, and therefore outcomes. However Laming (2003) reminds us that interpersonal communication between professionals promotes mutual understanding, which is lost through digitization of information sharing. Social workers also report that digitization has reduced direct work with families (Turney et al, 2011). Perhaps in this context the concerns of social work being dehumanized by technology find validation.

Digital technology is a neglected area in social work practice. Research shows that video games could be benefit direct social work practice (Stoll & Collett, 2013; Collins & Cox, 2013). Furthermore social workers engaging in play through video games, will gain new insights into their lived experiences and reduce the risk of poor outcomes (Van Deventer & White, 2002; Moyer, 2014; Horn & Reyes, 2014).

Due to similarities with PCIT, it is possible to suggest that evidence supporting PCITs ability to improve child-parent relationships through observations and feedback (Ware et al, 2003; Bjørseth & Wichstrøm, 2016), can be generalised to my VR intervention. However where it appears to be most powerful is in its ability to create empathy (Milk, 2015), which evidence would suggest facilitates a reduction in the risk child maltreatment (Ward et al, 2014). However the requirement for the parents to be recorded may inhibit the collection of useful footage (Police Foundation, 2013). This weakness may hinge on the parents desire to implement change.

Ultimately this project has explored digital technology through the lens of social work, focusing on training, assessment, and direct work. Throughout which my hypothesis has clearly been supported by evidence of digital technology being a valuable resource for social workers, however its full potential has not yet been realised. One must always be cautious to the claim that an over reliance on digital technology dehumanising social work practice where the very essence of social work is the opposite. I would finally emphasise all employers should consider the benefits digital technology can provide social work assessments and interventions.

References

Adams, J., & Leshone, D. (2016). *Active Social Work with Children with Disabilities*. St Albans: Critical Publishing

Asmussen, K. (2011). *The Evidence-based Parenting Practitioner's Handbook*. Abingdon: Routledge

Beresford, P. (2014). Personalisation: from solution to problem. In P. Beresford, *Personalisation* (pp. 1-26). Bristol: Policy Press

Bjørseth, A., & Wichstrøm, L. (2016). Effectiveness of Parent-Child Interaction Therapy (PCIT) in the Treatment of Young Children's Behavior Problems. A Randomized Controlled Study. *PLoS ONE, 11*(9). doi:10.1371/journal.pone.0159845

Bohil, C., Owen, C., Jeong, E., Alicea, B., & Biocca, F. (2009). Virtual Reality and Presence. In W. Eadie, *21st Century Communication: A Reference Handbook* (pp. 534-542). London: Sage

Botella, C., Serrano, B., Baños, R., & Garcia-Palacios, A. (2015). Virtual reality exposure-based therapy for the treatment of post-traumatic stress disorder: a review of its efficacy, the adequacy of the treatment protocol, and its acceptability. *Neuropsychiatric Disease and Treatment, 11*, 2533–2545

Brandl, K., Schneid, S., & Armour, C. (2015). Writing on the Board versus PowerPoint: What do Students Prefer and Why? *The FASEB Journal, 29*(1). Retrieved from http://www.fasebj.org/content/29/1_Supplement/LB465.short

Braye, S., & Preston-Shoot, M. (2016). Developing Research and Scholarship in Law Teaching for Social Work Education. In I. Taylor, M. Bogo, M. Lefevre, & B. Teater, *Routledge International Handbook of Social Work Education* (pp. 171-183). London: Taylor & Francis

British Association of Social Workers. (2016). *Social Work Careers*. Retrieved from British Association of Social Workers: https://www.basw.co.uk/social-work-careers/

Broadhurst, K., White, S., Fish, S., Munro, E., Fletcher, k., & Lincoln, H. (2010). *Ten pitfalls and how to avoid them: What research tells us*. NSPCC. Retrieved from https://www.nspcc.org.uk/globalassets/documents/research-reports/10-pitfalls-initial-assessments-report.pdf

Bronfenbrenner, U. (1986). Ecology of the family as a context for human development: Research perspectives. *Developmental Psychology, 22*(6), 723-742.

Buckley, R., & Caple, J. (2007). *The Theory & Practice of Training* (5th ed.). London: Kogan Page

Bunz, M. (2014). *The Silent Revolution*. Basingstoke: Palgrave Macmillan

Camphor, I. (2013). *The use of speech recognition tools could revolutionise the NHS, but departments are slow to adopt*. Retrieved from ITPro: http://www.itpro.co.uk/desktop-software/voice-recognition/20758/doctors-use-speech-recognition-cut-nhs-waiting-times

Candra, S., & Sharma, R. (2007). *Philosophy of Education*. Delhi: Atlantic

Centre for Child Protection. (2014). *Rosie1*. University of Kent. Retrieved from https://www.kent.ac.uk/sspssr/ccp/game/WorksheetRosie1Final.pdf

Children Act 1989. London: HMSO. Retrieved from http://www.legislation.gov.uk/ukpga/1989/41/contents

Cohen, S. (2011). *Folk Devils and Moral Panics*. Abingdon: Routledge

Coleman, J., & Hagell, A. (2007). The Nature of Risk and Resilience in Adolescence. In J. Coleman, & A. Hagell, *Adolescence, risk and resilience* (pp. 1-16). Chichester: John Wiley

College of Social Work. (2014). *Roles and functions of social workers in England: advice note*. London: College of Social Work. Retrieved from http://cdn.basw.co.uk/upload/

basw_115640-9.pdf

Collins, E., & Cox, A. (2013). Switch on to games: Can digital games aid post-work recovery? *International Journal of Human-Computer Studies, 72*, 654-662

Corcoran, J. (2000). *Evidence-Based Social Work Practice With Families: A Lifespan Approach.* New York: Springer

Dawson, C., Cragg, A., Taylor, C., & Toombs, B. (2007). *Video Games Research to improve understanding of what players enjoy about video games, and to explain their preferences for particular games.* London: British Board of Film Classification

Department for Education. (2013). *Digital technology in schools.* Retrieved from Department for Education: http://webarchive.nationalarchives.gov.uk/20130123124929/http://www.education.gov.uk/a00201823/digital-technology-in-schools

Diemer, J., Alpers, G.W., Peperkorn, H., Shiban, Y., & Mühlberger, A. (2015). The impact of perception and presence on emotional reactions: a review of research in virtual reality. *Frontiers in Psychology, 6*, 26. doi:10.3389/fpsyg.2015.00026

Dunn, S., Braddell, A., & Sunderland, J. (2014). *Digital capabilities in social care.* Leeds: Skills for Care

Easingwood, N. (2007). ICT in the Primary School. In J. Moyles, *Beginning Teaching, Beginning Learning: In Primary Education* (pp. 106-114). Milton Keynes: Open University Press

Edwards, A. (2012). *New Technology and Education.* London: Continuum

Eichberg, H. (2016). *Questioning Play: What play can tell us about social life.* Abingdon: Routledge

Entertainment Retailers Association. (2017). *Entertainment sales reached £6.3bn in 2016.* Retrieved from Entertainment Retailers Association: http://www.eraltd.org/news-events/press-releases/2017/entertainment-sales-reached-63bn-in-2016/

Epstein, L., & Walker, T. (2012). *Constitutional Law: Rights, Liberties and Justice* (8th ed.). Washington: Sage

Ferguson, C., & Kilburn, J. (2009). The Public Health Risks of Media Violence: A Meta-Analytic Review. *The Journal of Pediatrics, 154*(5), 759–763

Fitch, D., Canada, K., Cary, S., & Freese, R. (2016). Facilitating Social Work Role Plays in Online Courses: The Use of Video Conferencing. *Advances in Social Work, 17*(1), 78-92. doi:10.18060/20874

Fontes, L. (2008). *Child Abuse and Culture: Working with Diverse Families.* London: Guildford Press

Frick, T. (2016). *Designing for Sustainability: A Guide to Building Greener Digital Products.* Farnham: O'Reilly

Fromberg, D., & Bergen, D. (2006). Introduction. In D. Fromberg, & D. Bergen, *Play From Birth to Twelve : Contexts, Perspectives, and Meaning* (2nd ed., pp. xv-xii). Florence: Routledge

Gegenfurtner, A., Quesada-Pallarès, C., & Knogler, M. (2014). Digital simulation-based training: A meta-analysis. *British Journal of Educational Technology, 45*(6), 1097–1114

Goldstein, J. (2012). *Play in children's development, health and well-being*. Brussels: Toy Industries of Europe

Guo, R., Dobson, T., & Petrina, S. (2008). Digital Natives, Digital Immigrants: An Analysis of Age and ICT Competency in Teacher Education. *Journal of Educational Computing Research, 38*(3), 235-254

Haaster, K. (2014). *Youth Care Knowledge Exchange through Online Simulation Gaming: Designing and appreciating online simulation games to enhance youth care knowledge exchange*. Netherlands: Gildeprint

Harvey, A. (2015). *Gender, Age, and Digital Games in the Domestic Context*. Oxon: Routledge

Health and Care Professions Council. (2012). *Standards of proficiency for Social workers in England*. London: Health and Care Professions Council

Health and Care Professions Council. (2016). *Social Work Education in England*. London: Health and Care Professions Council. Retrieved from https://www.hcpc-uk.org/assets/documents/10004ED2SocialworkinEnglandreport-FINAL.pdf

Health and Social Care Information Centre. (2013). *Digital technology essentials guide*. NHS. Retrieved from http://systems.digital.nhs.uk/qipp/library/techessentials.pdf

Henderson, N., Selwyn, N., & Aston, R. (2015). What works and why? Student perceptions of 'useful' digital technology in university teaching and learning. *Studies in Higher Education*, 1-13. doi:dx.doi.org/10.1080/03075079.2015.1007946

Hill, A., & Shaw, I. (2011). *Social Work and ICT*. London: Sage

Hobart, M. (2012). Learning from Myself: Avatars and Educational Video Games. *Current Issues In Education, 15*(3), 1-16

Home Office. (2014). *Multi Agency Working and Information Project: Final Report*. Home Office. Retrieved from https://www.gov.uk/government/uploads/system/uploads/attachment_data/file/338875/MASH.pdf

Horn, P., & Reyes, V. (2014). Child-Parent Psychotherapy with infants and very young children. In S. Timmer, & A. Urquiza, *Evidence-Based Approaches for the Treatment of Maltreated Children: Considering core components and treatment effectiveness* (pp. 61-80). London: Springer

Horne-Moyer, L., Moyer, B., Messer, D., & Messer, E. (2014). The Use of Electronic Games in Therapy: a Review with Clinical Implications. *Current Psychiatry Reports, 16*(12), 520. doi:10.1007/s11920-014-0520-6

Inoue-Smith, Y., & Wang, S. (2016). College-based case studies in using PowerPoint effectively. *Cogent Education, 3*(1). doi:10.1080/2331186X.2015.1127745

International Data Corporation. (2016). *Worldwide Revenues for Augmented and Virtual Reality Forecast to Reach $162 Billion in 2020, According to IDC*. Retrieved from International Data Corporation: http://www.idc.com/getdoc.jsp?containerId=prUS41676216&utm_source=Triggermail&utm_medium=email&utm_campaign=Post%20Blast%20%28bii-apps-and-platforms%29:%20Google%27s%20app-install%20ad%20business%20hits%20growth%20spurt%20%E2%80%94%20Global%20VR%20and%20A

International Federation of Social Workers. (2014). *Global Definition of Social Work*. Retrieved from International Federation of Social Workers: http://ifsw.org/get-involved/global-definition-of-social-work/

Ipsos MORI, & British Medical Association. (2011). *Trust in Professions 2011* . Retrieved from Ipsos MORI: https://www.ipsos-mori.com/researchpublications/researcharchive/2818/Doctors-are-most-trusted-profession-politicians-least-trusted.aspx

Jerald, J. (2016). *The VR Book: Human-Centered Design for Virtual Reality*. London: Morgan and Claypool

Kadushin, G., & Kadushin, A. (2013). *The Social Work Interview*. Chichester: Columbia university Press

Kare-Silver, M. (2011). *How the Digital Technology Revolution Is Changing Business and All Our Lives*. Palgrave Macmillan. Retrieved from http://books.google.co.uk/books?id=9jPbShBONzUC&dq

Kolb, D. (2015). *Experiential Learning: Experience as the Source of Learning and Development*. New Jersey: Pearson Education

Kutner, L., & Olson, C. (2008). *Grand Theft Childhood: The Surprising Truth About Violent Video Games and What Parents Can Do*. New York: Simon and Schuster

Laming, L. (2003). *The Victoria Climbé Inquiry*. Retrieved from http://www.dh.gov.uk/prod_consum_dh/groups/dh_digitalassets/documents/digitalasset/dh_110711.pdf

LaValle, S. (2017). *Virtual Reality*. Cambridge University Press. Retrieved from http://vr.cs.uiuc.edu/vrbook.pdf

Lincoln, M. (2008). *Higher Order Thinking through ICT: What do middle years teachers think really matters?* Brisbane: Queensland University of Technology. Retrieved from http://eprints.qut.edu.au/29054/1/29054.pdf

López-Soler, C., Castro, M., Alcántara, M., & Botella, C. (2011). The virtual reality system EMMA-Childhood in the psychological treatment of a minor with posttraumatic stress disorder. *Revista de Psicopatología y Psicología Clínica, 16*(3), 189-206. Retrieved from http://revistas.uned.es/index.php/RPPC/article/download/10361/9899

Loveless, A. (2002). ICT In The Primary Curriculum. In A. Loveless, & B. Dore, *ICT in the Primary School* (pp. 3-22). Buckingham: Open University Press

Luckock, B., & Lefevre, M. (2008). *Direct Work: Social Work with Children and Young People in Care*. London: British Association for Adoption & Fostering

Macleod, S., Hart, R., Jeffes, J., & Wilkin, A. (2010). *he Impact of the Baby Peter Case on Applications for Care Orders*. Slough: NFER

Margaryan, A., Littlejohn, A., & Vojt, G. (2011). Are digital natives a myth or reality? University students' use of digital technologies. *Computers and Education, 56*(2), 429–440. doi:http://dx.doi.org/10.1016/j.compedu.2010.09.004

Martin, R. (2010). *Social Work Assessment*. Exeter: Learning Matters

Mason, R. (2007). Working with abused children and adolescents. In A. Freeman, *Cognitive Behavior Therapy in Clinical Social Work Practice* (pp. 235-260). New York: Springer

McNicoll, A. (2016). *One fifth of social workers failed accreditation pilot role play*. Retrieved from Community Care: http://www.communitycare.co.uk/2016/07/07/one-fifth-social-workers-failed-accreditation-pilot/

Mellon, M. (2016). *Have parents become the enemy in social work?* Retrieved from Community Care: http://www.communitycare.co.uk/2016/02/19/parents-become-enemy-social-work/

Milk, C. (2015). *Chris Milk: How virtual reality can create the ultimate empathy machine.* Retrieved from https://www.ted.com/talks/chris_milk_how_virtual_reality_can_create_the_ultimate_empathy_machine#t-607232

Misurell, J., Springer, C., Acosta, L., Liotta, L., & Kranzler, A. (2014). Game-based cognitive-behavioral therapy individual model (GB-CBT-IM) for child sexual abuse: A preliminary outcome study. *Psychological Trauma: Theory, Research, Practice, and Policy, 6*(3), 250-258. doi:10.1037/a0033411

Morgan, N., & Department for Education. (2016). *Nicky Morgan unveils plans to transform children's social work.* Retrieved from GOV.UK: https://www.gov.uk/government/news/nicky-morgan-unveils-plans-to-transform-childrens-social-work

Munby, J. (2016). *15th View from the President's Chambers: care cases: the looming crisis.* Retrieved from Family Law: http://www.familylaw.co.uk/news_and_comment/15th-view-from-the-president-s-chambers-care-cases-the-looming-crisis#.WChZQ8lGThM

Munro, E. (2011). *The Munro Review of Child Protection.* London: Department for Education

Nancarrow, M., & Rifkin, W. (2012). Reflective cycles and reflexive learning principles: teaching ethics from learner outward. In C. Wankel, *Handbook of Research on Teaching Ethics in Business and Management Education* (pp. 387-412). Hershey: IGI Global

NASA Advanced Supercomputing Division. (n.d). *Virtual Reality: Definition and Requirements.* Retrieved from NASA Advanced Supercomputing Division: https://www.nas.nasa.gov/Software/VWT/vr.html

Newman, J. (2013). *Videogames.* Abingdon: Routledge

Nuance Healthcare Solutions. (2015). *Accuracy & completeness of clinical documentation Understanding the clinician, patient and economic implications in NHS England acute trusts.* Nuance Communications. Retrieved from http://images.marketing.nuance.com/Web/Nuance/%7B12edfca6-8d45-4ab5-9a78-c6cf4df76289%7D_UKClinDocResearchReportJune2015v1_web.pdf?elqaid=2706&elqat=2&elqTrackId=4dd9e6b3bd004fa9804f60c881c3ad59

Ofcom. (2016). *Children and parents: media use and attitudes report.* Retrieved from https://www.ofcom.org.uk/__data/assets/pdf_file/0034/93976/Children-Parents-Media-Use-Attitudes-Report-2016.pdf

Parker, J. (2008). The process of social work: Assessment, planning, intervention and review. In M. Lymbery, & K. Postle, *Social Work: A Companion to Learning* (pp. 111-122). London: Sage

Paton, G. (2008). *Bad behaviour in classrooms is blamed on indulgent parents.* Retrieved from The Telegraph: http://www.telegraph.co.uk/news/uknews/1582451/Bad-behaviour-in-classrooms-is-blamed-on-indulgent-parents.html

Peachey, K. (2016). *Facebook blocks Admiral's car insurance discount plan.* Retrieved from

BBC News: http://www.bbc.co.uk/news/business-37847647

Peters, O. (2001). *Learning and Teaching in Distance Education : Analyses and Interpretations from an International Perspective*. London: Taylor & Francis

Police Foundation. (2013). *Self-Awareness to Being Watched and Socially-Desirable Behavior: A Field Experiment on the Effect of Body-Worn Cameras on Police Use-of-Force*. Police Foundation. Retrieved from https://www.bja.gov/bwc/pdfs/130767873-Self-awareness-to-being-watched-and-socially-desirable-behavior-A-field-experiment-on-the-effect-of-body-worn-cameras-on-police-use-of-force.pdf

Prensky, M. (2001). Digital Natives, Digital Immigrants. *On the Horizon, 9*(5), 1-6

Prensky, M. (2011). Digital Wisdom and Homo Sapiens Digital. In M. Thomas, *Deconstructing Digital Natives: Young People, Technology, and the New Literacies* (pp. 15-29). New York: Routledge

Pritchard, A. (2009). *Ways of Learning* (2nd ed.). Oxon: Routledge

Reeves, J. (2016). Training Child Protection professionals through gaming and simulation technologies. Retrieved from https://www.youtube.com/watch?v=KE5jtt2f10Y

Reeves, J., Drew, I., Shemmings, D., & Ferguson, H. (2015). 'Rosie 2' A Child Protection Simulation: Perspectives on Neglect and the 'Unconscious At Work'. *Child Abuse Review, 24*(5), 346–364. doi:10.1002/car.2362

Reilly, L., & Dolan, P. (2015). The Voice of the Child in Social Work Assessments: Age-Appropriate Communication with Children. *British Journal of Social Work, 46*(5), 1-17

Reinecke, L. (2009). Games and recovery: The use of video and computer games to recuperate from stress and strain. *Journal of Media Psychology, 21,* 126-142. doi:10.1027/1864-1105.21.3.126

Salajan, F., Schönwetter, D., & Cleghorn, B. (2010). Student and faculty inter-generational digital divide: Fact or fiction? *Computers and education, 55*(3), 1393-1403. doi: 10.1016/j.compedu.2010.06.017

Scharer, R. (2015). *Should parents be allowed to record child protection meetings?* Retrieved from Community care: http://www.communitycare.co.uk/2015/12/10/parents-allowed-record-child-protection-meetings/

Smale, G., Tuson, G., & Statham, D. (2000). *Social Work and social Problems*. London: Macmillan

Social Care Institute for Excellence. (2007). *Assessment in social work: a guide for learning and teaching*. Retrieved from Social Care Institute for Excellence: http://www.scie.org.uk/publications/guides/guide18/natureofassessment/riskassessment.asp

Stein, S. (2016). *We tried Snapchat Spectacles -- here's what it's like*. Retrieved from Cnet: https://www.cnet.com/uk/products/snapchat-spectacles/preview/

Steyaert, J., & Gould, N. (2010). Social Work and the changing face of the digital divide. In V. Cree, *Social Work: A Reader* (pp. 58-63). London: Routledge

Stoll, N., & Collett, K. (2013). *Video games and wellbeing*. We Are What We Do. Retrieved from https://mindfulnessinschools.org/wp-content/uploads/2013/09/video-games-and-wellbeing.pdf

Tait, A., & Wuso, H. (2012). *Direct work with vulnerable children: Playful Activities and*

Strategies for Communication. London: Jessica Kingsley

The College of Social Work. (2015). *Review of the Professional Capabilities Framework (PCF)*. The College of Social Work. Retrieved from https://www.basw.co.uk/pcf/pcfreview2015.pdf

Turney, D., Platt, D., Selwyn, J., & Farmer, E. (2011). *Social work assessment of children in need: what do we know? Messages from research*. DfE. Retrieved from https://www.gov.uk/government/uploads/system/uploads/attachment_data/file/182302/DFE-RBX-10-08.pdf

Unison, & Community Care. (2014). *Social Work Watch: inside an average day* in social work How social work staff support and protect people , against all the odds*. Unison and Community Care. Retrieved from https://www.unison.org.uk/content/uploads/2014/06/TowebSocial-Work-Watch-final-report-PDF1.pdf

University of Kent. (2016). *The Centre for Child Protection*. Retrieved from Child Protection Simulations: https://www.kent.ac.uk/sspssr/ccp/simulationsindex.html

Van Deventer, S., & White, J. (2002). Expert behavior in children's video game play. *Simulation & Gaming, 33*(1), 28-48. Retrieved from http://gblenvironments.pbworks.com/f/VanDeventerandWhite2002.pdf

Vogel, J., Vogel, D., Cannon-Bowers, J., Bowers, C., Muse, K., & Wright, M. (2006). Computer Gaming and Interactive Simulations for Learning: A Meta-Analysis. *Journal of Educational Computing Research, 34*(3), 229-243. doi:10.2190/FLHV-K4WA-WPVQ-H0YM

Vogel, M., Kaisers, W., Wassmuth, R., & Mayatepek, E. (2015). Analysis of Documentation Speed Using Web-Based Medical Speech Recognition Technology: Randomized Controlled Trial. *Journal of Medical Internet Research, 17*(11). doi:10.2196/jmir.5072

Ward, H., Brown, R., & Hyde-Dryden, G. (2014). *Assessing Parental Capacity to Change when Children are on the Edge of Care: an overview of current research evidence*. Department for Education. Retrieved from https://www.gov.uk/government/uploads/system/uploads/attachment_data/file/330332/RR369_Assessing_parental_capacity_to_change_Final.pdf

Ware, L., Fortson, B., & McNeil, C. (2003). Parent-child interaction therapy: A promising intervention for abusive families. *The Behavior Analyst Today, 3*(4), 375-382. doi:10.1037/h0099993

Wonnacott, J., & Watts, D. (2014). *Daniel Pelka review retrospective: deeper analysis and progress report on implementation of recommendations*. Coventry Safeguarding Children Board. Retrieved from http://cdn.basw.co.uk/upload/basw_93627-8.pdf

Wood, R. (2008). Problems with the Concept of Video Game "Addiction": Some Case Study Examples. *International Journal of Mental Health & Addiction, 6*(2), 169-178.

Woodford, C. (2006). *Digital technology*. London: Evans Brothers

Worsley, A., & Littler, L. (2013). Practice Education. In A. Worsley, T. Mann, A. Olsen, & E. Mason-Whitehead, *Key Concepts in Social Work Practice* (pp. 181-185). London: Sage.